DIFFERENTIATING DEVELOPMENT

Beyond an Anthropology of Critique

Edited by

Soumhya Venkatesan and Thomas Yarrow

berghahn

NEW YORK · OXFORD

www.berghahnbooks.com

Published in 2012 by
Berghahn Books
www.berghahnbooks.com

©2012, 2014 Soumhya Venkatesan and Thomas Yarrow
First paperback edition published in 2014

Library of Congress Cataloging-in-Publication Data

Differentiating development : beyond an anthropology of critique / edited by
Soumhya Venkatesan and Thomas Yarrow.
    p. cm.
    Includes bibliographical references and index.
    ISBN 978-0-85745-303-7 (hardcover) — ISBN 978-1-78238-674-2
(paperback) — ISBN 978-0-85745-304-4 (ebook)
    1. Applied anthropology. 2. Rural development. 3. Community
development. 4. International organizations. 5. International relations.
I. Venkatesan, Soumhya. II. Yarrow, Thomas, 1977–
    GN397.5.D54 2012
    301—dc23   2011037832

British Library Cataloguing in Publication Data
A catalogue record for this book is available from the British Library.

Printed on acid-free paper.

ISBN 978-0-85745-303-7 hardback
ISBN 978-1-78238-674-2 paperback
ISBN 978-0-85745-304-4 ebook

DIFFERENTIATING DEVELOPMENT

CONTENTS

ACKNOWLEDGEMENTS

The volume stems from a workshop bearing the same name, held in September 2008 funded by the Wenner-Gren Foundation for Anthropological Research and *Critique of Anthropology*. We would like to acknowledge our immense gratitude to both. We would also like to acknowledge the intellectual debt this volume owes to all the workshop participants, not all of whom were able to contribute directly to this volume. We are also grateful to the anonymous reviewers for their comments and encouragement. We also wish to thank Melissa Spinelli and Ann Przyzycki DeVita of Berghahn and Pax (P.X. Amphlett) for his preparation of the index.

Anthropology and Development

Critical Framings

Thomas Yarrow and Soumhya Venkatesan

A Development Impasse

Since the Second World War, concepts of 'development' have been used to describe and explain social and cultural differences on a global scale (Cooper and Packard 1997b; Mosse 2005). In the post-colonial world that began to emerge in the 1950s and 1960s, ideas of 'progress' with roots in earlier colonial and enlightenment thinking were reinvigorated. Embraced by Western leaders as well as by leaders of the newly emerging independent nations, development provided a utopian vision of a post-colonial future in which all could aspire to the socio-economic conditions experienced in the West[1]. These ideas provided the rationale for the creation of both the Bretton Woods institutions (IMF and World Bank) and the various United Nations agencies. In different ways, these and an expanding number of nongovernmental and multilateral organizations continue to pursue a broadly 'developmental' vision. Whilst the statist, technocratic and top-down ideologies that emerged in the 1950s and 1960s have subsequently been heavily criticized, neoliberal thinking predominant within development organizations over the last three decades remains wedded to the overarching goal of linear economic and social 'progress'.

Against these developmental visions, anthropologists have been central to the emergence of the 'post-development' critique (Cooper and Packard 1997a; Crush 1995; Sachs 1992). Arising from and feeding into a wider postmodern questioning of the superiority of Western forms of knowledge (Asad 2003; Fabian 1983), this has brought to light the often negative impacts of an ostensibly progressive developmentalist impulse. In particular the above critiques reveal how an overtly benign impulse to eradicate poverty and promote positive social change often ends up reinscribing the very forms of inequality 'development' purports to overcome. Thus it has been suggested that in their discursive construction of ideas of 'poverty', development institutions objectify an un-differentiated and passive 'third world', whose problems are erroneously attributed to the actions of the people living there. In this way development institutions justify their own activities by locating the 'solutions' in the supposedly superior forms of 'expertise' that Western development professionals bring (Escobar 1995; Ferguson 1994; Hobart 1993a; Long and Long 1992).

Although this post-development critique has pertinently highlighted how apparently 'neutral' and 'objective' developmental discourses often end up justifying political inequality, it has led to an increasingly acute impasse. In their wholesale rejection of 'development', these critiques have tended to foreclose consideration of how or whether it is possible to retain hope in the vision of a better or more just future (Porter 1995). Even in challenging the universal applicability of development knowledge and expertise, there has been a tendency to universalize the practices and processes through which development projects and programmes practically unfold. In particular, a prevailing concern with development as a form of 'discourse' leads to forms of analysis and description that ignore the particular ideas, relations and practices through which ideas of development are practically enacted (Friedman 2006; Li Murray 2007; Mosse 2005; Olivier de Sardan 2005). From this perspective a stark choice emerges between a disenchanted, rational 'development machine' (Ferguson 1994) and an equally dystopian future in which ideas of justice and democracy are abandoned.

This book attempts to move beyond this impasse, selectively building on the critical insights of the post-development critique whilst breaking with its predominantly discursive focus. By taking a more ethnographic approach, contributors aim to re-perceive and hence re-orient development practice as a potentially positive force for good. They do so by redirecting attention to the concrete practices through which development is enacted, and the specific social realities that ideas of development frame. In this vein, the book focuses on development as a mode of engagement that, like anthropology, attempts to understand, represent and work within a complex world. In doing so, it aims to pave the way for more reflexive and more ethnographically nuanced understandings of development.

Critical Framings

With the shift in the late 1980s and early 1990s from more applied forms of 'development anthropology' to a more detached 'anthropology *of* development', the relationship between anthropology and development was fundamentally redefined. Where previously anthropologists had largely confined themselves to studying the processes, relationships and dynamics by which development (or, inversely, underdevelopment) was to be understood, increasingly they were turning their attention to the very institutions and knowledge through which ideas of development were produced. From a self-evident if complex social and economic process, 'development' was increasingly apprehended as a Western 'invention' and the means by which its supposed superiority was tautologically reproduced. Arguably the very field of an 'anthropology of development' was founded on belief in the notion of critical deconstruction as a means of uncovering that 'myth'.

In different ways, Ferguson (1994) and Escobar (1995) made highly influential contributions in opening up this critical space. For both, this entailed moving from the kinds of narrow critiques that anthropologists had been making of particular development policies (normally from the perspective of applied studies of particular groups of people), to a wider critique of 'development' as a set of institutionally embedded processes. Rather than challenge particular projects or paradigms in the name of 'more' or 'better' development, the goal became the critical deconstruction of 'development' as such. Critics (anthropological and otherwise) advocating 'alternative' forms of development were thus chastised for a failure to sufficiently question the apparatus that was 'doing' the development.

This critique was hugely significant in bringing to light the mechanisms by which the industrialized 'West' has continued to exercise control over processes of global change in a postcolonial world. In particular, post-development scholars revealed how ostensibly neutral technocratic and market-based discourses have acted to depoliticize and hence justify the often partisan interventions of economically powerful states (e.g., Cooper and Packard 1997b; Ferguson 1994; Sachs 1992). In a related way, various post-development scholars have shown how development organizations define 'problems' in ways that justify their own forms of 'expertise' and thereby marginalize the insights and understandings of other groups of people (Apthorpe 1997; Escobar 1995; Fairhead and Leach 1997; Grillo and Stirrat 1997). Another strand of this critique reveals how development resources are often used to bolster the position of educated elites, who exploit their politically and socially privileged positions to the detriment of the poor they are supposed to help (e.g., Ferguson 1994).

From the start, the subject and object of this critique was somewhat ambiguous. As early anthropologists of development were quick to acknowledge, any critique of development was also necessarily a critique of anthropology (Escobar 1995; Ferguson 1994; Hobart 1993a). Anthropological knowledge has been used as a means of practically facilitating particular colonial and post-colonial attempts to enact social 'improvement' (Gardner and Lewis 1996). Moreover, both anthropologists and development practitioners have shared similar understandings about the evolution of societies. Thus for Escobar (1995), critique was seen as the means by which anthropologists could shed light on the practices and assumptions that both anthropology and development shared. In other words, liberating anthropology from its own colonial past was inextricably linked to the liberation of anthropology from the space mapped by the 'development encounter'.

Nonetheless, it is hard to escape the conclusion that in practice anthropological critiques of development have been underpinned by an asymmetry. In general, anthropologists have commented 'on' development from a position of superiority that has tended to be assumed rather than elucidated. Anthropological critiques have largely taken shape on the basis of ethnographic expertise. This has meant that anthropologists have tended to align themselves with the particular groups they study, and by extension a generalized non-Western 'other'. On this basis, knowledge of particular groups of people has been used as a means of highlighting the shortcomings of particular development projects and the limitations of 'development' practice more generally. In the stark terms in which Hobart (1993b) puts it, anthropology's knowledge of the complexities of particular social and cultural realities thus becomes the means of criticizing development's 'ignorance' of these facts. As Green (2003) has recently argued, anthropologists have therefore largely imagined themselves outside of and untainted by the development sector. Anthropology's increasing sense of itself as a discipline that has moved beyond its colonial past, has taken shape by reference to development's apparent inability to make the parallel move.

Yet if anthropological critiques have thus assumed superior *empirical* knowledge, anthropologists have also criticized development on the basis of greater *theoretical* sophistication. In this vein, various theoretical insights have been seen as the basis upon which anthropologists are able to see more about the world of development than are the various people who occupy that world. The early emphasis by Escobar and Ferguson on Foucauldian theories of power has been paradigmatic in framing subsequent engagements. If power is driven by disguise, then the role of critical scholarship is taken to be a critical unmasking of the political relations that underlie surface representations (Yarrow 2011). This approach has driven influential critiques of development policy (Apthorpe 1997, Shore and Wright 1997). Shore and Wright's (1997) work has been particularly ground-breaking in this respect, highlighting the 'mobilizing metaphors' and 'linguistic strategies' through which, they suggest, policy operates. Anthropologists have, then, focused on the historical conditions through which development policies are produced and the 'inventedness' of policy's 'taken-for-grantedness' (Shore and Wright 1997: 15). In all these respects we suggest that anthropological critiques of development have been founded on the belief that anthropologists *see* more than various development because they *know* more. More or less explicitly, the basis of much of this knowledge (and hence vision) has been imagined as theoretical.

While the movement from more applied forms of development anthropology to a more critical anthropology of development can to some extent be seen as a temporal evolution, debates have persisted through the 1990s and 2000s between anthropologists with different views about the extent to which the application of anthropological ideas is a desirable or achievable aim. Thus Gardner and Lewis's (1996) influential book can be seen as an important attempt to reappraise the forms of critical deconstruction that pervaded the 1990s. They suggest that whilst post-structural influences lead to significant insights, too frequently these forms of critique end up in outright condemnation of development. This negates the potential for anthropologists to bring insights that positively affect the way in which development projects are undertaken. Hence they suggest that a more constructive relationship will emerge if anthropologists use their knowledge to actively inform, if not transform, development practice. In particular the book highlights the potential for anthropologists to counter the Western bias of development policies, to moderate the relationships between development institutions and the groups they seek to help, and hence to link 'micro' and 'macro' processes.

This perspective constituted an important corrective to some of the more critical elements of anthropology. Yet in certain respects the call for more sensitive and productive forms of anthropological critique leaves intact the assumption that such critiques would form the underlying basis of anthropological engagements with development. Whilst advocating a less adversarial approach, Gardner and Lewis leave implicit many of the assumed epistemological and theoretical asymmetries of the anthropologists they take to task.

Questioning Critique

What would it mean to move beyond these critical framings, and why might that move be productive? Although post-development critiques have certainly been productive, their asymmetries have led to a number of problems. An assumption of the superiority of anthropological knowledge has tended to preclude consideration of how anthropological knowledge could itself be illuminated by various forms of development practice. Such critiques have also tended to negate nuanced ethnographic understanding, since the complex, diverse and often contradictory ideas that emerge in relation to development are frequently reduced to their assumed role in perpetuating inequality.

Since the advent of Malinowskian fieldwork, anthropologists have sought to understand the beliefs, practices and social relations of other groups of people as a means of shedding light on the beliefs and assumptions that anthropologists – and often by extension 'Westerners' – hold. In this way, a commitment to understanding other people's lives on their own terms led to what Strathern (1987) has termed 'routine reflexivity'. By this, she refers to an underlying mode of anthropological knowledge production rather than to recent attempts to highlight the individual subjectivity of the ethnographer in the construction of anthropological knowledge. According to Strathern, suspension of the kinds of criticism that animate routine forms of ethnocentrism constitutes the very grounds on which anthropologists have critically apprehended their own theories and ideas about the world. Anthropology has grown through increasing differentiation of its own analytical concepts as these have been applied to different groups of people (Strathern 1991).

From this perspective, the kinds of critical scholarship that have characterized anthropological engagement with development over the past two decades lead to a troubling inversion. Where anthropologists have turned their attention to development practice, assumptions about anthropology's theoretical, epistemological and empirical superiority have tended to militate against the forms of 'routine reflexivity' that have acted as a driver of theoretical innovation. In attempting to use anthropological insights to highlight development shortcomings, anthropologists have largely neglected to reflect upon what such encounters might teach *us*. Where anthropology is construed as a set of analytic or methodological resources to be *applied* in illuminating development contexts, the potential for those contexts to illuminate, challenge or extend anthropological thinking is therefore foreclosed.

A related problem with prevailing forms of critique is that they tend to *assume* anthropology to be a set of practices and relationships that are self-evidently distinct from those that operate within various development contexts. Critical comment is thus premised upon a break between subject (anthropology) and object (development). Such assumptions preclude a more reflexive understanding of the concepts and practices through which anthropology works. By construing development's difference from anthropology in terms of a deficit, these critiques have largely overlooked the extent to which anthropologists and development actors in fact engage in distinct forms of epistemological practice oriented towards distinct ends. In other words, the assumptions that frame and reproduce understandings of anthropology as critical resources to be applied to development work against a symmetrical (Latour 1993; Green this volume) treatment of anthropology and development as subjects of critical scrutiny in the same analytic terms. Assuming the superiority of anthropological knowledge thus forecloses sustained consideration of ways in which expertise and knowledge are constructed within anthropology and development in distinct, if overlapping, ways (cf. Li Murray 2007: 2).

If the critical framing of anthropology's encounter with development has tended to preclude anthropological reflexivity (Lewis and Mosse 2006, Yarrow 2008b), it has also precluded nuanced ethnographic understanding for precisely the same reasons. Here we join with other anthropologists who have recently pointed to the forms of ethnographic reductionism that prevailing approaches have produced (Bornstein 2003; Englund 2006; Friedman 2006; Lewis and Mosse 2006; Mosse 2005; Yarrow 2008a). Mosse (2005), for example, points to a neofunctionalist logic whereby the decisions and beliefs of particular development actors are reduced to their purported role in reproducing political inequalities. As such, he suggests, much of the anthropology of development has had the unfortunate effect of dissolving its object of study in the process of describing it. If all statements are taken to be dissembling acts, we lose a sense of the beliefs, ideas and voices of particular development actors (see also Fechter and Hindman 2011a). Where analysts assume that the discourses and practices of development are driven by the disguise of power, the beliefs, meanings and actions that development actors themselves privilege are overlooked. In this respect the language of disguise itself disguises important aspects of actors' own realities (cf. Reed 2003)

Beyond Critique

In attempting to move beyond the forms of critical deconstruction that have characterized anthropological engagements with development over the past two decades, we do not propose a break with critical scholarship per se. Rather we seek to unsettle some of the asymmetries that such critiques have both assumed and reproduced. We do this in the hope of producing more nuanced ethnographic accounts and hence more critical reflection on anthropology's own ideas and practices.

In attempting to reorient anthropology in a direction that is simultaneously more ethnographic and more critically aware of its own analytic and theoretical limitations, we take inspiration from a small but significant body of work within anthropology. In particular Lewis and Mosse (2006) have called for a more ethnographic approach to development, one that stands apart from normative and instrumental ideologies, in order to better appreciate the complexities of particular contexts in which ideas of development become ethnographically meaningful (cf. Bornstein 2003; Ferguson 2006; Li Murray 2007; Pigg 1997). Rather than the ideologically informed critical deconstruction characteristic of mainstream anthropological approaches, their call is for *methodological* deconstruction. By this, they refer to the capacity for ethnography to highlight how apparently coherent policies and programmes emerge through the unscripted actions of heterogeneous actors. Instead of focusing on the analytic shortcomings of particular policies, anthropologists should seek to reveal the 'hidden transcripts' that coexist alongside the 'public transcripts' that development practitioners produce. Although framed in somewhat different terms, this move parallels our own insistence that anthropological accounts can usefully produce critical commentary only from the basis of ethnography that does not in the first instance take critique as its aim (Yarrow 2008b).

Neither critical nor neutral, this book thus constitutes an explicit attempt to reveal the moral and social worlds in which ideas of development are made meaningful, without becoming apologists for those that we study. Rather than critique generalized 'development practice', our collective aim is to shed light on particular development contexts (however defined) in the knowledge that particular critiques may usefully emerge from such understandings (see Friedman this volume). In this sense critical engagement with development practice is regarded as a negotiated outcome of development practice, rather than the a priori assumed mode of engagement.

Thus the innovation of the volume emerges in the ways that contributors extend and reconfigure existing theories by applying them to particular ethnographic contexts. In this respect, three main themes emerge, each of which speaks to existing debates whilst taking these in new directions. These are explored in the following three sections, which focus respectively on the ethnographic differentiation of 'development', the differentiation of different modes of anthropological engagement with development, and the ways in which various anthropologists and development practitioners have thought about the relationship between acting and understanding.

Development Multiple

The book attempts to differentiate development as an object of study by ethnographically exploring the various meanings and practices that exist in the name of 'development' (cf. Mitchell 2002; cf. Olivier de Sardan 2005). Development has often been presented as a monolithic, Western set of ideas and practices. By contrast, this book reveals the diversity of ways in which ideas of 'development' are imbricated in the practices and relationships of otherwise socially, culturally and geographically distinct groups of people.

Arce and Long (2000) suggest the need to overcome a global-local dichotomy in anthropological theorizations about development, through a focus on the 'counter-tendencies' through which global development discourses are locally embedded and resisted. This focus importantly highlights the diversity of ways in which ideas of development become meaningful. However, a focus on 'counter-tendencies' and 'resistance' assumes that diversity and difference are located only at the level of 'the local'. In contrast, a number of the contributors to this volume show the heterogeneity of thought and practice that exists in the name of 'development'. In practice, ostensibly 'global' discourses emerge as nego- tiated outcomes of practices that entail specific forms of relationship and understanding. Thus, Jensen and Winthereik highlight how globally ubiquitous ideas of 'partnership' emerge through specific organizational practices. Similarly, Obeid shows how ideas of 'participation' become meaningful in the context of development NGOs that emerged within a very particular historical moment in Lebanon. In both cases, ostensibly 'global' forms of discourse emerge through the practices of particular actors. At the same time, international development discourses provide the means by which people negotiate and frame social, cultural and polit- ical differences. In other words, development workers construct ideas of development and are in turn constructed by them. By demonstrating the diversity of ways in which this happens, contributors reveal the problems of conceptualizing development workers as a sociologically unified group (see also contributors to Fechter and Hindman 2011b).

In a related way, contributors to this book question the tendency for anthropological studies to conflate 'development' with a narrow focus on the activities and ideas of international development organizations. Indeed, not all development projects are international or 'Western' in origin. Mathur's study of bureaucrats employed in implementing an ambitious Government of India project is a timely reminder of the fact that large development projects may well be national, and that we need to differentiate the local in our analyses. For Baviskar, this entails the need to broaden analyses of development to include the processes of capitalist accumulation that entail extraction, disposession and displacement – and also, paradoxically, trigger demands for development.

Other contributors to the volume differentiate the concept of development by revealing how these ideas are integral to forms of practice that do not on the surface appear to be primarily 'about' development. In this way Kelly demonstrates how scientific practice in The Gambia is framed in terms of ideas of 'progress'. Trundle similarly questions the separation between 'development' and 'charity'. This has been central to delimiting not only the activities of organizations working in the 'third world' from those working in the West, but also the literatures that have arisen in relation to these activities. Yet as Trundle shows, this is a separation that conceals important parallels.

Differentiating Anthropology

If anthropologists of development have tended to imagine 'development' in relatively homogeneous terms, there has also been a parallel tendency to neglect the different forms that anthropological engagements with development take (cf. Gardner and Lewis 1996). As well as differentiating 'development' as an object of study, contributors to the volume draw out the multiplicity of ways of being anthropologists with interests in development. In particular these highlight the different kinds of relationships and engagements that can result from different methodological and theoretical standpoints. This diversity is evident in the different positions from which the various contributors to the volume narrate their accounts.

At one end of the spectrum, Green exemplifies a wider trend for anthropologists to work in large donor organizations as consultants or specialists, with particular forms of expertise. She notes the impossibility of sustaining commitment to the epistemological practices of both simultaneously in such contexts. Although it is possible to be an anthropologist and a development 'practitioner', one cannot hold both identities at the same time, since each works through a form of knowledge that eclipses the other (Riles 2001). Jensen and Winthereik's analysis is also concerned with the overlapping forms of knowledge through which anthropology and development work, but their account is told from the rather different position of wanting to understand the practice of international development organizations through a process of ethnography. As ethnographers studying the material effects of discourses of 'partnership', they describe how their own interests became folded into this trope. In order to gain access to the field, they were required to do so as 'partners', producing knowledge that would be useful for the development practitioners they were interested in studying.

Arguably at the other extreme, Gledhill and Hita and Baviskar demonstrate the possibility for anthropologists to act as advocates for the socially and politically marginal groups they have conventionally studied. From this perspective, nuanced understanding of particular practices and beliefs of 'beneficiary' groups reveals the shortcomings of the neoliberal approaches that have so often been favoured by international finance institutions. In contrast to top-down development, as described by Baviskar, is bottom-up development, or initiatives that originate from the grass roots. Taylor and Rousseau came to think about 'development' because Vanuatuan actors' own interests in reorienting their lives presented a situation in which the ethnographic ubiquity of 'development' made it difficult to ignore. Likewise, Mathur's essay focuses on the desire for development (or *vikas*) in a marginal region of India and the workings-out of development in government offices committed to implementing an ambitious plan while simultaneously recognizing its problems.

Taken in the round, these accounts demonstrate how different points of entry into the field lead to very different kinds of analyses. The subject positions we occupy determine not only the questions that we ask but also the answers that we get. Questions concerning the kinds of relationships that anthropologists have with their subjects are not only methodological but frame the very terms in which 'development' can be thought about and theorized. As Jensen and Winthereik point out, the elements of 'development' that come into view do not depend simply on the theoretical perspective adopted by the analyst or researcher, but on where and how they move through organizations and contexts. If development actors and interests are folded into anthropological practice in a multitude of ways, then we need to be aware of the diverse forms that anthropological engagements with development issues and practices can take.

The relationship between anthropology and development has often been conceived in relatively abstract terms, as a theoretical issue of how to reconcile different kinds of knowledge. By contrast, contributors to this volume emphasize the importance of understanding the social and institutional contexts in which such encounters concretely take place. In particular, Green highlights how an anthropological belief in the power of textual critique negates understanding of different regimes of knowledge through which anthropology and development work. If the usefulness or applicability of such texts (whether anthropologically authored or otherwise) is socially constructed through specific practices of development, then anthropologists' own reification of textual forms of critique to some extent miss the point. In different ways, contributors highlight the need to take seriously the kinds of relationships that anthropologists sustain in the field, not simply as a means to the end of 'better' knowledge, but as ends in their own right. Whether such relationships entail NGO and development workers, or communities in which development projects are undertaken, these concrete interactions themselves entail forms of engagement that have potentially transformative effects.

Conceived in abstract terms, the relationship between anthropology and development has often seemed intractable. While anthropologists frequently chastise development workers for their lack of social and cultural knowledge, development workers at times regard this knowledge as unnecessarily complex and point to the difficulty of applying it. Yet if, as contributors to this volume suggest, anthropology and development are both highly heterogeneous forms of practice, then their relationship must also be understood in more nuanced and differentiated terms. Rather than talk of 'the' relationship between anthropology and development, it might be more useful to talk of *relationships* between anthropologists and various groups of people with interests in development. Although these relationships may entail tension and misunderstanding, they often have productive outcomes. Indeed, the productivity of such relations often depends on the ontological and epistemological differences these engender (cf. Englund 2011; Venkatesan 2010).

Whilst contributors to the volume question monolithic visions of anthropology and development by paying attention to heterogeneity within both, they also question the tendency to assume that anthropology and development are necessarily categorically opposed projects. Rather than assume an opposition between anthropology and development as the self-evident starting point of analysis, contributors take the issue of how these practices may be similar or different as an open question. Understanding how anthropology and development use knowledge differently requires understanding both sets of practices *in the same terms* (Green this volume). This leads to a more nuanced account of overlapping ways in which both anthropologists and development workers operate.

Acting and Understanding

The volume brings to light a more reflexive understanding of anthropological practice by moving beyond the forms of critical engagement that have characterized anthropological commentaries on development. As Green (this volume) suggests, this critical stance amounts in Latourian (Latour 1987, 1993, 1999) terms to an asymmetry, since only one half of the categorical divide – development – is subjected to critical scrutiny. Where anthropologists have assumed the superiority of anthropological knowledge as more complex and sophisticated, they have tended to overlook the ways in which development practices may in fact shed light on the assumptions and practices through which anthropologists work. In particular, contributors to the volume reveal how development practice sheds light on the relationship between understanding and action in anthropology.

Within the anthropology of development (e.g., Gardner and Lewis 1996; Olivier de Sardan 2005), as in anthropological studies more generally (e.g., Fortun 2001; Tsing 2005), the question of how anthropology is to have more impact on the world on which it comments has become increasingly central. Anthropologists of development have thus been vexed by their critiques' lack of tangible impact. This perceived inability to produce tangible changes in practice has often been taken as a stimulus to produce more, better or different forms of critique. Perhaps it should be unsurprising, for anthropologists whose own actions are routinely directed at the production of texts, that a failure to produce desired impacts should be taken as a failure of those texts. Arguably this turns on a misguided belief in the capacity of texts to act in and of themselves.

Throughout this book, accounts of the relationship between acting and understanding call into question any straightforward opposition between anthropology and development as one between understanding and acting. Rather than imagine 'action' as a self-evident domain of practice, various contributors reveal 'action' as a form that orients practice in particular ways. Thus in the context of an Episcopal food bank in Florence, Trundle elucidates how charity workers' commitment to 'doing' emerges as a particular 'aesthetic'. In this way she describes how charity workers direct attention to the means rather than the ends of 'action'. In the very different context of international development practices in Tanzania, Green makes a parallel point, highlighting the social practices through which development workers make knowledge 'act'. Her suggestion is that development knowledge, in contrast to academic knowledge, is itself understood as a form of 'action'. Unlike academics, development practitioners are concerned to make ideas work – to make concepts have effects. This is not simply a matter of using more applied forms of knowledge, but of orienting social and institutional practices in such a way that their effects are made apparent. In other words, it is not only that anthropologists and development practitioners have different ways of doing knowledge, but also that they have different ways of representing knowledge within their own practices.

In this way, contributors to the volume produce a more nuanced understanding of the importance of 'action' in development, by questioning the taken-for-granted status of the term in much development practice. At the same time, ethnographic engagement with these ideas and practices leads to a reconsideration of the ideas and practices through which anthropologists themselves operate. Despite the reflexive turn that has reoriented anthropological analyses since the 1980s, anthropologists have been reluctant to apprehend their own disciplinary practices anthropologically (Green this volume). As such, 'reflexivity' has tended to refer to a heightened attention to anthropology's modes of representation, both textually and as they have emerged in relation to fieldwork. By contrast, contributors to this volume highlight in different ways how understanding development practice sheds new light on the social relations and practices that underpin anthropological work.

In particular, contributors highlight how anthropological practice is underpinned by a break between field and desk (cf. Mosse 2006). In this vein, both Green and Kelly suggest that anthropology routinely separates understanding from action, abstracting anthropological theories and 'knowledge' from the specific social relations through which they emerge. Seen from this perspective, fieldwork is the means to the end of knowledge, just as social relations established through participant observation are imagined as the means to the end of textually elucidated theory. This insight is used by Green to highlight the mutually eclipsing forms of knowledge through which anthropology and development operate.

Seen from this perspective, anthropology has largely failed to impact upon development practice not because it has failed to produce sufficiently compelling critiques, but because anthropologists misunderstand the social practices through which development workers make knowledge 'act', or at least appear to do so. Yet an appreciation of the different ways in which anthropologists and development workers use knowledge also has potentially more positive applications. Thus Kelly proposes that scientific trials in The Gambia might offer anthropology a way of reorienting its own fieldwork practices. Although these practices may appear problematic, they bring to light how social relations are both the practice and the product of social research. This suggests the possibility that anthropologists need to reappraise the role and importance of such relations, not just as the means to the end of knowledge, but as sources of insight and transformation in their own right. Similarly, Green suggests that if anthropologists and development workers are to come together, this will not simply take place through new forms of knowledge, but through new forms of social relationship. At the same time, anthropologists do already sustain many different kinds of relationships with development workers and beneficiaries. Hence we also need to pay more attention to relationships that are already in existence but rarely explicitly valued.

Although various contributors thus highlight the problems of a naïve belief in the transformative potential of academic critique, this does not amount to an outright dismissal of critical scholarship as a potential basis for action. Rather, the volume moves beyond the relatively abstract terms in which post-development theorists have dismissed 'development', in order to produce more differentiated forms of critique. As Friedman insightfully points out, if we shed the post-development conception of development as a product of Western knowledge and power, we not only produce a more nuanced understanding of development practice, but in doing so create spaces for different, more creative and more flexible types of intervention. It is perfectly possible for anthropologists to support particular development projects on the basis of ethnographic understanding of the situation in which these emerge, without supporting Western knowledge and power per se. By the same token, anthropological critiques are more likely to shape development practice when they emerge in relation to specific projects, programmes or discourses.

Contributors also highlight the need to be aware of the different contexts in which their own knowledge circulates. In the context of anthropological dealings with development organizations, abstractly framed academic critiques may have limited purchase – not because they are academically problematic, but because of the different ways in which development organizations and academics construct knowledge. Yet in seeking to bring about social transformation or improvement, direct relationships with development institutions are not the only means available. Thus Gledhill and Hita highlight the potential for anthropologists to undermine neoliberal visions of development by lending direct support to those who are negatively impacted by them. By the same token, Baviskar writes of displaced and dispossessed groups of people in India with an eye to employing the experience of subalterns to critical effect. Although it is unlikely that such anthropological interventions can entirely ameliorate the deleterious effects of the processes they write about, this does not mean that such interventions cannot be useful or transformative. How or whether they are so does not depend upon their academic validity in a narrow sense, but on their success in enrolling support. In the context of Brazil, Gledhill and Hita thus draw attention to the potential importance of collaborations with NGOs and community organizations. In the context of India, Baviskar illuminates how the success of academic critiques in part depends on their effectiveness in enrolling media support.

Conclusion

If what unifies the contributors to this volume is precisely their commitment to ethnographic engagement, it should not be surprising that the chapters themselves provide a startlingly diverse set of descriptions and analyses. Through these, development is differentiated as both (and simultaneously) an ethnographic and a theoretical concern. Yet beyond the different perspectives encompassed, this heterogeneity of ethnographic and theoretical perspectives makes its own point. Collectively the essays do not simply add up to a new perspective within the anthropology of development, but expose the limits of a project framed in those terms. Our suggestion is not that new theories or insights are needed to reenergize this sub-discipline of anthropology, but that the very terms in which it is set up need rethinking. Broadly speaking, we have pointed to three main problems with the anthropology of development: that 'development' has been imagined in insufficiently differentiated terms; that correspondingly there has been a failure to appreciate the diversity of ways in which anthropologists engage in/with 'development'; and that the anthropological imagination of this relationship in asymmetrical terms leads to a problematic application of anthropological theories 'to' development contexts.

By contrast, the approaches represented within this book are more accurately summarized as 'anthropologies with development in them'. In one sense this admittedly cumbersome term captures a shift signalled by others from an analytic concern with development to a more ethnographic understanding of the meanings and resonances that the term acquires in particular social contexts (e.g. Olivier de Sardan 2005; Venkatesan 2009, 2010). At another level and perhaps more profoundly, the term also points to a need to frame such ethnographies as much through the lens of a wider regional and anthropological literature as in relation to other studies of 'development' (see Yarrow 2011). By locating issues of development more squarely in relation to mainstream anthropological concerns, our hope is not only that a more nuanced understanding of the different ways of imagining and defining the concept of 'development' will result, but also (consequently) that in the process, anthropology will grow through extension and refinement of its core concepts. Our suggestion is that this can only happen when anthropologists relinquish the belief that critique should provide both the means and the ends of engagement with development issues.

At the start of the chapter we alluded to the paradox that the critical unmasking of 'development' brought about by over two decades of sustained deconstruction erases hope in the prospect of positive social change. This volume reveals a level of ethnographic complexity from which it would be churlish to argue for the replacement of this predominantly 'negative' vision of 'development' with a more 'positive' one. Yet a genuinely ethnographic understanding of the contexts in which ideas of development are made to matter does at least open up spaces for hope (Miyazaki 2004; Yarrow 2010). As contributors show, development is not one thing but many, and not all of them are bad. It is only by moving beyond the ideologically charged rhetoric that has attended many of the anthropological critiques of development, that we will come to see what development can mean in a more nuanced and perhaps more productive light. Whilst it is certainly not our intention to produce applied solutions to development problems, in different ways the chapters open up new understandings of what development is and might mean. It remains our hope that these provide the grounds for imagining different, more varied, humane and just kinds of future.

NOTES

1. A key argument of this book is that it is unhelpful to understand development as a form of 'western' knowledge, constituted, as it is, through highly heterogeneous practices and relations that render the category analytically meaningless. We use the terms 'West' and 'Western', in a purely descriptive sense when referring to broader debates in which the terms have featured. Specifically, these terms are used to refer to a mode of thinking and operating that posits that planned intervention in line with certain 'universal' values is both possible and desirable.

BIBLIOGRAPHY

Apthorpe, R. 1997. 'Writing Development Policy and Policy Analysis Plain or Clear: On Language, Genre and Power', in C. Shore and S. Wright (eds), *Anthropology of Policy: Critical Perspectives on Governance and Power*. London: Routledge, pp. 43–58.

Arce, A. and N. Long (eds). 2000. *Anthropology, Development and Modernities: Exploring Discourses, Counter-Tendencies and Violence*. London: Routledge.

Asad, T. 2003. *Formations of the Secular: Christianity, Islam, Modernity*. Stanford, CA: Stanford University Press.

Bornstein, E. 2003. *The Spirit of Development: Protestant NGOs, Morality and Economics in Zimbabwe*. New York and London: Routledge.

Cooper, F. and R. Packard. 1997a. *International Development and the Social Sciences: Essays in the History and Politics of Knowledge*. Berkeley, Los Angeles, London: University of California Press.

———. 1997b. 'Introduction', in F. Cooper and R. Packard (eds), *International Development and the Social Sciences: Essays on the History and Politics of Knowledge*. Berkeley, Los Angeles and London: University of California Press, pp. 1–41.

Crush, J. 1995. *Power of Development*. London and New York: Routledge.

Englund, H. 2006. *Prisoners of Freedom: Human Rights and the African Poor*. Berkeley: University of California Press.

———. 2011. 'The Anthropologist and His Poor', in E. Bornstein and P. Redfield (eds), *Forces of Compassion: Humanitarianism between Ethics and Politics*. Santa Fe, NM: SAR Press: 71–93.

Escobar, A. 1995. *Encountering Development: The Making and Unmaking of the Third World*. Princeton: Princeton University Press.

Fabian, J. 1983. *Time and the Other: How Anthropology Makes Its Object*. New York: Columbia University Press.

Fairhead, J. and M. Leach. 1997. 'Webs of Power and the Construction of Environmental Policy Problems: Forest Loss in Guinea', in R. Grillo and R. Stirrat (eds), *Discourses of Development: Anthropological Perspectives*. Oxford: Berg, pp. 35–57.

Fechter, A-M., and H. Hindman. 2011a. 'Introduction', in A-M. Fechter and H. Hindman (eds), *Inside the Everyday Lives of Development Workers: The Challenges and Futures of Aidland.*, Sterling: Kumerian Press.

Fechter, A-M., and H. Hindman. 2011b. *Inside the Everyday Lives of Development Workers: The Challenges and Futures of Aidland.*, Sterling: Kumerian Press.

Ferguson, J. 1994. *The Anti-Politics Machine: 'Development', Depoliticisation, and Bureaucratic Power in Lesotho*. Minneapolis and London: University of Minnesota Press.

———. 2006. *Global Shadows: Africa in the Neoliberal World Order*. Durham and London: Duke University Press.

Fortun, K. 2001. *Advocacy After Bhopal: Environmentalism, Disaster, New Global Orders*. Chicago and London: University of Chicago Press.

Friedman, J. T. 2006. 'Beyond the Post-structural Impulse in the Anthropology of Development', *Dialectical Anthropology* 30: 201–225.

Gardner, K. and D. Lewis. 1996. *Anthropology, Development and the Post-Modern Challenge*. London and Sterling, VA: Pluto Press.

Green, M. 2003. 'Globalizing Development in Tanzania: Policy Franchising through Participatory Project Management', *Critique of Anthropology* 23: 123–143.

Grillo, R. D. and R. L. Stirrat (eds). 1997. *Discourses of Development: Anthropological Perspectives*. Oxford and New York: Berg.

Hobart, M. 1993a. *An Anthropological Critique of Development: The Growth of Ignorance*. London and New York: Routledge.

———. 1993b. 'Introduction: The Growth of Ignorance?' in M. Hobart (ed.), *An Anthropological Critique of Development: The Growth of Ignorance*. London and New York: Routledge.

Latour, B. 1987. *Science in Action: How to Follow Scientists and Engineers Through Society*. Cambridge, MA: Harvard University Press.

———. 1993. *We Have Never Been Modern*. London: Harvester Wheatsheaf.

———. 1999. *Pandora's Hope: Essays on the Reality of Science Studies*. London: Harvard University Press.

Lewis, D. and D. Mosse. 2006. 'Theoretical Approaches to Brokerage and Translation in Development', in D. Lewis and D. Mosse (eds), *Development Brokers and Translators: The Ethnography of Aid and Agencies*. Bloomfield, CT: Kumerian, pp. 1–27.

Li Murray, T. 2007. *The Will to Improve: Governmentality, Development and the Practice of Politics*. Durham and London: Duke University Press.

Long, N. and A. Long. 1992. *Battlefields of Knowledge: The Interlocking of Theory and Practice in Social Research and Development*. London: Routledge.

Tsing, A. L. 2005. *Friction: An Ethnography of Global Connection*. Princeton: Princeton University Press.

Mitchell, T. 2002. *Rule of Experts: Egypt, Techno-Politics, Modernity*. Berkeley and Los Angeles: University of California Press.

Miyazaki, H. 2004. *The Method of Hope: Anthropology, Philosophy and Fijian Knowledge*. Stanford, CA: Stanford University Press.

Mosse, D. 2005. *Cultivating Development: An Ethnography of Aid Policy and Practice*. London: Pluto Press.

———. 2006. 'Anti-social Anthropology? Objectivity, Objection and the Ethnography of Public Policy Professional Communities', *Journal of the Royal Anthropological Institute* 12: 935–956.

Olivier de Sardan, J.-P. 2005. *Anthropology and Development: Understanding Contemporary Social Change*. London and New York: Zed Books.

Pigg, S. L. 1997. '"Found in Most Traditional Societies": Traditional Medical Practitioners between Culture and Development', in F. Cooper and R. Packard (eds), *International Development and the Social Sciences*. Berkeley, Los Angeles and London: University of California Press, pp. 259–290.

Porter, D. J. 1995. 'Scenes from Childhood: The Homesickness of Development Discourses', in J. Crush (ed.), *Power of Development*. London and New York: Routledge, pp. 63–86.

Reed, A. 2003. *Papua New Guinea's Last Place*. New York and London: Berghahn Books.

Riles, A. 2001. *The Network Inside Out*. Ann Arbor: The University of Michigan Press.

Sachs, W. 1992. *The Development Dictionary: A Guide to Knowledge as Power*. London: Zed Books.

Shore, C. and S. Wright. 1997. 'Policy: A New Field of Anthropology', in C. Shore and S. Wright (eds), *Anthropology of Policy: Critical Perspectives on Governance and Power*. London and New York: Routledge, pp. 3–39.

Strathern, M. 1987. 'Out of Context: The Persuasive Fictions of Anthropology', *Current Anthropology* 28: 251–281.

———. 1991. *Partial Connections*. Savage, MD: Rowman and Littlefield.

Venkatesan, S. 2009. *Craft Matters: Artisans, Development and the Indian Nation*. Hyderabad: Orient Blackswan.

———. 2010. 'Learning to Weave; Weaving to Learn . . . What?' *Journal of the Royal Anthropological Institute* 16: S158–S175.
Yarrow, T. 2008a. 'Life/History: Personal Narratives of Development in Ghana', *Africa* 78: 334–358.
———. 2008b. 'Paired Opposites: Dualism in Development and Anthropology', *Critique of Anthropology* 28: 426–444.
———. 2011. Development Beyond Politics: Aid, Activism and NGOs in Ghana. Basingstoke: Palgrave Macmillan. .

PART I

Anthropology and Development Reconsidered

CHAPTER 1

On Text and Con-text

Towards an Anthropology in Development

John T. Friedman

This chapter addresses the fields of international development and anthropology in their relation to one another. The set of concerns that set it in motion implicate development practitioners and anthropologists alike. With respect to the former, it is difficult not to overlook the tendency of those working in the development field to offer rather simplistic, static and monocausal explanations for the shortcomings (or complete failures) of their projects. In this sense, and quite ironically so, many development practitioners explain away the limited effects of their projects by pointing a finger at the very conditions they set out to address. Accompanying this inclination to deflect responsibility, practitioners also tend to overestimate the importance of development more generally. As Crewe and Harrison point out, 'it is easy to forget that, for many intended to be on the receiving end, the effects of what developers do are peripheral or even entirely irrelevant' (1998: 1).

Since its formalization as a field of international practice, the development sector has remained sceptical of anthropology's ability to help ameliorate the conditions associated with global poverty and inequality. The turn towards a more holistic human welfare approach in development has helped reduce apprehensions within some agencies, but anthropology's marginal standing within the wider development landscape continues.

In those few instances when agencies have striven to bring anthropology to bear on development outcomes, the efforts have yielded only limited success. In part, this lacklustre performance relates to the fact that development's *modus operandi* rarely, if ever, accommodates the

Notes for this section begin on page 40

needs of a vigorous anthropology. The development anthropologist is thus forced to make significant methodological compromises. Not only is the customary 12–24 months of participant observation reduced to a mere 2–4 weeks within the scope of a development project, but also the more open-ended anthropological approach is replaced by a rigid and outcome-oriented research strategy. The insights that result from such efforts are often relatively shallow, limiting the extent and impact of their application.

These ways of 'doing' anthropology in the development sector are also one of the main reasons why, in relation to the wider field of anthropology, development anthropologists are often viewed as being much more *of development* than *of anthropology*. The other reason why so many academic anthropologists continue to treat their colleagues in development as disciplinary pariahs relates to the moral and normative mandates that accompany them to the field. Many academic anthropologists feel uncomfortable with any non-culturally relative approach.

If anthropologists have been forced to make significant methodological compromises in the practice of development, then what might be said of those on the academic side of the discipline? Though there are some noteworthy exceptions that resonate with the position to be adopted herein (e.g., Long and Long 1992; Olivier de Sardan 2005), during the past quarter-century the anthropology of development has remained closely tied to the post-structuralist paradigm. Inspired by the work of Michel Foucault, this perspective asserts that through the institutional production of development discourse Western countries dominate, manage and exploit the 'third world'. These critics call for the dismantling of development discourse as the only way to transcend development's domination and exploitation (e.g., Crush 1995; Escobar 1995; Ferguson 1990; Grillo and Stirrat 1997; Rahnema and Bawtree 1997).

Any honest assessment of anthropology's post-structuralist critique of development must acknowledge its important contributions. The critique has generated awareness about development discourse's ability to shape and construct global poverty, and it has helped us realize the extent to which the industrial West exerts control over processes of global change. In a nutshell, the approach has forced us to recognize the important relationship between poverty, knowledge and power. For these reasons, the post-structural critics have moved us beyond development's failed outcomes and imperfect practices in order to challenge an all too normative and self-evidently taken world view. But despite generating such critical awareness – and herein lies the problem – there is little evidence to suggest that the post-structuralists have contributed much to the improvement of the material realities of the world's poor and disenfranchised. In the end, then, this line of critique has revealed itself as mostly an intellectual exercise. As I will argue more extensively below, the anthropology of development's continued over-reliance on post-structuralism has ultimately limited the discipline's ability to contribute positively to the lives of those in the so-called developing world.

From both the academic and applied sides of our field, we are then left with a rather stark contradiction about anthropology more generally. How can a field of study that is so fully committed to humanity have such difficulties when it comes to acting in ways that improve the conditions under which that humanity exists? The burden of this problem rests on the backs of both anthropologists and development practitioners. As for the former, it is high time to re-balance the anthropology of development's overly structural interpretations, ones that privilege structure over agency, hegemony over dialectics, and text over context. By conceiving development as a dialectical encounter, rather than only a hegemonic one, and by returning to participant-observation and long-term fieldwork in grass-roots settings, rather than continued discourse analysis, anthropologists can engage more fully, understand more comprehensively and, most importantly, contribute more effectively to improving the quality of life for people in the 'third world'. For their part, development professionals need to recognize and accept the value of anthropology in development. Thus, this chapter also stands as an attempt to urge development practitioners and their agencies to embrace the field of anthropology, but to do so on anthropology's, rather than development's, own terms.

There is indeed some scope for a more productive and progressive relationship between development practice and the anthropology of development. In what follows, I present an ethnographic account of a high-profile case of development in northwest Namibia as a means to reflect on the dynamics of development more generally. The nuanced understanding of 'development' that emerges out my analysis of the proposed Kunene River Hydropower Scheme suggests the opportunity for a more significant anthropological contribution in the field of development practice. In trying to forge a productive synthesis between knowledge and practice, between an 'anthropology of development' and a 'development anthropology', I aim to chart a possible path forward towards a more efficacious anthropology *in* development.

On Text

Post-structuralism is premised on the fact that we live in a world shaped by language. Written and oral texts afford us the opportunity to communicate about things in specific ways, and they contribute to the constitution of discourses that govern our knowledge, and thus our actions. In relying on this particular insight, the post-structuralist critique of development establishes both its theoretical and methodological orientations. Theoretically, the critique argues for the power and strength of development discourse, and specifically for its ability to expand and perpetuate global poverty while simultaneously excluding the possibility of any alternatives. Here, development discourse defines and creates non-Western peoples as 'under-developed', thereby actually creating the conditions of poverty that it purports to address. As for the central methodological component, this body of scholarship asserts that if we are to understand how development discourse works, then we need to deconstruct its texts so as to unpack meaning. Discourse deconstruction is also meant to create the space to imagine alternatives to development.

As already mentioned, the post-structuralist critique of development has a great deal of merit. However, it also has a number of very significant shortcomings. For example, the critique views development discourse as monolithic, asserting the existence of a single, hegemonic discourse when there are in fact multiple discourses of development in circulation. Furthermore, it is overly structural in its orientation, and, as a result, it has a problematic relationship with issues of agency. Also (and quite ironically), this anthropologically driven approach takes its methodological point of departure from the top, that is, from the view of planners and institutions instead of the so-called targets of development. Since many scholars have addressed these and other problems elsewhere (e.g., Everett 1997; Kiely 1999; Rossi 2004), there is no need to rehearse them all again.

In order to make the connection between the anthropology of development's lacklustre set of material results and its continued overreliance on the post-structuralist paradigm, it is useful to emphasize one of the critique's most limiting shortcomings. The problem referred to is this: even though the post-structuralists have effectively linked power to poverty, their critique remains fundamentally apolitical. The reason why these anthropologists have a difficult time translating their insights into action is because they embrace an overly romanticized version of cultural relativism. Such an uncritical acceptance of 'the local' also leads these anthropologists to quickly dismiss outsiders' genuine attempts at promoting change as inherently neo-colonial. But it is more than just a simple unwillingness to act on the part of these anthropologists; there is also a great degree of incapacity involved. Since the post-structuralist critics conceive 'development' as a product of the deployment of

'Western' knowledge as power, they cannot simultaneously articulate their own set of alternatives for development and/or take part in development practice without falling prey to their own critique. Constructive intervention or action would open these anthropologists up to the charge of deploying their own knowledge as power. It is this conundrum that ultimately limits a great number of progressive academic anthropologists in making practical inroads in the field of development practice.

* * * * *

Located in Namibia's Kunene Region, the vast area known as Kaokoland is home to approximately 30,000 people. Most of the region's inhabitants reside in small settlements and villages where they earn a livelihood from semi-nomadic pastoralism, small-scale agriculture and the collection of wild foods. Governmental and other services are distributed sparsely throughout the region, and outside the regional capital of Opuwo (population 6,000) few spots are connected to telephone, electricity and water distribution networks. In comparison to the other twelve regions in Namibia, Kunene Region as a whole receives the country's second lowest per capita development budget (United Nations Development Programme 2000).

In Southern Africa, Kaokoland's reputation is also built upon a less empirically based inventory, upon a discourse that has been termed 'the Kaoko myth' (Miescher and Henrichsen 2000). Ever since German colonial times, written and oral accounts of the region have depicted the landscape as wild, exotic, harsh and isolated; meanwhile Kaokolanders themselves have been constructed as traditional, even 'natural', and as a people who are threatened by the debilitating onslaught of modernity.

Kaokoland also has a distinctive reputation among those who take an interest in, or work on, development-related activities in the region: ministerial personnel, national politicians, foreign aid workers, journalists, missionaries, local community leaders and ordinary Kaokolanders themselves. These commentators tend to share the view that the development work in Kaokoland is particularly challenging. And though the different stakeholders agree on the nature of their work, they differ substantially in their attempts to account for the difficulties. Just as modernization theorists argued half a century ago, a set of these 'texts' contends that local tradition and culture present the main obstacle, and that Kaokolanders are inherently conservative. Some practitioners point towards a lack of education as the main difficulty, or Kaokolanders' obsession with cattle ownership; meanwhile other observers attribute Kaokoland's development challenges to the physical constraints of geography. As for the residents of the region, many of them lay the blame on politicians for denying this opposition stronghold its rightful share of the national development budget.

From a personal standpoint too, after having lived and researched in the region, it is difficult for me to deny the overriding observation that the Kaokoland development process is indeed a challenging one. Throughout the past decade I have witnessed a number of promising projects fall apart, while other genuine initiatives never managed to move beyond the planning stages. The most notorious of these projects is my main case in point. To date, the proposed Kunene River Hydropower Scheme, known more popularly as the Epupa dam project, has to be classified as a development failure. In the late 1990s, the Namibian government spent US$5 million on an incomplete feasibility study that yielded little more than controversy and continued uncertainty for those who would be affected. Thus, from my vantage point as a former Namibian development worker turned anthropologist, I observe similarly: developing Kaokoland is indeed challenging.

Like others, I wish to extend beyond observation alone by offering my own explanation as to why many of these challenges exist and persist, an analysis that emerges out of my anthropological research in and on the region. For the remainder of the chapter, the focus remains on the evolution of my learning as it relates to (Kaokoland) 'development'. In detailing this research process, I convey an anthropological view on the development challenges facing Kaokolanders, and I distil a wider set of conclusions relating to the nature of both development practice and the anthropology of development more generally. Both sets of insights, I will argue, might be constructively fed back into the ways that we 'do anthropology in development', both in Kaokoland and elsewhere.

* * * * *

My first attempt to understand the development process in Kaokoland began in 1999 when I undertook a small research project on the dynamics of the proposed Kunene River Hydropower Scheme (Friedman 2000). The data sources for this initial study involved an extensive literature review and a period of interviewing and fieldwork in Namibia, though *not* in Kaokoland itself. By that time, the Namibian government's proposal to dam the Kunene River was already notorious. Like most large dams, the proposal drew the attention and involvement of a wide range of actors at the local, national and international levels.

This early study of the Epupa project was an attempt to understand how these various interest groups in the debate asserted their respective positions. The Namibian government and numerous Kaokolanders themselves were supporting the project on the grounds that it would lead to modernization, economic growth, and regional and national development. These project supporters tended to construct their Epupa opponents as backward, traditional, conservative and in need of development. Those who opposed the dam – environmental and indigenous rights organizations, as well as many of those living in northern Kaokoland – based their arguments on the negative ecological, social and cultural impacts of the project.

What I conveyed through that first research project was a view of the Epupa development process that privileged the dominant discourses emerging out of it. In other words, this was an analysis that showcased the voices that were making themselves heard in the voluminous amount of text that had been generated in response to the project. This set of sources was very valuable indeed, but it is important to emphasize that it contained many silences, many absences. My analysis was only one view on the Epupa process, and it was quite a limited one at that, precisely because I did not research the topic among ordinary Kaokolanders themselves. Here, then, is where the value of anthropological fieldwork comes in: it was not until after I had lived and researched in Kaokoland that I began to understand the dynamics of Epupa development in a very different light.

On Con-text

The opportunity came my way in 2000/01 while I was undertaking fieldwork in the region for what I thought was a completely unrelated research project. But after having lived there for a couple of months an interesting problem emerged. My interest in customary law eventually led me to the offices of Paulus Tjavara, the 'Chief of Kaokoland', or so I was told. As head of the Otjikaoko Traditional Authority, the chief oversaw a number of headmen, most of whom adjudicated in Kaokoland's traditional courts. Chief Tjavara soon introduced me to a few of these local leaders, and they, in turn, offered me the opportunity to observe and discuss court proceedings with them. What began in a most promising fashion, however, soon gave way to frustrations and doubts. During the ensuing weeks, I gained access to neither traditional courts nor the leaders that presided over them.

But then one afternoon I muttered some innocent words to an Otjikaoko representative: 'I would be interested to hear the history one of these days.' That was all it took, just the one sentence. Over the next few days, leaders of the Otjikaoko group became available. There were no more delays, or transport problems, or 'other matters to attend to';

instead, 'the history' began to flow. Here, then, was my anthropological problem: Why did these leaders display such an intense need to unload 'the history'?

I continued researching this question, and during the ensuing weeks I began learning about a local political dynamic that lay hidden to me and to other outsiders who lacked the requisite socio-political context. Chief Tjavara, I came to realize, was not the only 'Chief of Kaokoland', nor was the Otjikaoko Traditional Authority the only authority in the region. There were also Chief Kapuka Thom and the Vita Thom Royal House, whose supporters looked to them as the region's rightful traditional representatives.

As my time in Kaokoland passed, I came to understand the depth of the rivalry between these two groupings. The contest appeared to shape all matters of local politics, and it seemed to structure the relationship between Kaokolanders and the state more generally (Friedman 2005, 2011). But the chieftaincy dispute reached well beyond the realm of politics proper. The factional dynamic also manifested itself with respect to ethnicity, kinship, ritual and economy. Most importantly for my purposes here, I also came to recognize the extent to which the dispute became entangled in, and often derailed, planned development projects. It was this observation that eventually led me back – quite unexpectedly – to the so-called Epupa dam project.

* * * * *

In detailing this case of development I will not begin my exposition as one might anticipate – in the mid 1990s, when planning for the Epupa project started in earnest. Instead, I now venture into the colonial archives, the place where I was led in my efforts to better understand the historical contexts underlying the present political moment in Kaokoland. My point of departure is thus nearly a century ago in 1917, a year that was marked by two important events for the residents of Kaokoland.

First, in that momentous year Vita Thom and his group of followers left Angola to settle in Kaokoland. There, Thom's group found a number of others already resident in the region, including a community under the leadership of Muhona Katiti (whose descendents would help constitute the present-day Otjikaoko group). The second major event unfolded only a few months later, when Major C. N. Manning undertook the South African colonial regime's first official tour of the region. This expedition marked the beginning of *de facto* colonial rule in Kaokoland.

During his tour, Manning spent most of his time investigating the 'hostile dispute'[1] between Thom and Katiti, both of whom were native Otjiherero speakers. The observations Manning made during this tour went on to shape a set of policies that would, some eighty years later, intricately affect the Epupa development process. In particular, Manning could not detect the distinctive, geographically bounded tribes he had been conditioned to look for, but only groups of individuals who ascribed to the authority of specific leaders, of whom Thom and Katiti were the two most prominent. Most importantly, though, Manning observed a number of personal differences between these two influential figures. According to him, Thom was an 'enlightened character' and 'a highly intelligent native' who wore Western-style clothing, maintained a relatively settled lifestyle and had command of some European languages. In contrast, Katiti was seen as 'a real savage'. Manning concluded his tour by appointing immigrant Vita Thom as chief over northern Kaokoland.[2]

These two local leaders remained arch-rivals until Katiti's death in 1931, and Thom continued to (indirectly) rule the region until his own death in 1937. That latter event offered the then Native Commissioner the opportunity to consolidate government control through the introduction of a tribal council. This supposedly more democratic method of rule was meant to represent the interests of all Kaokolanders. However, all of its members were drawn from Thom's group, while those who had been under the authority of the deceased Katiti found none of their leaders sitting on this ruling body.[3]

The colonial archives reveal that up until the early 1950s South Africa's administrators continued to look towards these select Thom group leaders to rule over all Kaokolanders. In 1952, however, members of Katiti's group began objecting publicly to what they perceived as Thom group domination.[4] During the ensuing two decades, issues relating to headman appointments, animal disease control, court verdicts, and grazing and water rights sparked rounds of hostilities, and even a few cases of violence, between the two groups. As Namibia moved towards independence throughout the 1980s, the conflict also began to seep into national party politics.

Namibia's independence in 1990 brought a new set of policies relating to the country's traditional leaders. Among other things, the new government chose to pursue a policy of formally recognizing the country's traditional authorities. The government's decision to recognize one of Kaokoland's competing chieftaincies would certainly strengthen that group's political position, and at all levels. As one might imagine, then, the new government's policy stimulated a new round of strategic manoeuvring in Kaokoland and simultaneously rekindled the century-old factional animosities.

For Namibia's traditional leaders and their constituencies, official government recognition offers a host of political and economic benefits. The leaders from both sides were keenly aware of the stakes, and thus throughout the 1990s they worked tirelessly to establish the legitimacy of their respective chief. These efforts took numerous forms, including the construction and dissemination of origin myths, the 'revival' of royal lineages, and the formalization of oral history through the production of written documents. In attempting to assert their legitimacy, the Thom and Otjikaoko groups opted to bury their deceased leaders in the symbolically powerful regional capital, rather than in the village as custom would dictate; they redefined their political party alliances; and they tried to entrap unsuspecting anthropologists to their cause.

It was precisely within this local historical and political context that planning for the Epupa dam project began in earnest, and therefore it is in this light that the dynamics of this particular case of development should be understood and analysed. The main point of what may seem like a historical tangent is this: when the Namibian government proposed its plans to build the Epupa dam, the initiative was in no way being introduced into a neutral, history-less or apolitical social field. Rather, when the project's planners began their work, they unknowingly inserted themselves into a Kaokoland that remained embroiled in a 75-year-long factional dispute. Thus they had to contend with local leaders who were busy positioning themselves as 'the chief of Kaokoland' in an effort to capture the prize of government recognition.

* * * * *

With this context in place, I now shift to the Epupa project more directly. Here, I aim to show the extent to which the development process in Kaokoland was shaped inextricably by the region's internal socio-political landscape and, in particular, by the dynamics surrounding Kaokoland's long-standing factional dispute. Given the fact that a very significant amount of human and financial resources continue to be invested in this proposed project, it is quite relevant to highlight that not a single planning document or project report has ever even acknowledged the existence and/or influence of the local dispute.

The first insight that anthropological research afforded me was quite an accidental one. In broaching the Epupa project in discussions with leaders and ordinary Kaokolanders from both sides of the factional divide, I began to realize that a person's position on the dam correlated with his/her traditional authority affiliation. In almost all cases, the leaders and constituents of the Otjikaoko group opposed the project, while almost all affiliates of the Thom group supported it. I wondered if these sociological alignments might be a product of the local conflict.

My initial inquiries on the subject yielded only the standard public discourses, those with which I was already familiar from my previous research. For example, leaders of the Otjikaoko group pointed to the lack of local employment benefits from the project, the need for resettlement, and the cultural importance of graves that were to be flooded. Members of the Thom House expressed their position of support in familiar terms as well, speaking mostly of the project's development benefits.

As my time in the field progressed, though, I began mapping the events relating to Epupa, the recognition process and the factional dispute, one over the other, whereupon it soon became evident to me that these three issues were indeed bound tightly together. Local leaders, it seemed, were not assessing the merits of the proposed Epupa dam based on a strict cost-benefit development analysis. Instead, leaders from the two groups established their collective position, first and foremost, in reaction to the stance of their adversaries. A close Thom group informant eventually explained:

> Whoever said 'yes' first, the other party said 'no', from the start. The Thoms immediately supported the project because the Otjikaoko Traditional Authority opposed it, even without having arguments in favour of the project. Later on, both sides gave reasons for supporting or opposing it, reasons which were immaterial.

An Otjikaoko group insider offered a slightly different exposition, but the implications of his accounting remained quite the same:

> Because the Thom House and the Otjikaoko House are always in conflict, when one supports, the other opposes. Otjikaoko first hesitated in taking a position, while the Thoms supported Epupa from the beginning. But after the Thoms supported it publicly, then Otjikaoko opposed it publicly. . . . With respect to the graves, land and grazing issues as the reason for . . . [Otjikaoko's] opposition to the project, that all came from the feasibility study, not from the people.

In treating development as a means to 'manage and control, and, in many ways, even create the Third World' (Escobar 1984: 384), post-structuralist critics direct their analyses towards what might be thought of as the development sector's 'hidden transcript' (Scott 1990). In the Epupa case, however, the hidden transcript belongs to the so-called subjects of development themselves. The Epupa debate is indeed a debate about development, but only at one level. Within Kaokoland, and thus among those who will be most directly affected by the project, the debate is but another round in the long history of struggle over power and authority in the region. Here, 'development' is as much the outcome of internal socio-political processes as it is the product of a hegemonic developmentalist discourse. The factional dispute and the Epupa project feed and shape one another; they are both part and parcel of the dialectical processes of development.

Towards an Anthropology in Development

How might this ethnography reflect on the relationship between anthropology and development more generally? What implications does this particular case of Namibian development have for anthropologists? In what ways does it 'speak' to development professionals working in Kaokoland and elsewhere? Here, I address these questions in an effort to create the space for a more efficacious anthropology *in* development.

The case of development detailed in this chapter leads me back once again to anthropology's dominant post-structuralist critique, and in particular to the ways it impinges upon anthropologists' ability to act on poverty and suffering in the world today. In denying the polysemic character of development, post-structuralist critics have eliminated the agency of both the subjects of development *and* anthropologists alike. However, the Epupa case reveals the development process as something quite different, which suggests to me a possible path forward via two interventions that might help move us beyond our current post-structural impasse. Here, I suggest a simultaneous theoretical reorientation and methodological reclamation in the anthropology of development.

The theoretical reorientation proposed takes its lead from analyses of the relationship between social practice, historical process and culture in the colonial encounter. In particular, Jean Comaroff (1985) has invoked an understanding of the present as being the product of a 'dialectical process in a double sense'. In her account, the ethnographic present emerges out of the interplay between social structure and human agency on the one hand, and the dominant and subordinate in the colonial encounter on the other. It is two distinct dialectical relationships in dialectical relation with one another. This move allows Comaroff to explore her subjects 'as determined, yet determining, in their own history; as human beings who, in their everyday production of goods and meanings, acquiesce yet protest, reproduce yet seek to transform their predicament' (1985: 1).

Might our understanding of contemporary 'development' benefit by being treated in a similar manner, but with different dialectical variables?

Thus, we could view 'development' as the product of the interplay between *localized* social and political forces on the one hand, and the dominant and subordinate in the *global* development encounter on the other. The development encounter, like the colonial encounter, becomes the product of two dialectical relations – one local, one global – in a dialectical relation with one another.

This alternative conception of 'development' is useful precisely because it makes space for what is denied by the post-structuralist position. As the product of such a dialectical process, 'development' still retains the importance of a dominant discourse, but it also makes way for the influence of local agency. It thus limits the structural over-determination of the post-structural critique by balancing it with the recognition that local beneficiaries of development also play a critical role in the process. With this slight theoretical realignment, then, 'development' is no longer simply the product of a hegemonic and all-determining Western-led discourse, but rather the result of a much more complex dialectical interplay.

The proposed theoretical reorientation achieves something else in its wake. By limiting the role of the knowledge/power nexus in the development encounter, this model of development also eliminates the apolitical burden placed on the post-structuralist anthropologist. If 'development' is taken as more than the deployment of Western knowledge in the management of the 'third world', then critically aware anthropologists need not be so self-effacing when it comes to proposing their own development interventions. 'Development as dialectical encounter' allows anthropologists to opt for action *and* engagement. It frees them to not only articulate their imaginations about development, but to also act upon those imaginations. The form that such action may take must be left to the anthropologist him- or herself, but in any case it should be an anthropologically informed engagement. What is most critical here is that anthropological knowledge of development be put into circulation with constructive, rather than only deconstructive, aims.

We should recognize too that the post-structuralist critique's failure to acknowledge local agency in the development process results also from its own methodological shortcomings. With a focus on discourse and its deconstruction, post-structuralists are limited in their scope of analysis because the only discourse amenable to deconstruction is that which makes itself known; in other words, that which is generated by the dominant forces in society. This is why the post-structuralists cannot help but offer us a top-down view of development. Given this additional concern, and as part and parcel of the proposal for a theoretical reorientation, I suggest a concomitant methodological reclamation in the anthropological study of development. If we are to craft a more effectual anthropology in development, then we might also fruitfully begin by reclaiming our defining methodology.

Two central aspects of our discipline's methodology seem most pertinent here. First, long-term fieldwork in a respective community of study (with its associated social and cultural immersion) produces a unique form of knowledge. We should not forget that anthropologists distinguish themselves as fieldworkers, not discourse analysts or literary critics. Second, in their commitment to 'thick description', anthropologists aim to do much more than just observe and record. The ethnographer must also interpret and contextualize in such great depth that meaning can be grasped then conveyed. This is anthropology's concern with the finer textures of everyday life. On this count, however, post-structuralist anthropologists of development come up short, as their studies often prove ethnographically 'thin' (Ortner 1995).

As a way to help move our anthropological engagement with development beyond this post-structural impasse, I suggest that anthropologists of development need to return to the discipline's time-honoured ethnographic methods. I am convinced that the way forward rests in these defining disciplinary strengths. In order to better comprehend the complex dialectical processes associated with the development encounter, anthropology can do more to illuminate the perceptions, experiences and socio-political processes surrounding the so-called targets of development. This requires that we shift our attention from the top back to the bottom, and from the thinness of discourse and its deconstruction to the thickness of process, practice and lived experiences.

* * * * *

In late 2011, a transformed global economic and political landscape is helping generate new contexts for dam development in northwest Namibia. Among other things, the so-called 'new scramble' for Africa has introduced additional sources of foreign aid to the continent, and the recent global energy crisis has re-directed national priorities. As a result, the Namibian government is again moving ahead with the construction of a dam on the Kunene River.[5] In light of these recent developments, I direct another set of remarks towards those working in the name of Kaokoland development.

In my view, the challenging nature of development work in Kaokoland is not the result of traditionalism, conservativeness, remoteness, or any other essentialist attribute of the people or the region, but is rather the product of the ongoing political conflict. It is a point that is missed by outside development agencies and their workers. I certainly support continued calls by developers and Kaokolanders alike to address the pervasiveness of poverty and marginalization in the region through improved education, health care, employment opportunities and technical services. My concern, however, is that the dispute will continue to compromise initiatives aiming to achieve such goals. From my anthropological perspective, then, it is the recalcitrant conflict that remains Kaokoland's most important development issue. My hope is that those setting out to re-plan the dam can first recognize the extent to which this persistent, divisive political dynamic negatively affects all Kaokolanders. Development initiatives such as the Kunene River Hydropower Scheme could succeed in helping to meet the material needs of Kaokolanders and other Namibians, but only after the interested stakeholders confront and transcend the deep roots that lie beneath the local conflict.

The specific lessons gleaned from this anthropological engagement with the development process have broader implications as well. In particular, the case presented here suggests the need for development workers to significantly reconfigure *their* notion of 'development'. In this sense, anthropology can help practitioners to recognize that their work always takes place within a dynamic social system, within a set of specific social, political and cultural contexts. Anthropology also reminds us that these contexts are historically contingent, and not just at the global level of analysis. Effective development work requires historical awareness, and anthropology can help development practitioners address their so-called targets as people *with* history. But the question and challenges still remain: how might we integrate such anthropological insights about the processual nature of development into programmes that aim to ameliorate global poverty and inequality?

Conclusion

I have been trying to argue that a fruitful beginning requires mutual commitment from both anthropologists and development professionals. From the anthropological side of the equation, I have proposed a path beyond the post-structural impasse. In light of the Epupa case, I have argued for a theoretical reorientation and methodological reclamation in the anthropology of development. 'Development' is not nearly as hegemonic as the post-structuralists claim. To the contrary, our case shows the extent to which 'development' is always historically, politically, socially and culturally contingent. By theorizing 'development' as a dialectical encounter, rather than a hegemonic one, anthropologists can push beyond the post-structural impasse; and they can open up the

space to make new and significant contributions to the study and practice of development.

If we wish to fill the new spaces opened up by such a theoretical
reorientation, then we also need to shed our over-reliance on discourse
analysis. Anthropological accounts of development institutions and their
texts are very important indeed, but if we are to locate the most anthropologically significant sites of the encounter, then we should be looking
beyond the offices of the World Bank. The suggestion for a methodological reclamation is thus a call for anthropologists to revert to the discipline's traditional methodological strengths: a commitment to 'thick
description' through long-term fieldwork and participant-observation in
localized, grass-roots settings.

The proposed theoretical reorientation and methodological reclamation can help anthropologists of development transcend the post-structural impasse in a number of ways. It will help us see development as
'a meeting point of different and distinctive narratives' (van den Berg
and Quarles van Ufford 2005: 209), rather than simply the product of
a single, all-determining *discourse*. The proposed adjustments will help
us explore the complex ways that people challenge, co-opt and re-form
development in line with their own interests. 'Development' as dialectical encounter re-balances an overly structural account of development
with the agency of local actors. The development process is no longer
the product of a reified discourse, but rather of the dynamic interplay
between conscious, living, acting subjects. We *all* actively contribute to,
and create, 'development'.

Lastly, and perhaps most significantly, the proposed interventions
open up the theoretical and moral space for anthropologists to *also* introduce their own agency into the development encounter. Mainstream
anthropologists have been on the sidelines of development far too long,
finding solace in ivory towers and taking comfort in post-structuralism's
inability to engage politically with the material issues of global poverty.
In shedding our understanding of 'development' as discourse, we can
be certain that our own political and practical engagements with the
material issues of global inequality are but one of many dialectical components in a much more complex process of social change.

From the other side of the equation, development professionals might
look more wholeheartedly towards anthropology as a means to better
contextualize their practices and interventions. Anthropologists have
more on offer than simply deconstruction and/or criticism. To this end,
some have argued that anthropology programmes need to begin teach-
ing a different set of skills, ones more amenable to the requirements of
the development sector (Nolan 2002). Though I obviously see a need

for academic anthropology to search its soul in relation to its (in)ability to act on global suffering, here I suggest something quite different. In trying to claim more space for anthropology in development, the field of anthropology need not become more 'developmentalized'. Instead, it is now high time for development to become more 'anthropologized'.

* * * * *

In this case of Kaokoland development, then, as with any other possible project, the post–post-structuralist anthropologist is left with many more possibilities. An anthropologically informed opinion may lead one to oppose the dam. Anthropologists of development might choose to write scholarly and popular articles in opposition to the project; they could direct advocacy campaigns in their own countries; or they might wish to support local opponents of the dam in ways they deem useful. Similarly, though, as long as anthropologists are adequately informed by the products of their own field research, then there is no reason why they should feel reluctant to support any such dam through similar means. Sometimes it is indeed warranted for an anthropologist to assert the interests of an entire country over those of a small community. The point is that by not saying or doing anything, anthropological knowledge fails to take its rightful place in the dialectical development encounter. As for my part, anthropological research on this proposed dam leads me to try and address what I see as the most pressing development issue in Kaokoland. For me, a strategy to help resolve the century-old conflict begins by excavating, understanding and communicating its underlying deep roots.

Since a new set of developers are planning a dam on the Kunene River yet again, they might try to embrace anthropology in new ways. Especially in the early phases of a project such as this one, a serious exchange between developers and anthropologists might be one way to begin. In this sense, narrow regional-based conferences and working groups could be an ideal vehicle through which to initiate constructive dialogue. Developers could work closely with groups of anthropologists who already possess knowledge in the respective project's topical and geographical areas of focus. In this case it would mean bringing together developers with anthropologists who have worked in Kaokoland, but also with those who have researched large dam projects in other locations. Another possible avenue for constructive collaboration might be the institutionalization of a sector-wide development projects peer review process. Especially at the design stage, anthropologists of development could be asked to offer blind reviews of proposals and other planned interventions, an approach that would mirror the process of peer review in the production of academic scholarship. Finally, and in specific relation to those overseeing the hydroelectric project in Kaokoland, developers might wish to integrate forums for local dispute resolution into the project framework itself. Building a dam and resolving the long-standing dispute in northwest Namibia should go hand in hand, as should anthropology and development more generally.

NOTES

This chapter is a revised synthesis of two previously published articles that appeared in *Dialectical Anthropology* (Friedman 2006) and the *European Journal of Development Research* (Friedman 2009) respectively. It is based on fieldwork undertaken in Namibia during 1999, 2000/01 and 2008. I would like to express my appreciation to the numerous Kaokolanders who have shared their time and knowledge with me, especially Mike Kavekotora and Jekura Kavari. The Wenner-Gren Foundation, the United States National Science Foundation, and various bodies associated with the University of Cambridge supported the research financially.

1. NAN [National Archives of Namibia] ADM 156 W32, 'Report on Kaokoveld by Major C.N. Manning', 1917.
2. Ibid.
3. See NAN NAO 020 11/1 (Vol. 11).
4. NAN NAO 061 12/3, 'Minutes of Meeting Held at Ohopoho from 7th to 16th April, 1952'.
5. After more than a decade of negotiations, Namibia and Angola finally reached an agreement for the construction of the dam in late 2008. The two governments chose a new site for the project (Baynes, rather than Epupa) and commissioned a new feasibility study team. At the time of publication, the Baynes feasibility study had yet to be released.

BIBLIOGRAPHY

Comaroff, J. 1985. *Body of Power Spirit of Resistance: The Culture and History of a South African People*. Chicago: University of Chicago Press.

Crewe, E. and E. Harrison. 1998. *Whose Development? An Ethnography of Aid*. London: Zed.

Crush, J. (ed.). 1995. *Power of Development*. London: Routledge.

Escobar, A. 1984. 'Discourse and Power in Development: Michel Foucault and the Relevance of His Work to the Third World', *Alternatives* 10(3): 377–400.

———. 1995. *Encountering Development: The Making and Unmaking of the Third World*. Princeton: Princeton University Press.

Everett, M. 1997. 'The Ghost in the Machine: Agency in "Poststructural" Critiques of Development', *Anthropological Quarterly* 70(3): 137–151.

Ferguson, J. 1990. *The Anti-Politics Machine: 'Development,' Depoliticization, and Bureaucratic Power in Lesotho*. Cambridge: Cambridge University Press.

Friedman, J. T. 2000. 'Mapping the Epupa Debate: Discourse and Representation in a Namibian Development Project', in G. Miescher and D. Henrichsen (eds), *New Notes on Kaoko: The Northern Kunene Region (Namibia) in Texts and Photographs.* Basel: Basler Afrika Bibliographien, pp. 220–235.

———. 2005. 'Making Politics, Making History: Chiefship and the Post-Apartheid State in Namibia', *Journal of Southern African Studies* 31(1): 23–51.

———. 2006. 'Beyond the Post-Structural Impasse in the Anthropology of Development', *Dialectical Anthropology* 30(3/4): 201–225.

———. 2009. 'Context and Contestation in the Development Process: Lessons from Kaokoland (Namibia)', *European Journal of Development Research* 21(3): 325–343.

———. 2011. *Imagining the Post-Apartheid State: An Ethnographic Account of Namibia.* New York and Oxford: Berghahn.

Grillo, R. and R. Stirrat. (eds). 1997. *Discourses of Development: Anthropological Perspectives.* Oxford: Berg.

Kiely, R. 1999. 'The Last Refuge of the Noble Savage? A Critical Assessment of Post-Development Theory', *The European Journal of Development Research* 11(1): 30–55.

Long, N. and A. Long (eds). 1992. *Battlefields of Knowledge: The Interlocking of Theory and Practice in Social Research and Development.* London: Routledge.

Miescher, G. and D. Henrichsen. 2000. 'Epilogue', in G. Miescher and D. Henrichsen (eds), *New Notes on Kaoko: The Northern Kunene Region (Namibia) in Texts and Photographs.* Basel: Basler Afrika Bibliographien, pp. 237–245.

Nolan, R. 2002. *Development Anthropology: Encounters in the Real World.* Boulder: Westview Press.

Olivier de Sardan, J. 2005. *Anthropology and Development: Understanding Contemporary Social Change.* London: Zed.

Ortner, S. 1995. 'Resistance and the Problem of Ethnographic Refusal', *Comparative Studies in Society and History* 37: 173–193.

Rahnema, M. and V. Bawtree (eds). 1997. *The Post-Development Reader.* London: Zed Books.

Rossi, B. 2004. 'Revisiting Foucauldian Approaches: Power Dynamics in Development Projects', *The Journal of Development Studies* 40(6): 1–29.

Scott, J. 1990. *Domination and the Arts of Resistance: Hidden Transcripts.* New Haven: Yale University Press.

United Nations Development Programme. 2000. *Namibia: Human Development Report 2000, Gender and Violence in Namibia.* Windhoek: UNDP.

Van den Berg, R. and P. Quarles van Ufford. 2005. 'Disjuncture and Marginality: Towards a New Approach to Development Practice', in D. Mosse and D. Lewis (eds), *The Aid Effect: Giving and Governing in International Development.* London: Pluto, pp. 196–212.

CHAPTER 2

Framing and Escaping

Contrasting Aspects of Knowledge Work in International Development and Anthropology

Maia Green

A t first sight international development and anthropology have much in common – a shared concern with social transformation in the world's poorer places and similar histories as disciplines evolving through particular colonial and postcolonial conjunctures of knowledge and power (Escobar 1995; Ferguson 1997). The interdisciplinary sweep of development knowledge, combined with the emphasis in international development practice on evidence-based policy making, makes it perhaps surprising that knowledge produced by anthropology remains largely peripheral to development practice (Green 2005). This chapter considers some of the reasons for the problematic relationship between anthropology and international development, or more specifically, between the kinds of knowledge produced by development and the kinds of knowledge produced by anthropology. The exclusion of anthropological knowledge from international development is a consequence not merely of the latter's preference for quantification, but of the social relations between anthropology and development, and of their different knowledge forms and practices. Social development, as the policy discipline that claims to render the social intelligible for development interventions, may claim ancestry in anthropology but is a radically different enterprise, its intellectual concerns determined by policy priorities and its methodologies by the need to manage (Green 2005).

Notes for this section begin on page 55

The absence of anthropological knowledge from development practice is not a matter of the relation between different kinds of knowledge but between different ways of doing knowing and the different professionals contracted to provide knowledge expertise. Making knowledge work in development is not a straightforward matter of acquiring knowledge relevant to an issue and devising actions to address it. Anthropological knowledge cannot simply be 'applied' to a development context. In this chapter, I show how development constructs knowledge as relevant to interventions within particular paradigms around expertise and community-generated knowledge forms. The application of what is counted as knowledge within development relations is constituted within the organization of development itself. Relevance and evidence in international development are socially constituted within development relations. Both produce different kinds of knowledge about particular contexts, often within the same programme. Conventions about which knowledge is relevant for what mean that these forms are never brought into a relation with each other to create new knowledge. As the sociology of science has demonstrated, conventions around knowledge and relevance operate in all knowledge domains, delimiting what counts as knowledge and the ways in which this is constituted (Latour 1987). International development is no exception. Consequently, anthropological knowledge, which adheres to very different conventions, struggles to occupy a place within development knowledge forms.

Understanding why development and anthropology use knowledge differently and recognize different knowledge entails apprehending both anthropology and international development in the same terms. In approaching international development and anthropology in terms of what development practitioners and anthropologists actually do and how certain kinds of things are categorized as knowledge, it becomes clear that their knowledge practices are not only distinct and dependent on different forms of representation, but essentially concerned with different rules about what kinds of knowledge can be brought into particular relations. What we are dealing with is not only different *kinds* of knowledge and different ways of *doing* knowledge, but practices that make, and make use of, different representations of knowledge within their own systems of organization (Bowker and Star 2000; Strathern 2005; Woolgar 2004: 453–454). Understanding knowledge in anthropology or development does not, then, rest on what knowledge is represented as being, but on how practice is constituted around knowledge production – on the modalities of 'epistemic conduct' that are associated with each domain (Osborne 2004: 436).

In much anthropological work, apprehending knowledge is problematic. Informants' categories of knowledge do not map onto our analytical ones. Ethnographic accounts of knowledge, even in so called 'knowledge societies', routinely conflate knowledge as a category with other categories such as culture and meaning (Osborne 2004; Hastrup 2004). Studying international development knowledge systems does not present this problem to the same extent. Knowledge is a distinct category within international development and in anthropology. Indeed, both anthropology and international development are premised on distinct representations of the category of knowledge and its place within particular orders.

My arguments about knowledge practices are based on my experience of being a participant in the systems of two disciplines simultaneously: as a practitioner contracted to undertake knowledge work in international development organizations, and as a professional anthropologist producing anthropological knowledge in a university setting. My work in international development organizations over the past decade has not been in the capacity of an anthropologist in that I have not been employed to undertake ethnography or the work of cultural translation. I have worked in varying capacities as a social development specialist, a poverty adviser and social policy analyst in a range of organizations for assignments of between several weeks and just over one year. I have undertaken this kind of work for the U.K. government's Department for International Development, for several international nongovernmental organizations, for a multilateral organization within the UN system and for the government of a recipient country, Tanzania. Most of the country-based work I have undertaken has been in Tanzania, the country where I undertook my doctoral fieldwork as an anthropologist (Green 1993, 2003b). Reflection on the different styles of epistemic conduct and epistemic forms in anthropology and in development enables an account in which knowledge forms can be apprehended socially. It is my contention that the reason international development organizations do not make use of anthropological knowledge is not that development knowledge brokers are ignorant of the insights of anthropology or its potential to engage, but that the epistemic form of anthropology and the epistemic conduct of anthropologists do not 'work' within the organization of development.

Development Work

International development refers to the system of organizations that define themselves as existing in order to achieve whatever are currently defined as international development objectives, as with the Millennium Development Goals (MDGs), for example. The international development system includes a range of agencies and organizations, from small-scale civil society networks to international organizations with a global purview. Implementation of development objectives is achieved through dissemination of policy through influence and the brokering of policy ideas, and through spending (Green 2007; 2011). These dimensions of development practice are distributed among different organizations and actors. The image of an international development system as coherent and encompassing is largely representational, an effect of the ways in which it is promoted by those claiming recognition as constituent actors. This is achieved through images and motifs of the global and the network, and the vertical tiers of local to regional – imagery that facilitates the encompassing imaginary of the international system (Gupta and Ferguson 2002; Riles 2001).

International development as a system of organization is as much conceptual as it is material. Much effort in development practice is oriented towards categorical organizing – the reorganizing dimensions of policy change, for example, or the ordering of reforms. This is supported through financial organizing, i.e., the resource transfers that support international development interventions and the financial reforming that is a central component of the international development order (Green 2007, 2011). Development professionals are not concerned with conceptual ordering alone but must also deal with managing spending as the means to realizing reforms. The conceptual repertoire of international development and public policy provides the architecture through which the effects of aid can be programmed and projected through scalable concepts applicable at micro or macro levels of imagination and analysis. This permits, in the abstract at least, the representation of cause and effect, and hence programmability in relation to spending (Craig and Porter 1997). Practices of legibility and homogenization are necessarily central to governing, as anthropologists writing from the perspective of criticism have shown in relation to the extension of state power (Scott 1998; Tsing 1993). They are, however, necessary techniques of government, of organizing means and ends, things and people in certain ways to achieve certain objectives (Foucault 2002; Lemke 2001; Murray Li 2007).

Unlike anthropology, which seeks to unpack and dissemble through critique and deconstruction, competency in development entails doing the opposite: using concepts constructively in order to model and realize policy worlds (Green 2007). Knowledge in development is a form of action within an associated form of social organization. There is no 'useful knowledge' (Strathern 2006b) outside the social relations of development (Mosse 2006). What counts as knowledge within international development, as in government more generally, is institutionalized within and through specific epistemic and organizational forms. This institutionalization is shown clearly by the example of a development process in Tanzania that demarcates and allocates knowledge institutionally in what are fairly standard ways. These ways are not unique to that particular context or programme, but are in fact generalizable across development interventions in different places. The Local Government Reform Programme (LGRP) is a paradigmatic development intervention, a product of the phase of governance reforms that have been globally implemented. Running for just over a decade, it has adapted to the international policy shifts that are redrawing development as an outcome rather than an adjunct of government. What were previously organized as stand-alone programmes are now in the process of being 'mainstreamed', that is absorbed into government systems to be funded through government budgets, something made possible by new modalities of development financing. This process of absorption dissolves the boundaries between development and government while leaving intact the relations of development premised on the fundamental inequality between developer and developee, donor and beneficiary, external donor government and recipient government.

Local government reform programmes in most countries receiving development assistance tend to be a mix of the public sector and governance reform packages that have been widely implemented over the past fifteen years (Falk Moore 2001). Local government reform is not merely an endeavour aimed at improving the process of government at district level but a discrete project situated within Tanzania's network of ongoing projects supported by donors in various sectors including health, education, public services and the economy. As a project tied to a specific budget and time frame, LGRP is both a bundle of resources and social relations subject to management techniques (Green 2003a) and a set of contractual obligation between implementers and donors and between contracted staff and clients. Social relations tied to resources and time frames are units of management, conceptually in that they can be represented as manageable, and socially as a means of connecting the people and things that must be brought into relation for certain outcomes to happen (Craig and Porter 1997: 231; Green 2003 a). The Tanzania local government reform programme as a development project brings together people who are concerned with it in different capacities, some temporarily and some more or less permanently. Because development as a form of social organization maps over other forms of social organization in which actors are enmeshed, certain roles and obligations have to be tightly specified. Those more formally engaged with the organization are officially involved in it via the offices they hold, while the roles of short-term consultants are clearly demarcated in terms of the time they are associated with a project, their scope of work and with whom they will interact in order to complete it.

As projects of government within government and as projects of management, development social relations entail particular forms of knowing and of representing what comes to have status as 'knowledge' (Goldman 2005) that Thomas Osborne has called *epistemic forms* and *modes of conduct* (Osborne 2004: 436). Two in particular characterize contemporary development organizations. The first, *expertise*, with the two components of evidence and evaluation, is a practice of contemporary government that is premised on a rational use of resources. Appraisal, audit and evaluation are necessary to government practices represented contractually. This is not a mere matter of accounting but of selectivity in interventions (Murray Li 2007; Rose 1996: 53). What is categorized as knowledge about what works and what is programmable, assumes status as a driver of policy choice within this paradigm. Because expert knowledge is fundamental to the practice of government, the space for expertise is designed into a programme. The role of expert is an office within the social organization of a project.

The second knowledge form now incorporated into development organizations is also institutionally formalized. *Participatory* knowledge refers in practice to what is represented as the product of participatory processes or techniques for obtaining knowledge, which can then be applied to problems that have emerged as outcomes of the knowledge production process. Participatory processes have evolved from the initial hybrid of activist-inspired action research and participant-observation to include not only research methodologies such as Participatory Rural Appraisal and Participatory Learning and Action, but participatory project management and national-level institutions such as participatory poverty assessments (PPAs) (Cornwall 2006; Green 2000). Participatory methods and the knowledge they generate are no longer the preserve of populist movements that claim to speak with or through the 'voices of the poor'. Participation is institutionalized across the majority of what are perceived to be credible nongovernmental organizations and within certain programmes and practices of agencies such as the World Bank.

The Tanzania local government reform programme as a project formally incorporates participatory knowledge production as an institution within reformed local government organizations and expertise in the form of contractual relations with experts hired to evaluate and improve an evolving programme. What is categorized as 'participation' within the reform programme does not only take the form of democratic participation through the electoral process for local government elections. It also extends to encompass new forms of participatory knowledge that can become the basis of decision making about the allocation and use of resources within and between levels of government. Initially piloted as part of the reform programme, the local government system now incorporates a form of participatory knowledge production as a routine component of the local government planning cycle (Green 2010).

Doing Expertise

I have a long-term involvement with the Tanzanian Local Government Reform Programme in different capacities, initially as an observer from a distance, as reform processes got underway through district development programmes in the 1990s, and later as a representative of a major donor organization, hence as a key stakeholder in the initial appraisal process. My official placing within the programme itself is more limited. I write here as an ex-expert, someone contracted to provide expertise within a specialism for a limited time frame as part of a team of experts undertaking an evaluation of the whole programme. Our team comprised a mix of individuals who were deemed to have distinct specialisms relevant to the core areas of the programme. Specialist knowledge was not an adequate basis for recognition as having sufficient expertise to undertake the evaluation. Additional competencies were required, which meant having had similar experience applying expertise in cognate processes or programmes. It was my background in public sector reform in Tanzania and in social policy analysis for a bilateral donor that provided the required knowledge for the evaluation, not my academic competency in anthropology, even if it was in the anthropology of rural Tanzania.

My contracted area of expertise for the evaluation was in governance, not as defined academically within political or social science, but as specified in the programme documentation as concerned primarily with participation and accountability, a common take on governance concerns within the development field. The areas of the programme that I was required to address were set out in the contract that constituted the basis of my official involvement in the programme. In development contracting, this is effected through the Terms of Reference (ToR), which position the expert in relation to required expertise and to the kind of knowledge required by the programme (Stirrat 2000). Terms of reference provide a map in which consultants situate themselves in relation to what is deemed relevant to the piece of work they are contracted to undertake. This can include project history, the policy context, its relation to other projects, and people occupying significant roles in relation to the wider development organization or who have important knowledge claims about the project issues. Following the map orients the process of knowledge production the project requires, constituting the expert who makes the relevant connections – social and textual – through the listed persons, institutions and documents. The role of the expert here is not to make connections relevant, but to make the relevant connections. Competent experts know what counts as evidence and how to make evidence count. This is not an objective property of certain information or knowledge but depends on the social context in which it is brought to have status as such (Hastrup 2004; Lambert 2006).

Producing expert knowledge of this sort is not so much about the knowledge that is produced as it is about the social process of dialogue that generates what is acceptable as relevant knowledge. Because acceptability necessitates the performance of some kind of consensus, this generally involves collective events and workshops where the findings of experts can be presented, debated and amended. The knowledge product is usually a text addressing the issues, contracted through the terms of reference and structured in a particular way often specified within the original contract (Stirrat 2000). As an 'expert' on governance for the evaluation, I was familiar with the kind of epistemic conduct I was expected to perform. I followed the map of relevant connections with others in the team. We discussed issues with persons to consult, conducted meetings, read documents and policy papers. We met with officials from ministries, departments and agencies, and with representatives of nongovernmental organizations and donor governments. We visited local government authorities and talked with councillors, local government staff and the officers who provide a link between village and district tiers of government. As an evaluation team we made the connections between persons, documents and issues relevant by ensuring their relation to one another, and we all produced reports that represented our collectively agreed perspectives.

Expertise here, as in all consultancies, required a certain form of epistemic conduct that framed what was to be known and the form the knowledge should take. While the knowledge product, in the form of a series of reports, was a contracted outcome of the process of engagement with the programme, what was more important was the process of dialogue with persons and documents to consult, so that evaluation became a social process around establishing a shared interpretation about the value of certain interventions and activities (cf. Mosse 2004: 658, 2006: 940; Harper 2000). Experts' reports are not simply accepted by programme teams and other stakeholders. Like presentations at workshops they are reviewed, altered, contested. Evaluation, as the term implies, is about values. Interpretation matters (Mosse 2004: 658, 2006: 940).

Participatory Knowledge

The epistemic form of expert knowledge and its epistemic conduct presents a contrast to the other paradigmatic form of knowledge institutionalized in development organizations. Participatory approaches in development originate in the practices of agricultural research – hence their representation as alternative ways of conducting scientific research premised on an idea of applying knowledge to address specific problems, with both knowledge and problem to be determined through participation. The generalization of participatory methods through standardization with other sectors and activities has been achieved through sustained activist pressure and the professionalized promotion of participation, with the resultant consolidation of a realm of expertise. Participatory approaches are made to stand in contrast to expert knowledge because of the stated claims about the valorization of local and insider perspectives. Paradoxically, because these perspectives cannot be accessed without the specialized frameworks provided through participatory methods, participatory approaches cannot be operationaliseized without specialist expertise (Cleaver 2006; Green 2000; 2010; Mosse 1999; 2005; Cleaver 2006).

The discursive construction of participation within development, and to an extent outside it, rests on an imposed boundary between qualitatively different kinds of knowledge. Expert outsider knowledge is categorized as less valid than knowledge generated by insiders. Insider status is conceptualized geographically, so that insiders are local and occupy positions within another bounded entity, community (Brosius 2006; van der Riet 2008). Participatory methods thus work to elicit the knowledge of local communities, and this knowledge is valid because it is relevant. Relevance as a moral attribute of knowledge is claimed to render participatory knowledge legitimate and useful. Participatory knowledge, like expertise, derives its relevance and usefulness from its situation within the development organization. Local knowledge cannot exist in a meaningful way outside the programme for which it is relevant (cf. Mosse 2004: 649).

In the Local Government Reform Programme, a system of participatory knowledge production called Opportunities and Obstacles to

Development (O and OD) provides an institutional form through which what counts as participatory knowledge can be generated. O and OD has much in common with other participatory approaches used in development settings within Tanzania and internationally (Green 2010). These explicitly delineate the local as context, performing the community whose knowledge is represented as product in the documentation produced through participatory exercises. Established participatory techniques include transect walks around the territory occupied by a community, seasonal diagrams, event histories and mapping of community areas and boundaries. These performative strategies of community making are objectified through representational devices associated with participatory techniques – the pictorial strategies devised to provide explicit contrast with the narrative orientation of expertise. They are objectified again through articulation in group discussions that are then written up in the form of community reports. Ranking and voting feature prominently as participatory techniques to produce facts based on 'what everybody knows' (Campbell 2001). Local knowledge as 'facts' does not require supplementation by other kinds of knowledge. Indeed, other knowledge is not relevant because it is neither locally produced nor applicable to the locality. Evaluations of participatory knowledge accept this ring fencing off locally produced knowledge, assessing the process of knowledge production but not the quality of knowledge produced, which in being local is morally unassailable, literally beyond criticism.

Writing up – the representation of representations – is the point at which local knowledge is formally appropriated into a product through expertise. Specialists produce reports of participatory processes and facilitate the process of knowledge production. The expert here is contracted to feed knowledge into a project, but what this knowledge is enabled to do is framed through its localization. Knowledge produced through participatory processes is bounded knowledge, knowledge that is made to operate as information about certain people and places–to perform work as knowledge about the community for programme use. Products of participatory knowledge thus become checklists of community characteristics, problems or needs, or in the case of the LGRP as prioritizations of demands that can be represented in forward plans as budget lines. Participatory process does not simply provide a facilitated discursive space in which people can potentially express views about what is relevant to the community. It constitutes both community and relevance through the delineation of this space: practically, within the exercise through its demarcating methodologies; and representationally, through the format of reporting, which provides a portfolio of local knowledge.

Evaluating Knowledge

Just as knowledge workers in development are situated relationally through contracting and a fixed place in the project order, knowledge in development is intentionally bounded. The place of knowledge is structurally and temporally demarcated within the development organization, rendered useful at certain points in a programme cycle, sourced from certain individuals, adopted by others and operationalized, or not, through the plans and budgets that represent the project in a future-oriented, organizational form. Expertise and participatory knowledge are made relevant by their situation within the social organization of development projects. The situation of participatory knowledge as concerned with beneficiaries as objects of impact renders participation peripheral as a project object. If the power of expertise rests in its place in the social ordering of projects, rather than content, it potentially derives additional power from its place as a mediator or knowledge broker within development organizations. This is achieved through the social relations sanctioning what can be counted as evidence within policy communities and the boundary between expertise and other kinds of knowledge. The special status of expert knowledge is not an attribute of a kind of knowledge but of the situation of the individuals as knowledge agents who are contracted to produce it.

Participatory knowledge and expertise apply to different spheres and achieve different ends within the project organization. Different kinds of knowledge within development are related to each other through the social relations of the project, yet they are not brought into a relation with each other in ways that could generate new knowledge. Neither kind of knowledge comes into a relation with the other in terms of content. Expert knowledge about a topic or a location is not brought into a relation with participatory knowledge, except when experts evaluate participatory processes , that is when they assess the epistemic conduct of participation. What is counted as knowledge within the organization of development is tightly bounded, creating the possibility of an instrumental relation between knowledge and action. It is not that development knowledge is applicable to problems in development and hence is inherently instrumental; it is, rather, that development is organized in such a way as to include knowledge in a specific relation with projects. As I have shown, the kinds of paradigmatic knowledge it incorporates at present are expertise and participatory knowledge, which are in fact specific social institutions within development organizations. Different kinds of knowledge about something – a problem or a project – are not brought into a relationship with each other in order to become applicable because problem and applicability are already contained within the different knowledge paradigms and practices.

Conclusion

The rigidity of the specification of knowledge practices within development, including the terms of their relation with other kinds of knowledge (Strathern 2005), restricts the potential ways in which more open-ended knowledge can be brought into development organization (cf. Friedman this volume). This is recognized by academics and development practitioners alike when they speak of either the rigidity of certain knowledge forms, or the irrelevance or 'uselessness' of academic knowledge. If two distinct kinds of knowledge within development, even within the same programme, do not inform each other, knowledge in development is evidently not a matter of facts. Making anthropological knowledge relevant to development is not then a question of applying anthropological knowledge to development or rendering anthropological findings visible. The institutional space simply does not exist in development for the incorporation of anthropological knowledge. This is partly because of the current organization of what counts as knowledge within the organization of development. It is accentuated by the radically different knowledge practices of anthropology. These centre on the prioritization of the emergent properties of knowledge, in which the object of investigation is always changing as new knowledge is brought into relation to the anthropological subject.

Anthropology as a discipline resists foreclosure, both in its approach to the field through ethnography and after, when new knowledge in the form of texts can be brought into new relations with other kinds of knowledge and applied to the product of field investigation (Strathern 2005: 85; 2006c) . The porosity associated with anthropological knowledge renders it endlessly forward-looking; it can accommodate new problematics and possibilities (Strathern 2004: 7, 2006b: 200). The openness of anthropology to new knowledge, not only from within the discipline but across other disciplinary frames, accords anthropology a certain epistemological advantage over other forms of knowledge when it comes to addressing the unanticipated. But these attributes also contain the parameters of the inapplicability of anthropology – its escape from frames renders it difficult to corral and render useful, in the sense of useful knowledge. Rather, like the good policy that Mosse describes as 'metaphor not management' (2004: 666), being hence impossible to implement because of its vagueness and fluidity, anthropological knowledge resists application to templates and grids. It is this attribute of anthropological knowledge that makes it so importantly 'useless' in terms of its utility to other disciplines (Strathern 2006b: 78, 87).

The fixity and coherence of boundaries are essential, not only to management and implementation in project worlds but also to *representing* social order in a more general sense in the constant effort to confront flux (Douglas 1986; Tilly 1998). The representation of anthropological knowledge as creative and open-ended is partly borne out representationally, in the domain of text. Although the formalities and framings of development as rendering certain knowledge practices useful in turn restrict the range of knowledge products that can be incorporated, generally excluding anthropological knowledge, anthropological texts lend themselves to excludability by refusing to be useful, opening endless possibilities, resisting facts and declining the status of evidence (Hastrup 2004; Strathern 2006b). The openness of anthropology here imposes a different kind of boundary, a boundary that is maintained by the disciplinary practices of anthropology (Strathern 2004).

Our claim as anthropologists to openness and innovation may be borne out by the questions we address through fieldwork and the range of categories that we subject to ethnographic interrogation. It is less evident in our epistemic conduct – in what and how we do. And while anthropological fieldwork may have transformed itself since the crisis of representation and the insights of reflexivity, postcolonialism and postmodernism, this applies more to the focus of the ethnographic project than the practice of fieldwork. The location of the field has shifted and become less fixed. What persists is the tradition of the lone fieldworker and the status of fieldwork as the source of anthropological knowledge. Further, anthropology as a discipline has not innovated institutionally in terms of location beyond the field. It remains practically encapsulated within the academic sector, at least in the United Kingdom, within universities and scholarship in the humanities, and within the tradition of pure knowledge, which insists on the possibility of a separation of truth from power (Anderson 2003; Wolf 2001). Engagement with development occurs at the level of, and is confined to, texts – not the texts within development that are calls to action, but those outside it, and hence outside the relations and networks of development organization.

There is no doubt that anthropology's openness and creativity hold possibilities for development thinking and practice, just as international development's explicit recognition of the social practice of knowledge holds lessons for anthropology's quest for relevance (Latour 2005; Woolgar 2005; compare Kelly this volume). Relevance for anthropology within development requires changes on both sides: increased openness in development in terms of how to make knowledge work in less instrumental ways, and change within anthropology in terms of new ways to work outside the academy. This is not simply a matter of institutional placing or organizational reform but of altering the ways in which we as anthropologists work, experimenting with reconstruction after deconstruction, with positive criticism – what de Laet and Mol call 'love' (2000) – and with working on shared projects of interpretation *with*, rather than *of*, others.

NOTES

This chapter is based on a presentation first given at the workshop on differentiating development in Buxton, United Kingdom in 2008. It benefits considerably from the inputs of workshop participants . Some of the arguments have since been developed further in Green (2009).

1. On framing as an epistemic strategy see Knorr Cetina (1999: 72) and Brenneis (2004: 47), and as an effect of project organizing, Craig and Porter (1997).

BIBLIOGRAPHY

Anderson, L. 2003. *Pursuing Truth, Exercising Power: Social Science and Public Policy in the 21st Century.* New York: Columbia University Press.

Bowker, G. and S. Star. 2000. *Sorting Things Out: Classification and Its Consequences.* Ann Arbor: MIT Press.

Brenneis, D. 2004. 'A Partial View of Contemporary Anthropology', *American Anthropologist* 106(3): 580–588.

Brosius, P. 2006. 'Seeing Communities: Technologies of Visualisation in Conservation', in Creed, G. (ed.), *The Seductions of Community: Emancipations, Oppressions, Quandaries.* Santa Fe: School of American Research Press. 227–254.

Campbell, J. 2001. 'Participatory Rural Appraisal as Qualitative Research: Distinguishing Methodological Issues from Participatory Claims', *Human Organization* 60(4): 380–389.

Cleaver, F. 1999. 'Paradoxes of Participation: Questioning Participatory Approaches to Development', *Journal of International Development* 11: 597–612.

Cornwall, A. 2006. 'Historical Perspectives on Participation in Development', *Commonwealth and Comparative Politics* 44(1): 62–83.

Craig, D. and D. Porter. 1997. 'Framing Participation: Development Projects, Professionals and Organizations', *Development in Practice* 7(3): 229–237.

De Laet, M. and A. Mol. 2000. 'The Zimbabwe Bush Pump: Mechanics of a Fluid Technology', *Social Studies of Science* 30(2): 225–263.

Escobar, A. 1995. *Encountering Development: The Making and Unmaking of the Third World.* Princeton: Princeton University Press.

Ferguson, J. 1990. *The Anti Politics Machine: Development, Depolitiicization and Bureaucratic Power in Lesotho.* Cambridge: Cambridge University Press.

———. 1997. 'Anthropology and Its Evil Twin: Development in the Constitution of a Discipline', in F. Cooper and R. Packard (eds), *International Development and the Social Sciences.* Berkeley: University of California Press.

Ferguson, J. and A. Gupta. 2002. 'Spatializing States: Towards an Ethnography of Neoliberal Governmentality', *American Ethnologist* 29(4): 981–1002.

Foucault, M. 2002. 'Governmentality', in *Power: Essential Works of Foucault 1954–1984*. London: Penguin, pp. 201–222.

Goldman, M. 2005. *Imperial Nature: The World Bank and Struggles for Social Justice in the Age of Globalization*. New Haven: Yale University Press.

Green, M. 1993. *The Construction of Religion and the Perpetuation of Tradition Among Pogoro Catholics Southern Tanzania*, PhD thesis. London, University of London.

———. 2000. 'Participatory Development and the Appropriation of Agency in Southern Tanzania', *Critique of Anthropology*, 20 (1):, 67–86.

———. 2003a. 'Globalizing Development in Tanzania: Policy Franchising through Participatory Project Management', *Critique of Anthropology* 23(2): 123–143.

———. 2003b. *Priests, Witches and Power: Popular Christianity After Mission in Southern Tanzania*. Cambridge: Cambridge University Press.

———. 2005. 'International Development, Social Analysis . . . and Anthropology? Applying Anthropology in and to Development', in S. Pink (ed.), *Applications of Anthropology: Professional Anthropology in the Twenty-first Century*. London: Berghahn Books, pp. 110–129.

———. 2007. 'Delivering Discourse: Some Ethnographic Reflections on the Practice of Policy Making in International Development', *Critical Policy Analysis* 1(2): 139–153.

———. 2009. 'Doing Development and Writing Culture: Knowledge Practices in Anthropology and in International Development', *Anthropological Theory* 9(4): 395–417.

———. 2010. 'Making Development Agents: Participation as Boundary Object in International Development', *Journal of Development Studies* 46(7):

———. 2011. Calculating Compassion: Accounting for Some Categorical Practices in International Development, in Mosse, D (ed) *Adventures in Aidland: The Anthropology of Professionals in International Development*, London, Berghahn, 33–58.

Harper, R. 2000. 'The Social Organization of the IMF's Mission Work: An Examination of International Auditing', in M. Strathern (ed.), *Audit Cultures: Anthropological Studies in Accountability, Ethics and the Academy*. London: Athlone, pp. 23–53.

Hastrup, K. 2004. 'Knowledge and Evidence in Anthropology', *Anthropological Theory* 4(4): 455–472.

Lambert, H. 2006. 'Accounting for EBM: Notions of Evidence in Medicine', *Social Science and Medicine* 62(11): 2633–2645.

Latour, B. 1987. *Science in Action: How to Follow Scientists and Engineers Through Society*. Cambridge, MA: Harvard University Press.

———. 2005. *Reassembling the Social: An Introduction to Actor Network Theory*. Oxford: Oxford University Press.

Lemke, T. 2001. 'The Birth of Bio-Politics: Michel Foucault's Lecture at the College de France on Neo-Liberal Governmentality', *Economy and Society* 30(2): 190–207.

Moore, S. F. 2001. 'The International Production of Authoritative Knowledge: The Case of Drought Stricken West Africa', *Ethnography* 2(2): 161–189.

Mosse, D. 1994. 'Authority, Gender and Knowledge: Theoretical Reflections on the Practice of Participatory Rural Appraisal', *Development and Change* 25: 497–526.

———. 2004. 'Is Good Policy Unimplementable? Reflections on the Ethnography of Aid Policy and Practice', *Development and Change* 35(4): 639–671.

———. 2006. 'Anti-Social Anthropology? Objectivity, Objection, and the Ethnography of Public Policy and Professional Communities', *Journal of the Royal Anthropological Institute* 12: 935–956.

Murray Li, T. 2007. *The Will To Improve: Governmentality, Development and the Practice of Politics*. Durham, NC: Duke University Press.

Osborne, T. 2004. 'On Mediators: Intellectuals and the Ideas Trade in the Knowledge Society', *Economy and Society* 33(4): 430–447.

Riles, A. 2001. *The Network Inside Out*. Ann Arbor: University of Michigan Press.

Rose, N. 1996. 'Governing "Advanced" Liberal Democracies', in A. Barry, T. Osborne and N. Rose (eds), *Foucault and Political Reason*. London: UCL Press, pp. 37–64.

Scott, J. 1998. *Seeing Like a State: How Certain Schemes to Improve the Human Condition Have Failed*, Newhaven, Yale University Press.

Stirrat, R. L. 2000. 'Cultures of Consultancy', *Critique of Anthropology* 20(1): 31–47.

Strathern, M. 2004. *Commons and Borderlands: Working Papers On Interdisciplinarity and the Flow of Knowledge*. Oxford: Sean Kingston Publishing.

———. 2005. 'Experiments in Interdisciplinarity', *Social Anthropology* 13(1): 75–90.

———. 2006a. 'A Community of Critics? Thoughts on New Knowledge', *Journal of the Royal Anthropological Institute* 12: 191–209.

———. 2006b. 'Useful Knowledge', *Proceedings of the British Academy* 139: 73–109.

———. 2006c. *Partial Connections*, updated edition. Walnut Creek, CA: Altamira Press.

Tilly, C. 1998. *Durable Inequality*. Berkeley: University of California Press.

Tsing, A. 1993. *In the Realm of the Diamond Queen: Marginality in an Out of the Way Place*. Princeton: Princeton University Press.

Van der Riet, M. 2008. 'Participatory Research and the Philosophy of Social Science: Beyond the Moral Imperative', *Qualitative Inquiry* 14(4): 546–565.

CHAPTER 3

Intersection

Economies of Knowledge

Veena Das

A major issue in both the chapters under discussion here centres around economies of knowledge and action in the fields of development and anthropology. Though there are some very interesting differences between the way Green and Friedman position themselves in relation to anthropology, both ask: Can the epistemic differences between anthropology and development initiatives be brought into a productive conversation? Or are the two incommensurable, separated by a criterial difference that no amount of good intentions can bridge? After all, as they note, both anthropologists and development experts call for political and social action to alleviate the conditions of the poor. How, then, might we understand the fraught relations between anthropologists located in academic institutions and development experts on questions such as what constitutes the necessary evidence and plan of action needed to increase income levels, ensure food security or create better opportunities for well-being?

This problem is not specific to anthropology's relationship with development – similar tensions straddle fields such as public health and anthropology, or policy and political theory. Green goes to the heart of the matter when she points to the tension between intervention and what is seen as the disinterested production of knowledge. Friedman specifically targets positions that he understands as 'post-structuralist' for their neglect of agency. However, I suggest that each author's diagnosis of the problem suffers from a readiness to assume that such terms as 'representation' and 'agency' are transparent and readily available for thought that does disservice to the complexity of the issues they raise.

First, let us consider the question of knowledge economies. Since the publication of Lorain Daston's (1995) seminal essay on the moral economy of science, there has been a veritable explosion of writings on moral economy – the expression taking on new dimensions in economics, political science and anthropology itself. Daston's point was that science stands today as the paradigmatic example of modernity in the public imagination, with its emphasis on rationality, objectivity and facticity. Nevertheless, she says, affects run deep within laboratories and inform scientific controversies, not as free-flowing emotions but as balanced systems of emotional forces with equilibrium points and constraints. Thus such values as quantification or mathematization become affect-saturated. Others (e.g., Haraway 1997) have argued that affects are carefully purged in the public record of science, since the model of detachment and disciplinary civility informs the picture of the scientist as a 'modest witness' to an objectified nature.

I leave for the moment the deep connections of modern science to Christianity and its picture of God who is no longer immanent in the laws of the world. Many others have noted such connections. Instead, I want to ask what implications Daston's separation of the moral economy of science from the historical literature on moral economy has for our understanding of the production of disciplines and the circulation of knowledge? Interesting debates have asked whether one can fruitfully detach the notion of moral economy from subsistence economies and extend it to cover the moral aspects of modern markets and states (see Das and Das 2010). From the perspective of understanding scientific practice, it means that the particular intersections of economy and science need to be scrutinized much more closely than is suggested by the ideal model of the laboratory as the disinterested space where science can create its objects independent of political or moral considerations. What are the implications for anthropology, with its claims to being a scientific discipline, and the more immediate debate at hand?

Both our authors present a picture of anthropology that has two characteristics. First, they argue that the final product of research, which circulates as anthropological knowledge in the form of either a monograph or a scientific essay, is written to 'represent' past actions of others as these were observed in the field. Second, they suggest that the actual practices on which anthropologists base their own knowledge are somehow erased from the anthropological text. The burden of the argument seems to be that anthropology is not only committed to the production of disinterested knowledge but also oriented to the past. In contrast, development agencies are interested in the kind of knowledge that could be oriented to the future – hence their knowledge is produced in the form of plans and project evaluations that could provide a blueprint for action and evaluate the impact of specific interventions.

While this contrast seems elegant and compelling at first sight, a closer look suggests far greater heterogeneity within the two forms of knowledge and not only between them. Anthropological texts are not seamless descriptions of norms and practices of the kind that could be rendered as propositional knowledge of the indicative kind – e.g., 'the Nuer believe that . . . '. In order to understand how such representations work, we would need to put the moral economy of science in conversation with political and moral economy of the state and the market. Indeed, the genealogical method, most famously associated with Nietzsche and Foucault, uses materials from dispersed discourses and practices but is not the same as discourse analysis of texts, as Friedman's references to post-structuralism seem to suggest. When the question is one of intervention, and accountability generates pressures that some kind of success story be told for funding agencies, anthropological concepts such as those of belief or personality types are stripped of complexity and made into discrete objects that can be manipulated for specific objectives. With regards to the category of representation as explored by Green, my own thinking is that there is no logical connection between representation and the category of the 'past' – provided our notion of the present is deep enough to include not only the actual but also the potential and the eventual, as I have argued elsewhere (Das 2007). I am struck by the dearth of studies on how programmatic interventions work in a community once the project is over, a direct consequence of paying little attention to the relation between the event of intervention and the eventual as it unfolds.

The anthropological text, I suggest, is much more than representations of the norms and practices of the other – nor is it profitable to think of simple oppositions, such as those of structure and agency, that are the staple of question papers for anthropology students. The very presence of surplus ethnographic description in anthropological monographs often points to regions of conflict, indeterminacies, strategies, betrayals, memories, aporia – in short, textures of what is not only defined as the social but also what might count as life (Fassin 2010). It is from this perspective that the actions of many development agencies come under suspicion especially because of the place that expert knowledge has in these projects. The recent critiques of humanitarianism in contexts of ongoing violence, for example, do not come from suspicion of *all* action, but of the way in which such forms of intervention manage to privilege concepts such as trauma or PTSD over routine economic hardships faced by inhabitants of these areas, or their demands for justice rather than empathy.

We have known since Hannah Pitkin's (1972) work that the relation between aesthetic and political representations is not transparent, so one way of formulating the question of how knowledge economies operate in academic anthropology and among development agencies is to ask how the forms popularized by development agencies in terms of targets, participatory mapping, project evaluations, etc., travel into anthropology and policy making. What impact, for example, will methods of quick appraisal have on fieldwork methods, or on the weight placed on monographs versus reports? Further, we need to ask how forms of presentation (e.g., Power Point presentations or lectures on YouTube) affect the content of anthropological knowledge. Will there be a place for the non-instrumental reasoning that often accounts for slow shifts in subjectivity? With regard to poverty, how might we receive such a view as that of Hannah Arendt (1963): that social questions pertaining to poverty should properly remain in the private realm of the household or in the administrative realm of government and should not be allowed to contaminate politics as a realm of free association between equals that is not driven by need. Is the desire to reopen a discussion on issues like these, which provide the taken-for-granted ground for policy making among elite agencies in the nexus of development institutions, to count as a call for 'disinterested' knowledge as opposed to action? Both these chapters offer a provocation to think beyond their own frame, and for that provocation, I am grateful.

BIBLIOGRAPHY

Arendt, H. 1963. *On Revolution*. London: Faber and Faber.
Das, V. 2007. *Life and Words: Violence and the Descent into the Ordinary*. Berkeley: University of California Press.
Das, V. and R. K. Das. 2010. 'The Moral Embedding of Economic Action: An Introduction', in *Sociology and Anthropology of Economic Life 1: The Moral Embedding of Economic Action*. Delhi: Oxford University Press, pp. 1–31.
Daston, L. 1995. 'The Moral Economy of Science', *Osiris* 10: 2–24.
Fassin, D. 2010. 'The Ethics of Survival', *Humanity* 1(1): 81–97.
Haraway, D. 1997. *Modest_Witness @ Second_Millennium*. London: Routledge.
Pitkin, H. F. 1972. *The Concept of Representation*. Berkeley: University of California Press.

PART II

Enacting Development

CHAPTER 4

The Progress of the Project

Scientific Traction in The Gambia

Ann Kelly

What place is made for science in development? How do the circulations of science – from laboratory to field station, metropolis to rural hospital – relate to the geography of social and economic progress? Over the past three decades, work in science and technology studies (STS) has unsettled understandings of experimentation, discovery and technological innovation (e.g., Barry 2001; Haraway 1991; Latour 1988). Following the production of 'facts' across institutional landscapes, ethnographers of science have illuminated the material practices, political negotiations and social conventions that underpin scientific legitimacy. These investigations have challenged the *placelessness* of science, demonstrating how specific localities matter – and matter differently – for epistemic claims (e.g., Henke and Gieyrn 2008; Raj 2007). The ordered and standardized character of the laboratory distances the bench sciences from the quotidian (Latour and Woolgar 1979); for the field sciences, the particularities of place serve to enhance the representative character of findings (Kohler 2002). *Where* experiments occur is a key element in the career of knowledge; places discipline a community of experts, display experimental practices for public ratification and link novel technologies to civic infrastructures (Shapin 1988).

The epistemic significance of 'place' to science resonates with the concerns that preoccupy development studies. Most broadly, 'Development' (big 'D', Amita Baviskar this volume) describes a configuration of policies and practices oriented towards social transformation. Developmental processes entail transfer; technologies invented *somewhere* are retooled and relocated to improve life *elsewhere*. Mirroring the analytical concerns of sociologists of technology and science, anthropologists of development have stressed the place-bound character of these initiatives, describing the role of particular 'contexts' in shaping the dynamics of modernization (e.g., Arce and Long 2000). Ethnographic attention to the ways in which development interventions are configured in political and physical space, reveals the diverse forms of knowing – whether they be understood as 'lay', 'indigenous', 'popular' or 'communal' – involved in the social trajectory of technologies. Like STS scholarship, anthropological interest in the locality has come to frame policy discourse: the current enthusiasm for participatory development attests to the widespread belief that local attitudes and activities are essential to the success of technocratic projects (Kumar 2003).[1] Thus, conversations between STS and development studies – when they have taken place – have tended to focus on the challenges and possibilities of engaging publics to guide innovation processes (e.g., Leach, Scones and Wynne 2005). The emphasis of this work is on modalities of involvement: how citizens can exert influence over the interventions and innovations that impact their lives.

But situating science offers other theoretical opportunities for the study of development. Calling attention to the specific locations of experimentation opens up the range of materials and spaces that constitute participation. Sociological analyses of medical research, such as those provided by Stefan Timmermans and Marc Berg (2003) and Catherine Will (2007), have described the accommodations made for the contextual dimensions of clinical care by trial design, noting how experimental protocols are embedded in the clinic. Rather than focus on the democratic process through which research agendas are set, these authors analyse the way research is done – the practical alignment of actors, institutions, resources, objects and practices that underwrite the production of medical knowledge. Abandoning the notion that research can be disentangled from the clinical contexts in which it takes place, these authors point to the ways in which investigative practice reorders and manages its object of study in order to improve it. Their open-ended empirical exploration of the entanglements of persons and things in the formation of facts demonstrates how proofs are simultaneously evaluative and transformative.

The purpose of this chapter is, first, to use this pragmatic understanding of knowledge production to conceptualize the role of international research projects in development.[2] Its focus is the Larval Control Project (LCP), a trial implemented by the UK Medical Research Council (MRC) from 2004 to 2007 in upcountry Gambia. As an experiment in malaria *control*, LCP did not measure the efficacy of an intervention

but piloted a programme of management. Drawing from the methodological example of the LCP, this chapter, like the contributions made
by Maia Green and John Friedman, reflexively considers the delimita-
tions of anthropological critique and engagement. During the trial, I was
asked to assess the operational feasibility of the collaboration between
village health workers and research nurses by using focus group discussions to elicit the experiences of participant mothers. Collaborating with
the team offered an opportunity to enhance my ethnographic intimacy
and to justify my presence. But what I believed was a straightforward
foray into applied anthropology became an unexpected and perplexing
entanglement with a fieldworker over the ethos of inquiry.[3] The friction
between my attempt to elicit communal views and the fieldworker's
countervailing efforts to mobilize communities pressed me to consider
the different ways through which knowledge practices – including my
own – can come to matter.

A description of place provides the entry point to this discussion. The
MRC's institutional location within The Gambia has considerable bearing on the slippage between a project of research and one of development that characterized the LCP. I then move into a deeper analysis of
the relevant places for the LCP, focusing on how its investigative practices reworked Gambian natural and therapeutic landscapes. Finally, I
describe my own role in the LCP and the tensions that emerged between
my approach to focus group discussions and that of the Gambian fieldworker with whom I worked. I suggest that what initially seemed instrumentalist understandings of the purpose of research was in fact a more
subtle coordination of the goals of research with local imperatives. His
pragmatic tactics, I believe, point to ways anthropologists might rethink
the substantive relationship between the social relationships they generate during fieldwork and the analyses they produce.

Medical Research Council (UK), The Gambia

As the UK's major medical research unit in a developing country, MRC
Laboratories has offered a site for field and laboratory-based work in
The Gambia since 1947. Its original purpose was to conduct nutritional
research on peanut planters, peanuts being the major export from the
colony. Tropical medicine and research were, therefore, tools to advance
the interests of the empire (e.g., Bonneuil 2001; Vaughan 1991). After
The Gambia achieved independence and joined the Commonwealth
in 1965, population welfare was reframed as a national concern; however, the institutional arrangements that belie scientific research in The

Gambia suggest that the relationship between knowledge and government is not moored in the state. Now, at the beginning of the twenty-first century, most Gambians live within potential MRC study areas, and a large proportion of the population have participated directly or indirectly in medical research. Their familiarity with research protocol makes Gambians an attractive population for large-scale trials. The MRC laboratories in The Gambia are a magnet for philanthropic funds and public-private partnerships. Much of what is known about tropical disease and its control has come out of The Gambia, which has been described as 'Africa's laboratory'.[4] Arguably, then, Gambian labour remains an asset to northern economies, though its value is linked to the data gathered from health experiments rather than from the peanuts picked on plantations. According to some, tropical research not only continues to provide the infrastructure for economic development but also enables a form of extraction particular to the global bio-economy (e.g., Petryna 2007).

Indeed, the intensity and duration of the MRC's operations, the sheer size of its field stations and the extensive resources that come through its gates stand in stark contrast to the country's weak economy and poorly resourced health system. In their investigation of mothers' engagement with a pneumococcal vaccine trial, Leach, Fairhead and Small (2004) emphasize the precarious nature of the choice to enrol in research. 'Being with the MRC' entitles participants to free medications – which, in accordance with global ethical protocol, the MRC offers to those enrolled in research. 'Joining involves transactions' (ibid: 1117); giving blood samples and receiving therapeutic care is an exchange embedded in the power imbalances and inequalities attendant on the global medical sciences and bioscience industry.

Upcountry MRC stations like Farafenni provide a point of contact for neighbouring communities, who become habitual hosts to research and repeated beneficiaries of clinical services. Some also become employees. Even modest research projects require large numbers of staff – to recruit participants, collect data and analyse samples but also to drive the cars, clean the labs and prepare meals for the staff. These jobs are a major source of employment for Gambians, second only to agriculture. While I was based there over the summer of 2007, the MRC's field station in Farafenni was an epicentre of social life. Auctions and parties were held on its grounds; MRC staff would use the laboratory facilities to freeze ice blocks for Ramadan. In the evening, a local soccer team ran drills across the station's central field and later would gather with the guards in the mess hall to watch Nigerian soap operas on TV (Kelly 2011).

Despite the enduring presence of MRC buildings, the limits between Gambian society and the institutional capacities of the MRC are sharply drawn. Therapeutic attention is given by specific projects to participants – it is contractual and periodic. The intermittent therapeutic attention to which participants have grown accustomed is mirrored by the staff's experience of employment. It is MRC policy not to hire anyone who has recently worked for the state. A waiting period of six months before contracting staff is meant to prevent direct competition with government hospitals. In the main, MRC employees are hired by a particular research project. It is not unusual to come across fieldworkers who have worked under the auspices of the MRC for twenty years or more but only on short-term contracts. While it provides the critical infrastructure for the outsourcing of trials into The Gambia, the MRC is not a clinic, nor do the innovations its trials produce speak to the interests of the state.[5]

Set within the institutional parameters of the MRC, research projects encompass two distinct modalities of benefit. The first, associated with work within the laboratory compound, yields potential advances – publications, research grants, innovative therapeutics – processed through ordered protocols and standardized spaces. This flow of information is continual, but effectively placeless (Kuklick and Kohler 1996). The second, entangled with the Gambian people and embedded in the landscape, provides immediate enhancements to Gambian well-being, such as health care or bed-nets or jobs, but is constrained to the resources of a research budget. Like trials before it, the Larval Control Project (LCP) was constrained by the countervailing temporal and material dimensions of medical research in a resource-poor setting.[6] However, what is distinct about the LCP is that this task of embedding the empirical in the context of experimentation is not framed in terms of an ethical commitment to the community, or indeed as a scaling of 'universal standards' to the 'personal realities of moral life' (Kleinman 1999: 70). The connections the LCP made to the community were methodological.

Larval Control Project (LCP)

The Larval Control Project (LCP) was a massive undertaking. Over the course of two years, microbial larvicide (*Bti*) was applied across four zones along the north and south banks of the Gambia River, each approximately 100km^2 (Majambere et al. 2007). Larval habitats, which are generally associated with human activity, are typically the sunlit pools formed by depressions made by animals or footprints that fill with rain or ground water. Because breeding grounds are transient and unpredictable, larval control programmes require exhaustive and continual surveys of the intervention area. With villages located between one and eight kilometres from the river, the study areas encompassed a wide range of microclimates from grassland to stream fringe, rice fields and mangrove forest. In contrast to DDT, the powerful (and belatedly controversial) insecticide *Bti* is safe for non-target organisms. It passes quickly through the ecosystem and thus is less likely to result in resistance, but because it has little residual activity it must be reapplied on a weekly basis. Equipped with heavy spray packs, larvae dippers and detailed maps, teams of fifteen or more fieldworkers walked transepts 2 kilometres long and 100 metres wide in an attempt to locate, record and treat all mosquito habitats from floodplain to brick-pit.

Establishing the *clinical* effectiveness of this locally coordinated method of mosquito surveillance added another layer of logistical complexity between experimental protocol and fieldwork. First, the LCP needed to recruit a paediatric research population of two thousand children – five hundred in each zone – aged six months to ten years. This initiative required lengthy discussions with village leaders and meetings with community members, some highly sceptical of MRC motives. Second, the impact of such a continuous and incremental intervention necessitated a measure of disease incidence – the number of malarial attacks in a set population over a given time. Thus, in addition to a biannual collection of blood samples, fieldworkers and nurses were stationed in villages during the rainy season to record cases of malaria, survey who had travelled and provide on-site care. Two nurses and one field assistant were stationed in key villages in each of the four LCP zones for the duration of the rainy season (May–November). During the day nurses waited for patients from the neighbouring homes, and in the afternoon they made visits to the farthest villages within their catchment area. If a study participant was considered too ill to treat on-site, he or she was assisted with transport to the hospital.

Village health workers (VHWs) played a critical function in this surveillance strategy. Initiated in the early 1980s, The Gambia's health care system is based on a three-tier system of referral, with local primary health care villages at its base, rural clinics operating at the district level and three national hospitals at its apex. The primary health care villages (of roughly 400 inhabitants or more) are managed by village development committees, a grass-roots institutional tier intended to encourage rural communities to become more proactive in the development process (Davis, Hulme and Woodhouse 1994). Village development committees select village health workers, who are given six weeks' training in preventative and curative medicine. Understood as a panacea for a weak and underfunded health system, the VHWs are unsalaried but expect compensation from members of the community who seek their care. Occasionally, VHWs receive nominal payments from research projects to serve as reporters, informing MRC staff of cases occurring in their villages that might be relevant for specific investigative purposes. In a similar capacity, they provide a contact point through which agencies can mount programmes in the village.

The role ascribed to the VHWs in the LCP protocol surpassed that of data capture. Because the LCP could only contract a few nurses, they were responsible for not only monitoring malaria events but also providing treatment coverage to the village. The VHWs did not make for the easiest of experimental collaborators. Few were able to read and write, and fewer still had any formal education. Beyond the six weeks of training the VHW workers received following their selection, the VHW handbook, which had not been updated since its release in 1980, was the only formal instrument of clinical support – and copies of that text were nearly impossible to find.[7] Moreover, in contrast to traditional birth assistants (TBAs), who historically occupied a role in the villages as healers, the VHWs were relatively recent actors in the political ecology (Cham et al. 1987). The appointment of a VHW often involved a process of negotiation between the research interests of the MRC and the interests of the powerful members of the community, who treated selection as a form of patronage. Thus, rather than facilitating community access, these political entanglements entrenched distrust of research, leading to high dropout rates.

Enrolling local Gambians in the day-to-day operation of the LCP had clear advantages: the village health workers' familiarity with their communities meant that they were alert to the health of the participants. These modes of participatory practice yoked technologies of disease assessment to site-specific techniques of disease control. However, by the beginning of the LCP's second year, the success of this partnership was uncertain. Did the VHWs' involvement in therapeutic delivery impact mothers' decisions to seek care from the nurses? How, moreover, were the different roles of the nurses and VHW understood? With these questions in mind, the Principal Investigator (PI) believed that a series of focus groups and interviews with the mothers of participant children might provide critical insight. In addition to revealing any programmatic errors in case detection, he thought the discussion would offer a good opportunity to forestall any misunderstandings about the benefits the mothers might expect from the research team in the future. Having worked in The Gambia before, the PI was aware of the potential for conflicts to arise when trials drew to a close. As the only social scientist on site, I was asked to devise a line of questioning that could illuminate

the mothers' understanding of the protocols of the LCP and their investigative (as opposed to therapeutic) purposes.

Communities on the Make

Though my interest in the operational efficiency of the LCP's clinical
strategy was rather limited, I welcomed the PI's request. The focus of my
ethnographic research was the work of local research assistants employed
by the MRC – how project fieldworkers negotiated the protocols of science and the demands of local health populations. With its large number
of staff, complicated protocols and labour-intensive research activities,
the LCP seemed an ideal site to explore these concerns. Embedding my
research *within* the project quieted my anxieties about drawing conclusions *about* it. Though the social relations of science may hold interest for
an academic audience – and possibly even for policymakers – this analytical preoccupation was at a remove from the investigative concerns of
the LCP. Working alongside health researchers and practitioners, I found
the tentative authority of my ethnographic claims (balanced as they
are between scientific method and literary craft) compounded by their
uncertain utility. Whether or not my observations of the LCP practices
were theoretically insightful sat awkwardly with the question of whether
or not they were relevant to the well-being of those involved.

One way anthropologists working in clinical settings reconcile the
pragmatic and theoretical dimensions of their work is to focus their
attention on the practices, experiences and understandings that 'expert'
knowledge excludes. Illustrative of science *in context*, ethnographic data
reveals the contingent and site-specific relations invisible to the universalizing and purifying gaze of medical science. The impact of anthropological evidence on personal and collective well-being has, therefore,
been understood in terms of the social and cultural dimensions it *adds
to* clinical research and practice. The corroborative potential of this perspective has been particularly evident in the treatment of mental illness,
for which patient narratives have a direct impact on clinical diagnosis
(e.g., Kleinman 1995; Young 1995); in the formation of public health
policy, insofar as local perceptions about health care are believed to
inform health-seeking behaviours (e.g., Hahn 1999; Helman 1994); and
finally, in the analysis of global inequalities, where fine-grained ethnographic accounts of individuals' struggles to gain therapeutic access are
used to reveal and challenge corporate agendas in the production and
distribution of pharmaceuticals (e.g., Biehl 2004; Petryna, Lakoff and
Kleinman 2006). As Thomas Yarrow and Soumhya Venkatesan argue

in this volume's introduction, the 'usefulness' of anthropological data to development has been conceived along similar lines: as cultural specialists, anthropologists help clarify the landscape of intervention and facilitate the implementation of technologies.

There are concerns to be raised over the instrumentalization of ethnography, not the least of which is that circumscribing anthropology to a singular outcome short-circuits the empirical resilience of the field. Writing field notes entails anticipation rather than prediction; anthropologists gather as much as possible with an eye to the very things they would take for granted, knowing that at some point they might prove relevant. However, I felt that as long as I could distinguish between modes of exegesis, this operational study would enhance the corroborative potential of my research without foreclosing more indefinite avenues of reflection. The significance of this focus group data was not fixed; the critical task was merely to recognize the ways in which qualitative observations were marshalled into evidence.

As a collaborator, I dutifully approached focus group discussions as occasions to gather 'viewpoints' on the trial. The focus group discussion is a pervasive instrument of social research; its authority rests on a rather different investigative arrangement than that associated with ethnography. As Javier Lezaun points out in his analysis of the epistemology of public opinion, though its format appears simple – a neutral space where opinions can be aired – the focus group entails a highly crafted art of mediation and a specific notion of political order (Lezaun 2007). A fundamentally utilitarian exercise, the focus group discussion produces value that is determined by the number and diversity of views that can be collected and contrasted. In this context, focus group discussions were intended to reveal health-seeking behaviours; the collective opinions they generated could predict whether participants were likely to seek help from a project nurse when their child fell ill. Producing these insights required a subtle negotiation of participants' prior experiences of being enrolled in MRC projects and their anticipation of the kinds of responses the clinical team might want to hear. It meant staying away from questions like 'what are the signs of malaria' or 'what are the purposes of this project', which might be taken as tests of knowledge, and instead eliciting personal narratives about participants' experiences with illness and research through inquisitive indirection and communicative exchange.

Focus group discussions were conducted in villages, either at the gathering place in the village's centre – the *bantaba* – or in open-air structures that functioned as clinics or schools. These were charged research spaces, used for explaining research purposes to the community and enrolling participants. The fieldworker, acting as my translator, informed me that he had considerable experience 'engaging communities', having been previously employed by the nongovernmental organization (NGO) Action Aid. While experimentation entails highly rigid and specific protocols, there is considerable overlap between the techniques through which populations are encouraged to participate in research and those used to galvanize political action or promote public health messages. This ambiguity is advantageous for the purposes of increasing enrolment, and I will return to this point. For the purposes of the focus groups, these instrumental associations made the naturalness of conversation fragile.

The fieldworker was an excellent facilitator. His tone was informal but authoritative. Under his direction mothers were vocal about their experiences; conversations were always lively and full of laughter. I left meetings with dense transcripts peppered with provocative quotations. But from the onset, it was clear that the fieldworker had a rather different sense of the purposes of these discussions. Rather than simply pursuing health-seeking behaviours – as per my instructions – he used these meetings as opportunities to teach mothers to recognize malaria symptoms. More troublesome was his tendency to conclude discussions by listing the duties of trial participation: to refrain from travel, to bring their children for finger-pricking and to be vigilant in their reporting of illness. He also continually emphasized the importance of community mobilization, whether it was for health checks or for group meetings, like the ones we were conducting. Try as I might to impress upon the fieldworker the need to keep questions open-ended, the tenor of the discussions inevitably turned didactic. On the very few instances when we were not met by mothers upon arriving at the village, he would begin meetings by chastising the mothers for their lack of 'group responsibility'. In this regard, villagers were described as 'good' or 'bad': the inhabitants of Dibba Kunda Woolof, for instance were deemed too 'individualistic' for research: 'People here do not yet understand how to take responsibility for the health of their community. . . . We must teach them to act together if things [are ever to] improve.'

The fieldworker's approach to 'community engagement' echoes recent ethnographic findings in the anthropology of development. In contrast to optimistic policy initiatives, anthropologists have questioned whether practices of 'participation' might in fact serve to diminish the civic potential of science by circumscribing the ways in which citizenship is imagined (Cooke and Kothari 2001). Though current medical research protocol may champion community engagement, anthropologists have shown the coercive character of participatory practices that force local partners to conform to formal management goals that systematically exclude those who do not. Indeed, I found it difficult to disassociate the fieldworker's approach to public consultation from the ends of data collection. To ensure the operational success of clinical trials, the MRC – in line with an increasing number of institutions engaged in global research – stresses establishing rapport and trust with local populations (e.g., Molyneux et al. 2005).

These – in my view, failed – focus group discussions confirmed this cynical understanding of the corroborative potential of local knowledge. The fieldworker's affective relationships with participants were used to enforce adherence to research protocol and thus transform 'bad communities' into 'good ones'. To my great dismay, at the conclusion of the final focus group the fieldworker commended our qualitative project thusly: 'after our work with these people, even the hardest villages, they are ready for us, for any project, and at *any time*.' Rather than a forum for deliberation, the focus group discussion was an instrument to generate future research subjects.

The End(s) of Research

But before we dismiss the experimental integrity of the focus groups entirely, let us consider this instrumentalist objective more closely. The fieldworker's insistence that his respondents would be prepared to participate in research '*any time*' reminds us of the distinct temporalities at work between a medical experiment, a public health project and ethnographic research. After three years of spraying, and a great deal of effort, the LCP found that clinical cases were not reduced by any significant degree. Spraying initiated at the end of the dry season and run throughout the raining season might help reduce transmission, but in the final analysis, targeted ground application of *Bti* was not an appropriate tool for areas with extensive flooding, where larva habitats are largely inaccessible by foot. In terms of policy, the trial's negative outcomes were merely suggestive; resources could be used more effectively for more targeted interventions.

These conclusions did not square with the participants' experience. During discussions, mothers emphasized their gratitude towards the LCP staff. As opposed to previous years, their children had remained in good health during the rainy season. Though some noted the lower number of mosquitoes, for the most part this positive change was attributed to the on-site clinical care made available by the presence of the nurse. The impact of these services was not limited to their children; the LCP had improved the health of the community overall. During one

discussion, a mother recalled how a nurse's intervention in a complicated delivery had saved her life and her baby's. She joked that she and
the other mothers had hatched a plan to marry him to one of the eligible
women in the village. But above all, mothers were distressed over the
upcoming close of the project:

> We are thinking now of the hardship we will suffer when the proj-
> ect ends . . . our message to the MRC is 'give us more future projects';
> there is much happiness and gratitude for their participation. We hope
> for a continual renewal extension of our contract.

In light of the project's negative results, statements like this underscore
the gross discrepancies between the ways in which science-society relations play out in The Gambia and the mechanisms of social accountability built into American and European policy environments (Nowotny,
Scott and Gibbons 2001). This mother's hope for 'future projects' is a
testament to the ways in which processes of technological innovation
in The Gambia provide only temporary infrastructures for social and
economic development. Progress is circumscribed to the time-space of
the experiment.

But there may be ways to re-imagine the social contract posed by
MRC and its Gambian publics. The mothers understood the benefits of
research in terms of the free health care that comes with participation
(Geissler et al. 2008; Leach and Fairhead 2007). But the therapeutic
benefits they experienced with the LCP were explicitly contrasted to
their expectations of those generally associated with the MRC. Many
had initially been reluctant to enrol in the trial, since they had heard
that nurses from previous projects would provide treatment only when
they came to collect blood. During the LCP, however, they found that
clinical services were available at any time and to anyone – an accessibility they attributed to the close relationship the LCP fostered between
nurses and VHWs. For mothers, the collaboration between the VHW
and the nurse meant that benefits of research were not wholly contingent on experimental practice: their improved health was also attribut-
able to the increase in local capacity. Though mothers conveyed concern
at the closure of the trial, they asked not for more research (and by
extension, more health care), but rather for a continuation of the MRC's
supportive role within the community:

> We are praying for the MRC not to leave but when they do leave let
> them continue to empower the village health worker, teach him and
> supply him with enough medication.

By locating its evidentiary context within the social and physical landscape, the LCP built connections between test setting and governmental intervention. Research protocol provided a template to train VHW workers and spray-men. In this way, the LCP united malaria research with the techniques to control transmission and the local partners responsible for its implementation. The scientific credibility of the facts produced in the LCP was a product of collaboration; the experimental contribution of non-experts forecast the effectiveness of an environmental management strategy and in so doing, demonstrated its sustainability. A model for future action, the LCP occupies a critical space within the landscape of public health. Rather than through a series of contractual extensions, the LCP's empirical *extensibility* turned the practice of demonstration into an engine of development (Miyazaki 2004).[8]

Conceptualized as a space of extensibility, the technology focus group becomes more creative than extractive. My anxieties of coercion notwithstanding, the fieldworker expressed a rather dim view of my insistence on neutrality. After a meeting in which the fieldworker chastised the mothers for their inability to organize themselves 'as a community', I suggested that perhaps it would be better if I worked with a fieldworker not directly involved in the LCP. A more detached moderator, I reasoned, would safeguard the genuineness of mothers' responses, enabling them to speak more candidly about the trial. The fieldworker was appalled. How, he retorted, did I plan to find the 'right' people to participate? Even if I happened to be fortunate enough to draw a 'good' group, without a recognizable member of the 'project' they would not understand the purposes of the discussion, and thus not take its messages to heart. Was not the larger goal to ensure that mothers understood the trial and the dangers of malaria? Pointing to my notebook, he asked: 'Are you trying to keep this knowledge for yourself?'

For the purpose of educational outreach, focus group discussions hinge upon the moderator's familiarity with the research setting. Conducted correctly with the 'right' people, these discussions could alter the health status of participant populations. The goal of the fieldworker was one of mobilization: he wanted to move participants, to affect their views, generate awareness, and most important, bring people together. Observed in this light, focus groups are not merely an instrument of knowledge but a critical assembling device, a form of collective action. Like the local spray-men working in floodplains, the fieldworker's familiarity with the place of research rendered it amenable both to investigation and to improvement. In the words of one mother: 'The fieldworker is here to mobilize us as a community to participate . . . we have responded and the health of our community has improved.'

The fieldworker's efforts to produce the public brought to light the disengaged character of my engagement. For anthropologists, relation-ships function both as objects and as heuristic devices; analysis oscillates between the abstract and the concrete. As Marilyn Strathern argues, 'one not only perceives relations between things but also perceives things as relations.' (Strathern 2005: 63). 'The relation' is therefore not only anthropology's heuristic and object, but also its field. Anthropologists use relationships (made with informants) to relate social orders (inter-personal relationships) to cultural logics (categorical relationships). But while attentive to that relation triplex, anthropologists tend to regard the problem of how to manage the particular relationships formed dur-ing fieldwork as of a different order than their interpretive decisions. The distinction is generally considered an issue of ethics as opposed to one of epistemology. However, one implication of investigating the place of science and the consequences of its emplacement is that such an inquiry forces anthropologists to recognize the empirical practices that drive the worlds we produce through analysis.

As a mode of research that reorganizes practice through the pro-cess of description, the LCP problematizes the formal distinctions an anthropologist implicitly draws between research, knowledge, ethics and agency. The fieldworker provides a fresh gloss on the dialectics of social and conceptual relations, showing how the techniques of inquiry can become mechanisms to promote social vitality. How anthropology might be reconfigured to cultivate a similar mode of intellectual com-munion requires a robust conceptualization of the epistemic value of our research associations. This returns us to the question of the scientific significance of location. To what extent, we might ask, can the anthropo-logical project, as a movement between fields, be thought of as belong-ing to a place? What role does *where* fieldwork happens have in shaping the insights that it produces?

Conclusion: Ethnography Put in Its Place

My approach to place in this chapter is cast in terms of how 'science' in the context of 'development' draws from practices generally under-stood as belonging to the latter. My discomfort with the fieldworker's approach to focus group techniques stemmed from the asymmetrical treatment of these two modalities of progress. Focused on the proto-cols and practices of *research*, I hoped to illuminate the social work and material practices that constitute scientific coherence. Underwriting this analytic was my commitment to preserving the open-endedness of fact. But as I became more deeply involved in the LCP, I came to regard that investigative agenda as inadequate. Documenting the social construction of science did little to illuminate what is at stake for those involved in the production of knowledge. The complex interactions between LCP fieldworkers, clinical staff, participants and research- ers were both normative and substantive; participation in the project was constitutive of the technical enhancement it sought to describe. By attending only to 'science', I had implicitly bracketed some of the other forms of connection and processes of signification advanced by the LCP.

The fieldworker's perplexity at the distinctions I drew between research and relevance brought these connections to light. In a place where the practices of science frequently yield more good than their outcomes, the fieldworker manipulates the protocols of research to aug- ment their immediate socio-material impact. Though no one knew it then, the LCP was to be one of the last trials to be hosted in Farafenni. In February 2009, a notice was put upon the station bulletin board informing the staff that the MRC head office in London had decided to shift its vision: rather than focus its investments in The Gambia, the MRC would support regional collaborations across West Africa; and in the upcoming five years, the MRC would cut the budget for their laboratories in The Gambia in half. The rationale was to create oppor- tunities to conduct multi-centred studies on a greater number of people and thereby enhance the quality of research and the speed with which it is conducted. As one might expect, this plan was not well received by Gambians. The former head of Farafenni station, now paid to moni- tor the empty buildings while the London office decides what to do with them, received hundreds of letters from neighbouring villagers protesting the closure. 'For the most part', he said, 'these people feel abandoned. Some feel betrayed. They had participated with the MRC because they believed it was a lasting commitment.'

The fieldworker's effort to ground research – to wrestle it out of its inevitable circulations from field laboratory to global metropolis – provokes some interesting questions about how anthropologists might productively engage with development. As I argued above, one way anthropologists have positioned themselves vis-à-vis practitioners is to see their work as complementary to their interventions. The corrobo- rative potential of ethnography is understood not simply in terms of its applied dimensions – say, in facilitating the communication of public health messages or tailoring interventions so that they can be more successfully implemented. Ethnography must also be understood as providing a voice for the underrepresented, a vehicle for revealing the local practices that expert discourses conceal. This complementarily rests on a notion of epistemic integrity: ethnography might be informed by the issues concerning the people studied, but ultimately it remains methodologically distinct from these engagements.

In his 2007 discussion of the ethical potentials of ethnography, Michael Parker interrogates the recent call for an ethnographically informed bioethics – the championing of the empirical as the foundation for universal ethical protocols. Parker takes issue with the assumption that ethnographic methods offer a privileged vantage on moral worlds and that simply by 'taking into account local everyday values', ethicists and philosophers might be better equipped to adjudicate what constitutes the good. This enfolding of the empirical into the ethical, Parker argues, neglects the profound ethical commitments (e.g., giving voice to the vulnerable, preserving traditions, respecting host communities, exposing the violence of colonialism or global capital) that undergird the anthropological project. The methodological centrality of radical otherness to anthropological research amplifies rather than resolves the tension between the values that structure everyday life and situations of moral concern. Ethnographic insight thus does not consist in revealing local values, but in balancing the interplay of empathy and difference, reflexivity and representation. In reminding us of that ethos, Parker situates anthropological engagement not merely as a moral-ethical negotiation of the field, but rather as a creative co-production of that field. In other words, taking seriously the social character of anthropological research means that the empirical and the epistemic emerge with and through the people anthropologists study. What we understand and how we understand it is forged in the moment of ethnographic encounter.

My experience with the LCP prompts me to expand Parker's point. For the fieldworker, the 'community' was not merely the beneficiary of research outcomes but rather its product. Social relationships were both the practice and the products of research practice. In the LCP the evidentiary context was protensive – its empirical power was built into the future connections those practices enabled. Rather than introducing cultural sensitivity to interventionist logics or critiquing the latter for a lack of situated vision, anthropology can explore the practical and intellectual extensions of our research. The question remains how to effectively use our empirical contiguity – being together in a space – to precipitate forms of continuity, a responsiveness and creativity to the evidence we generate. Understanding the tools we use as analogous to other methods of knowledge production may help us experiment with new and different ways to entangle the integrity of our projects with other forms of progress.

NOTES

I would first like to thank Pateh Bah, the fieldworker who taught me something about the value of social scientific methods. I am also grateful to my colleagues conducting research at the Medical Research Council Laboratories – Steve Lindsay, Margaret Pinder, Silas Mjamabere, Clare Green, Vas Louca and Emma Harding-Esch – who provided extensive support for this project. This piece benefited from the many insightful comments by Javier Lezaun, Alice Street and the editors of this volume. Finally I am grateful to the joint Gambian Government/MRC Ethics Committee for granting their approval for this study, and to the organizations that have supported it: the Wellcome Trust, the Brocher Foundation and the London School of Hygiene and Tropical Medicine.

1. These trends also speak to the bureaucratic value of ethnography, an institutional relocation of anthropological knowledge that is elegantly described in the introduction to this volume.
2. As an account of how we think that privileges practice over theory, pragmatism encompasses a variety of philosophical and political positions. My take on pragmatism draws from a concern with the performativity of scientific inquiry – an understanding that empirical facts constitute a convergence between inductive methods and the world they describe.
3. Callon and Rabeharisoa (2004) develop the notion of entanglement to describe the process by which certain links and relations are recognized within, and become part of, a shared moral framework. Entanglement is apposite for this discussion, as it describes the ways in which, by doing research in this place, I came to embrace a trajectory of anthropological knowledge defined by those with whom I was doing work.
4. Tom Paulson, "In steamy Gambia, frontline research into disease: Nation benefits from British lab founded in 1947 to keep farmers healthy and productive" Seattle Post-Intelligencer, Friday, March 23, 2001: http://www.seattlepi.com/africa/gambia23.shtml.
5. One particularly compelling example of the uneasiness of that partnership is MRC's silence with regards to President Jammeh's recent claim that he has found a cure for AIDS based on West African traditional practices. Despite heavy criticism from scientists working in country, the MRC's administration argued that its legitimacy depends on the degree to which it can distance itself from the government while not appearing hostile to its interests.
6. For an analysis of the ways in which these distinct modes of public benefit are and are not articulated by ethics, see Kelly et al. (2010).
7. I was only able to locate one copy, torn and in terrible condition, at the district health offices in Fajara, at the coast.
8. In information technology, extensibility refers to programmes that have a built-in capacity for growth; these are protocols that through use extend the system's capacity. Hirokari Miyazaki develops the term to describe the relationship between hope and knowledge he sees at work in indigenous Fijian gift-giving (2004). Miyazaki focuses on the temporal scheme of giving and how the expectation of reciprocity becomes an engine of social life; here, too, I want to argue that the value of the programme is linked to future civic capacity.

BIBLIOGRAPHY

Arce, A. and N. Long (eds). 2000. *Anthropology, Modernity and Development*. London: Routledge.

Barry, A. 2001. *Political Machines*. London: Athlone Press.

Biehl, J. 2004. 'The Activist State: Global Pharmaceuticals, AIDS, and Citizenship in Brazil', *Social Text* 22(3): 105–132.

Bonneuil, C. 2001. 'Development as Experiment', *Osiris* 14: 258–281.

Callon, M. and V. Rabeharisoa. 2004. 'Gino's Lesson in Humanity: Genetics, Mutual Entanglements and the Sociologist's Role', *Economy and Society* 25(1): 1–27.

Cham, K., C. MacCormack, A. Touray and S. Baldeh. 1987. 'Social Organisation and Political Factionalism: PHC in The Gambia', *Health Policy and Planning* 2(3): 214–226.

Cooke, B. and U. Kothari (eds). 2001. Participation: The new tyranny? London and New York: Zed Books

Davis, D., D. Hulme and P. Woodhouse. 1994. 'Decentralization by Default: Local Governance and the View from The Village The Gambia', *Public Administration and Development* 14: 253–269.

Fairhead, J., M. Leach and M. Small. 2004. *Childhood Vaccination and Society in The Gambia: Public Engagement with Science and Delivery*. Brighton, Sussex: Institute of Development Studies, University of Sussex.

Geissler, P. W., A. Kelly, R. Pool and B. Imokhuede. 2008. '"He is now like a brother, I can even give him some blood": Relational Ethics and Material Exchanges in a Malaria Vaccine "Trial Community" in The Gambia', *Social Science and Medicine* 67(5): 698–707.

Hahn, R. 1999. *Anthropology in Public Health: Bridging Differences in Culture and Society*. Oxford: Oxford University Press.

Haraway, D. 1991. *Simians, Cyborgs, and Women: The Reinvention of Nature*. New York: Routledge.

Helman, C. G. 1994. *Culture, Health and Illness: An Introduction for Health Professionals*, 3rd ed. London: Butterworth Heinemann.

Henke, C. R. 2000. 'Making a Place for Science: The Field Trial', *Social Studies of Science* 30: 483–511.

Henke, C. and T. Gieyrn. 2008. 'Sites of Scientific Practice: The Enduring Importance of Place', in E. J. Hackett (ed.), *The Handbook of Science and Technologies Studies*. Cambridge, MA: MIT Press, pp. 353–376.

Kelly, A. 2011. 'Remember Bambali: Evidence, Ethics and the Co-Production of Truth', in P. W. Geissler (ed.), *Evidence, Ethos and Experiment: The Anthropology and History of Medical Research in Africa*. Oxford: Berghahn Books, pp.120–135.

Kelly, A. M. Pinder, D. Ameh, S. Majambere and S. Lindsay. 2010. '"Like Sugar and Honey": The Embedded Ethics of a Larval Control Project in The Gambia', *Social Science and Medicine* 70(12): 1912–1919.

Kleinman, A. 1995. *Writing at the Margin: Discourse between Anthropology and Medicine*. Berkeley: University of California Press.

Kleinman, A. 1999. 'Moral experience and ethical reflection: Can ethnography reconcile them? A quandary for 'the new bioethics'. *Daedalus*, 128(4): 69–97.

Kohler, R. E. 2002. *Labscapes and Landscapes*. Chicago: University of Chicago Press.

Kuklick, H. and R. E. Kohler. 1996. 'Introduction', in H. Kuklick and R. E. Kohler (eds), 'Science in the Field', Special Issue of *Osiris* 11: 1–14.

Kumar, S. 2003. *Methods for Community Participation*. London: ITDG Press.

Latour, B. 1988. *The Pasteurization of France*. Cambridge, MA: Harvard University Press.

Latour, B. and S. Woolgar. 1979. *Laboratory Life: The Construction of Scientific Facts*. Princeton: Princeton University Press.

Leach, M., I. Scoones and B. Wynne (eds). 2005. *Science and Citizens: Globalization and The Challenge of Engagement*. London and New York: Zed Books.

Leach, M. and J. Fairhead. 2007. *Vaccine Anxieties: Global Science, Child Health and Society*. London: Earthscan.

Lezaun, J. 2007. 'A Market of Opinions: The Political Epistemology of Focus Groups', *The Sociological Review* 55: 130–151.

Majambere S., et al. 2007. 'Microbial Larvicides for Malaria Control in The Gambia', *Malaria Journal* 6: 76.

Miyazaki, H. 2004. *The Method of Hope*. Stanford, CA: Stanford University Press.

Molyneux, C. S., et al. 2005. '"Even if they ask you to stand by a tree all day, you will have to do it (laughter) . . . !": Community Voices on the Notion and Practice of Informed Consent for Biomedical Research in Developing Countries', *Social Science and Medicine* 61(2): 443–454.

Nowotny, H., P. Scott and M. Gibbons. 2001. *Rethinking Science: Knowledge and the Public in an Age of Uncertainty*. Cambridge: Polity Press.

Parker, M. 2007. 'Ethnography/Ethics'. *Social Science & Medicine* 65 (11): 2248–2257.

Petryna, A. 2007. 'Clinical Trials Offshored: On Private Sector Science and Public Health', *Biosocieties* 2(1): 21–40.

Petryna, A., A. Lakoff and A. Kleineman (eds). 2006. *Global Pharmaceuticals: Ethics, Markets, Practices*. Durham, NC, and London: Duke University Press.

Raj, K. 2007. *Relocating Modern Science*. London: Palgrave-MacMillan.

Shapin, S. 1988. 'The House of Experiment in Seventeenth-Century England', *Isis* 79: 373–404.

Strathern, M. 2005. *Kinship, Law and the Unexpected: Relatives Are Always a Surprise*. Cambridge: Cambridge University Press.

Vaughan, M. 1991. *Curing Their Ills: Colonial Power and African Illness*. Stanford: Stanford University Press.

Will, Catherine. 2007. 'The Alchemy of Clinical Trials', *Biosocieties* 2(1): 85–99.

Young, A. 1995. *The Harmony of Illusions: Inventing Posttraumatic Stress Disorder*. Princeton: Princeton University Press.

CHAPTER 5

Recursive Partnerships in Global Development Aid

Casper Bruun Jensen and Brit Ross Winthereik

Introduction

The notion of postdevelopment has become affiliated with a range of authors (Escobar 1995; Goldman 2005; Sachs 1992) who, inspired by postmodern critiques of knowledge/power, turned their attention to development practices. Rather than believing in development as an unquestioned good or viewing it as part of a global system of capitalism, these authors studied discourses of development to investigate how power and knowledge enmeshed in representations of the undeveloped. Although these were undoubtedly powerful and creative interventions, in a Latourian phrase (Latour 2004) they can be viewed as instances of 'critique run out of steam'. This is obviously not because global inequalities have diminished. Rather, the problem is that the hybrid configurations characterizing contemporary development practices cannot be adequately analysed with a predominantly discursive emphasis. Hence the need to challenge and redirect the assumptions held by 'postdevelopment researchers' has become increasingly evident (cf. Yarrow, 2011).

Postdevelopment studies had two prominent ancestors: Foucault on the one hand, and Marx on the other. In the literature it appears at first that Foucault has superseded Marx. This is suggested by the emphasis on discourses through which power/knowledge nexuses are articulated, prevalent in the work of Arturo Escobar and later writers (Crush 1995; Escobar 1995; Grillo and Stirrat 1997). For Foucault, discourse always operates as part of assemblages comprising many other elements (e.g., Foucault 2001; Jensen 2008). Together these make up practice. In postdevelopment, however, rather than an element among others, it sometimes seems as if discourse has a prioritized standing. It may, for example, become an analytical aspiration as such to show how the World Bank discourse *misrepresents* practice elsewhere (e.g., Mehta 1999). From our point of view, these analyses fail to ask with enough care the question of what such discourses accomplish, or to use Foucault's vocabulary, what they produce (Jensen and Lauritsen 2005). In our estimation this is largely because the operations of discourse are relatively unproblematized in this body of literature. Propagated by the powerful with little regard for the powerless, they perpetuate the long-standing critical interest in analysing systems of hierarchy and dominance, the only difference being that the key analytical concept for doing so has shifted to discourse.

It might obviously be that discourses are very powerful and their consequences harmful. As we see it, however, this is an open question, one that cannot be answered prior to close scrutiny of particular situations, projects or networks. Thus, if one assumes that discourses create homogeneously oppressive effects, the analytical sensibility towards the *surprising effects* or the *lack of effects* that discourse may have diminishes. Perhaps the discourses of the powerful are not themselves so powerful, at least not everywhere, or all of the time (Latour 1986). Perhaps, also, there are 'backflows' from the powerless to the powerful that destabilize established positions. This possibility directs attention to the links discourses make with specific practices and suggests that hierarchies of power are always precarious achievements.

What Comes after Postdevelopment?

It has been noted that postdevelopment is relentlessly critical (e.g., Corbridge 1998; Friedman this volume; Green this volume). We might suggest that the critical inclination indicates the point where Marx enters the picture and Foucault takes leave. Indeed, it is no exaggeration to suggest that discourse analysis often comes across as an updated form of ideology critique, based on rather simple assumptions of where knowledge and power reside and how they take effect. The problem is that this renders irrelevant the Foucauldian (and, arguably, ethnographic) task of unraveling the micropolitics of practices. It is perhaps for this reason that discursive critiques tend to come across as somewhat external to what they talk about. As well, they often fail to account for the relation between discursive representations, their modes of production and their concrete operations in different contexts. Ethnographic studies that suspend the presupposition of given power hierarchies and their relations to textual representation, might point to the entanglement of discourse and social practice, and offer a picture where the role of power is far more ambiguous (e.g., Bornstein 2005; Mosse and Lewis 2005).

Ferguson's famous study of development in Lesotho (1990) is often taken as an exemplar of critical postdevelopment studies (e.g., Corbridge 1998; Mosse 2004). Yet its emphasis was quite different from many of these studies because Ferguson's careful deconstruction of development discourse went hand in hand with specific analysis of what happened as this discourse hit the ground. As he showed, it was not just that development statistics and analyses were problematic in that they misrepresented the realities of Lesotho. It was also that the concrete activities that were implemented transformed in practice to the point where they were hardly recognizable to the development agents whose discourse had provided the impetus for those interventions.

David Mosse's work provides another especially interesting case. Inspired by science and technology studies (STS) scholar Bruno Latour, Mosse's work is based on the premise that contrasts 'between instrumental and critical views have blocked the way for a more insightful ethnography of development capable of opening up the implementation black box so as to address the relationship between policy and event' (Mosse 2004: 644). Mosse views Ferguson's approach as a primary instance of critical development studies and remarks that for Ferguson, the 'micro-physics of power occurs beyond the intelligence of the actors; although not that of the decoding anthropologist' (ibid.). He categorizes Ferguson's analysis as an example of what Bruno Latour (2005) has called the 'new functionalist' sociology, which substitutes false objects for real ones (e.g., development in concrete practice with social function or discourse in general). Mosse further follows Latour in arguing that this destroys, rather than elucidates, the object of analytical concern.

In Mosse's evaluation, the critical ambition and attendant explanatory substitution account for the fact that 'critics such as Ferguson spend so little of their time talking to development workers' (2004: 644). The contrast is with Mosse's own work, in which the ethnographic practice was directly implicated with development organizations and projects. Mosse argues that such an involved position enables the ethnographer to blur the boundaries between rational planning and domination frameworks, thereby creating a different space for critical analysis and intervention *from the inside*. It is, however, somewhat uncertain whether the clear boundary Mosse installs between Ferguson's mode of analysis and his own proposals for a new ethnography of development holds under close scrutiny – not least given his own sceptical conclusions, which might well be read as critical of actual efforts of development practice (and in fact have been read in this way by development practitioners).

But if Mosse's theoretical perspective is not necessarily as different from Ferguson as he claims, Mosse is certainly right in suggesting that his entry point into the field creates a quite different research set-up. This bears upon both the questions he could become interested in asking and be able to answer, and the questions he was prodded to become interested in *through* his active involvement with development practice. As anthropologists and other social scientists are, in fact–increasingly – enmeshed with their fields of study, this is a crucial point. If development actors and their interests and concerns are enfolded into research practice in new ways, then Mosse's suggestion is that this is not merely a methodological problem, but an issue of central analytical significance. In coming to terms with the entailments of this situation, Mosse suggests that insights from STS could provide analytical leverage. We agree with this estimation.

With an analytical disposition informed by STS, discourse does not vanish as one moves into practices of development but it is complemented by many other things. The elements of development that come into view vary, depending on where one goes: from World Bank officers, modern offices, organizational charts, spreadsheets and fax machines in some settings, to villagers, huts, water pipes, latrines and dusty roads in others. As this admittedly contrived list suggests, when one moves from discourse to practice, one also moves from broadly human-centred concerns to situations in which development actors and actions are always multiply mediated by organizational technologies.

One classical STS insight was to add materiality to social analysis, recognizing nonhuman actors as potentially capable of redefining and transforming human actions, intentions and discourses. An excellent illustration is found in Marianne de Laet and Annemarie Mol's study of the Zimbabwe bush pump (2000; see also Kelly this volume). In this article de Laet and Mol follow the transformations of technologies and African villages *in the same* process.

Given the interest in materiality, we suggest that if one prioritized metaphor in postdevelopment studies has been genealogy, then the corresponding term for STS-inspired approaches would be geology. Whereas Foucault conducted genealogies of the prison, the school, and so forth, thus putting an anthropocentric metaphor to use in understanding the emergence of modern institutions, STS-inspired anthropology can be said to conduct *geologies* of development in that they aim to dig into the multiple layers of organizational practice and technological infrastructure into which development practice is folded and through which it gradually transforms (cf. Deleuze and Guattari 1987; Tsing 2005). Geology is not invoked as a static structure that is opposed to dynamic process and lived experience, for geology is itself deeply temporal and transformative.[1] Considering geology as a handle with which to differentiate development, suggests a view in which development practices gradually change through many infrastructural means besides discourse and human interaction. They include performance measurements and indicators, organizational layouts, reporting formats and so forth.

Geologies of development encourage one to pay attention not so much to the social structures of power and domination said to guide or determine development discourses as to the dynamic infrastructures of development, their emergence, elements and consequences. In the following we discuss aspects of our preliminary geology of development, one that focuses on the forms of development currently coming into view under the banner of 'partnership'.

Partnerships on the Agenda and as Sites for Ethnographic Inquiry

Making partnerships is a salient feature of development aid cooperation – if not *the* prominent and dominant mode of contemporary development programmes and practice. The idea of partnership is not new, of course; cultural geographer Marcus Power suggests it first became popular with the publication of the 1969 Pearson report *Partners in Development* (Power 2003: 132). Since then the popularity of the term has waxed and waned, but partnership was again high on the agenda in the 1990s. As David Lewis documents, the term gained in ability to describe any set of development relationships: thus farmers can partner with farmers, but also with NGO field staff and researchers, who too can partner with each other (Lewis 1998: 108). NGOs can partner with each other, and with business, cooperatives or governmental institutions.

In this situation partnership ceases to belong to any particular level of interaction, becoming an encompassing form for all development activity. In *Reproducing the Future*, Marilyn Strathern suggested that in the culture in the 1990s, 'prescriptive consumerism dictates that there is no choice but to exercise choice' (Strathern 1992: 38). In this way culture is *enterprised-up* as actors are required to make endless new choices. Analogously, we argue, partnership has been enterprised-up: prescriptive development aid dictates that there is no choice but to partner. But partnership as a prescriptive and encompassing form has effects. They are what we aim to explore in what follows.

The Paris Declaration on Aid Effectiveness, signed in 2005 by 111 countries, is a central event in the newest turn of the partnership paradigm. The Paris declaration claims to lay down 'a practical action-orientated roadmap to improve the quality of aid and its impact on development' organized around five key principles: 'ownership, alignment, harmonization, managing for results, and mutual accountability', specified in fifty-six 'partnership commitments'. The model of partnership that the Paris declaration puts in play is based on transparency and accountability, especially with reference to the use of development resources. The aim is to ensure alignment of strategies between donor countries and recipients, harmonization of donor systems and procedures for ensuring mutual accountability between development partners. Donors and receiving countries have agreed to make efforts to make their strategies and actions transparent to each other. For example, donors have agreed to work towards standardized monitoring and evaluation systems, so partnering countries do not need to provide information according to multiple formats defined by individual donors. Also, donors have agreed to work towards aligning funding strategies with strategies and budgets in receiving countries. Governments in the receiving countries, on the other hand, have agreed to render budgets and planned decisions more transparent to donors and open for public scrutiny in their domestic environments.

Diverse consequences follow from this indication of trust in governments, some of which have been previously viewed as quite untrustworthy. It is not simply the case that large sums of money are now transferred 'freely' from donors to governmental partners; rather, new mechanisms are put in place to hold partners accountable for their use of these funds (Anders 2005). Thus new organizational formats and technologically mediated procedures are developed that enable governments to act in transparent and accountable ways. These include complicated organizational set-ups of supervisory meetings and negotiations as well as implementation of indicators facilitating M and E (monitoring and evaluating) practices. National governments are also required to implement systems through which funds can be distributed to local levels. In turn, local officials must gather the information and provide the documentation required for government to perform accountably – and perform accountability – in relation to international donors. As bureaucracies at all levels have to adapt their working procedures to be able to generate this information, partnerships gradually 'sediment' through the infrastructures of national government.

Partnerships are consequential not only within the bureaucratic systems of development aid recipients but also in, for example, the careers of international advisors. Technical experts hired by donors must partner with local-level bureaucrats in order to meet targets, collect data, and so forth. Nowadays international experts work next door to officials in local ministries. Similarly, nongovernmental organizations and local or international businesses are involved in concrete development tasks – laying pipelines or providing courses on hygienic behaviour change, for instance – as partners.

It may be true, as critiques of partnership have noted, that the term 'partnership' reflects a paradox (cf. Cooke and Kothari 2001). If developing countries can only be partners by engaging in capacity-building activities that will bring them 'to the level of' donor countries, this uncannily resembles former attempts to 'civilize' and casts a shadow on the project of making partnerships (Gould 2005). But this is only one version of what partnership might turn out to be. In some cases, it may be that an underlying agenda to 'civilize' is transformed into successful attempts to delegate control over disbursement of funds to recipients, which has positive effects on growth and development.

As a final example of how partnership is put on the agenda and enacted in development settings, we note that researchers are increasingly stimulated to 'make research relevant to policymakers'. As Sue Unsworth, a former advisor to the UK Department for International Development currently employed at Sussex University with the purpose of making research relevant, explained in a keynote speech at the annual conference for the Danish Association of Development Researchers in 2009, development researchers must learn to network with policymakers and write in a way that is comprehensible to them. Indeed, this demand for partnership also encompasses researchers interested in studying the performance of partnerships. In our own case, only by becoming partners was access to the field made possible. There is a distinct recursive, loop-like quality to the ways in which contemporary development partnerships encompass whatever comes into contact with them.

Partnership as Form

If every organization, institution or individual in development is a partner in the sense that he, she or it is supposed to be implicated, responsible and accountable, what are the empirical and analytical implications? We have suggested that partnership, while certainly a discursive construct, is not only that. Partnerships have functions other than infusing international declarations and visionary statements about the future of development. They also give form to specific modes of relation (Thévenot 1984). We suggest that there is a certain form to partnership, much as anthropologist Annelise Riles (2000) suggested that a particular aesthetic of collaboration is brought into being under the figure of the network (for other uses, see Kelly this volume; Trundle this volume).

Below we briefly consider how partnership is (per-)formed in three quite different contexts. The first relates to the organization of work at the National Audit Office, an institution carrying out audits of governmental organizations, including those responsible for foreign aid given by the state. The second example involves attempts by recipients of foreign aid (Vietnam and Cambodia) to discipline international donors by calling for adherence to partnership. The third has to do with our own efforts to 'enter' a research field site in Vietnam. These are situations that one might intuitively locate at quite different 'levels' of analysis. They have been chosen to emphasize that a differentiating feature of contemporary partnership is that it does pertain to any specific scale, but recurs across scales (see also Jensen 2007).

The three examples thus evoke a sense of how partnership provides an encompassing but highly varied form for making relations. Commenting upon the use of the notion of networks in her own study of international NGO collaboration, Riles notes that:

> The idea of the Network, as the term is used here and by the subjects of this study as a form that supersedes analysis and reality, might also be imagined to borrow from the reflexive turn in the social sciences – from the notion that there is no longer such a thing as dependent and independent variables, that causes and effects are all mutually constituted in an endless feedback loop. (Riles 2005: 263)

Just as it was inconceivable to Riles's informants to live outside networks, no one can possibly be against partnership. Like networks, partnerships promise to enable development actors with simply 'a technical device for doing what one is already doing, only in a more efficient, principled and sophisticated way' (ibid.). But as we intend to show in the following, the form of partnership produces other effects. Partnership manufactures 'desire through mundane 'technicalities,'; it has 'the activating power of unnoticed forms' (ibid.: 265).

Audit as Partnership: From Controller to Advisor

The National Audit Office is an independent institution under the parliament with the specific function of auditing ministries' and state organizations' budgeting and expenditure. This means both that the institution verifies that accounts are correct, and that it organizes comprehensive performance reviews that examine whether state funds are being used for the purposes decided by Parliament. Among its tasks the Audit of the State Accounts also makes performance reviews of the Ministry of Foreign Affairs and Danida, the development agency. It specifies documentation that must be provided from ministerial departments and collects and makes audits and performance reviews of the organization in question on the basis of this information. It also visits embassies and selected projects in developing countries as part of the endeavour to review performances.

The National Audit Office appears as an exemplary external agent, a non-partner. Indeed, it is crucial for the institution to be perceived as a provider of objective knowledge on accounting matters, as this is what legitimates its function in the parliamentary landscape. Nevertheless more interactive and collaborative forms of interaction between auditors and those they audit have made headway into organizational practices and ways of thinking. It is not simply that notions such as collaboration and mutual learning are used colloquially and informally: rather the language of partnership, if not the specific term, is adopted even in official reports. For example, the annual report for 2008 highlighted a new holistic concept for auditing, developed in order to *create value for businesses* by offering an overview of their strengths and weaknesses.[2] While the control function remains central, a partnership dimension is introduced through the emphasis on *value-creation* and *knowledge sharing about best practices*. It is also stressed that the office aims to strengthen cooperation with its clients.

In relation to the specific practices and challenges relating to the work of auditing and reviewing development aid programmes, international trends promote the devolution of managerial responsibilities from donors, such as the state, to governments in developing countries. This implies a gradual change from project-specific funding to budget support, where large sums of money are transferred directly to ministries in developing countries. One of the challenges faced by the National Audit Office is that such transfers render this money invisible to its auditing gaze. Asked whether budget support would not be the nightmare of the auditor general, a head of department explained:

> We tell ourselves that this [budget support] is something we do
> with eyes wide open. Somewhere there is a hope that it could be

better. Simply a hope. As the National Audit Office we know, of course, that there is a risk that more money will disappear. But presently it disappears into administration. Or so it has done. If you look at how much money in development projects is spent on salaries, you would be shocked. I have seen projects where 80–90 per cent of the expenses went to consultants and only the last few percentages to local aid. It all vanishes in internal bureaucracy. Administration, the writing of reports, evaluations, and all of these things. Instead you could hope for, well, if we deliver aid through the systems [administration] of the countries, and even if 20 per cent disappears there will still be more money left for the local population. (Interview, 9 January 2009)

One would perhaps imagine that the parliamentary mandate of the audit office – to ensure the proper use of Danish taxpayers' money – is put under pressure when funds are allocated through budget support. But if, according to the head of the department, development experts and politicians encourage budget support it is not the job of the audit office to judge the merits of this strategy. Instead, the task of the office is to develop monitoring systems that are good enough to both *measure actual effects* and *stimulate self-monitoring and learning inside these organizations*. Developing such systems, however, engages the office in a counselling role, where auditors provide advice. It may, for example, advise the Ministry of Foreign Affairs about how to monitor and evaluate in difficult and uncontrollable settings, such as alien bureaucracies

If we cannot count the number of wells that have been dug, or the number of hospital beds that Denmark has helped provide . . . what then? One thing I could think of for the future is to sit down and look at the fourteen partner countries and examine whether we see any relation between some of the indicators I talked about – corruption, good governance and development effects – or does it depend on who is the ambassador? (Interview, 9 January 2009).

Problems arise, however, when the office begin acting as a counsellor instead of as a controller, for example by scrutinizing whether the indicators highlighted by donors are precise enough to capture the sought-after effects, or perhaps even suggesting improvements in the monitoring systems used by the donors – not as part of an audit, but stemming from a wish to help improve the performance of the Ministry of Foreign Affairs preventively. As this happens, the office becomes potentially co-responsible for shortcomings in the organizations they audit. In such cases it can be accused of 'politicizing'.[3]

Partnership in the National Audit Office is exemplified by the gradual change from a controlling to a counselling role. What start out as studies of development partnerships gradually engage the Audit in partnership as the organization takes on the job of analysing relations between government policy, indicators and development effects. As briefly indicated, this is brought about through the implementation of new technical systems, such as the indicators that allow the Audit to gain partial insight into, say, good governance in developing countries supported by funds from development aid. But the loop-like quality of partnership brings into view the potential limits of the jurisdiction and legitimacy of presumably external organizations. In the same process it opens questions concerning the meaning of independent evaluation.

Governmental Partnerships: Mutual Accountability and Demands for Action

If the National Audit Office finds itself engaged in partnership-like modes of engagement somewhat in spite of itself, the same cannot be said of development collaboration between donors and aid-receiving governments. Partnership, as defined in the Paris declaration, explicitly targets these actors. Neither the Danish embassy in Hanoi nor the Vietnamese ministries (e.g., of agriculture and rural development or of planning and investment) doubt that they are involved in the making of partnerships. But the forms of collaboration this demands are still emerging and uncertain, subject to negotiation and revision. What are partnerships in these settings? What does it entail for the partners? Which demands can they make on one another? And what consequences do such demands have? A consideration of a report and interviews with a consultant from Australian Aid (AUSaid), three government officials at the Danish Embassy and a British consultant working for the Danida in Hanoi allow us to touch upon these issues.

In April 2008, government representatives from Laos, Cambodia and Vietnam met in Bangkok to conduct what was called the South East Asia consultation, an informal meeting leading to a report that was to be submitted as a contribution to discussions on mutual accountability between donors and partnering countries for the then upcoming Accra meeting – the third High Level Forum on Aid Effectiveness. The report was based on the assumption that a 'genuinely partner country–led contribution on mutual accountability' would be important, since mutual accountability was seen to have unclear implications both in theory and practice, being one of the 'least understood' principles of the Paris declaration. We point to the emerging form of partnership by looking at two aspects of the report. The first relates to the conditions for the consultation and the work related to it; the second to the conclusions it reached.

Prior to the High Level Forum, a variety of preparations took place. As an international development consultant from the Overseas Development Institute[4] explained in an interview, there was serious concern from the donors' side that not enough input was being generated by the partners, who were supposed to actively contribute to agenda-setting for the meeting. Since no such contributions appeared to be forthcoming, however, the initiative for the South East Asian consultation was taken not by the countries themselves but by a United Nations Development Programme representative. In turn the suggestion to have a consultation meeting was taken up quite differently by the invited governments. Whereas Vietnam saw an opportunity to set the agenda, Cambodia apparently showed little interest, perhaps because, we were told, they found out they were part of the consultation by reading the minutes of the meeting where the decision was made.

In the actual event, the South East Asian countries did make the most of the opportunity to provide input. They proposed to 'develop a set of recommended priority actions to remove obstacles' to the achievement of mutual accountability, arguing that the process in which they had participated provided a model for south-south capacity development. And the delegations agreed on a common platform of recommendations.

Considering the Vietnamese case, it is particularly instructive to note how 'obstacles to behaviour change' in relation to establishing mutual accountability among partners came to be understood by Vietnamese partners. In their interpretation, almost all problems were identified as relating to the donor side. Thus it was noted that: 'in spite of the government leadership on MA (mutual accountability), it appears that there has been very little guidance . . . from the donor headquarters to their local offices in terms of MA'. It was also indicated that the Vietnamese viewed some current measures of mutual accountability as residual 'conditionalities' belonging to the days of structural adjustment policies. The report further pointed out that 'no donors inform about their strength and the way of delivering aid (project and non-project types)', making it hard for the government to develop a coherent and rational framework for handling the inflow of money. Additionally it emphasized that although there existed a development aid database that aimed to be comprehensive, donors provided inconsistent data at irregular intervals. Finally, the problem of aligning the policies and strategies of recipients was likewise placed in the hands of donors, who should not wait 'until the partner countries reach international standard but align where the capacity exists'.

What is striking in this example is how, contrary to the presumptions and ideals of the Paris Declaration, for the Vietnamese delegation, partnership was not a benign and consensual format for collaboration. The aesthetic of partnership was present and enacted in the meetings held and in the documents that circulated prior to the Accra High Level Forum on Aid Effectiveness. But rather than a way of setting up a particular form of collaboration among donors and countries in the region specific to the High Level Forum, partnership became a platform for formulating new demands. These demands covered the collaborative evaluation formats among donors, their internal and external information and communication systems, and their budgeting and evaluation systems. Meanwhile, thanks to the existence of new technologies such as development aid databases, it became possible for the Vietnamese to make a strong argument that donors were not living up to their obligations. In this case new technology facilitated new discourse, rather than 'old discourse' promoting new technology.

For the Vietnamese delegation, partnership became a platform for formulating demands of donor countries' foreign policies at large. Obviously, it is an open question whether their demands will transform Danish development policies. However, the fact that these discussions now take place and that arguments are put forward in this manner, points to new, perhaps farther-reaching ways in which relations can be imagined and worked on under the form of partnership.

Researching Partnerships, Partnering Researchers

Our final example touches briefly upon how researchers also become caught up in partnerships. That this is not a voluntary matter suggests something about the limitations of the critical stance of postdevelopment theory, and about partnerships as a mode of collaboration and knowledge making.

In October 2008 we went on a preliminary field visit to Hanoi. We had arranged to meet with employees at the Danish embassy, whom we would interview about their work with Danish-Vietnamese aid. The aim was to start up a research project on accountability and partnerships in global development aid. We hoped to facilitate further contact with people in the Vietnamese ministries and find opportunities to visit village-level implementation sites. However, this turned out to be a rather complicated affair, and the issue of partnership was significant in that regard. Employees at the embassy repeatedly stressed that getting access to interviewees and field sites would be very difficult. They explained that they did not want to put pressure on their partners or bother them with researchers who conducted studies unrelated to the immediate goals of the programme. Previously this might not have been a problem, they indicated, but under the form of partnership it was, not least since a side effect of partnering was that government officials and embassy employees were busier than ever, implementing monitoring and evaluation systems and arranging meetings.

We were repeatedly told that it would be far easier to conduct our project in Africa. There, apparently, partnerships did not prevent donors from dictating what governments should do. But in Vietnam, partnership had provided an effective platform for recalcitrance towards demands that would place the country in the role of passive recipient. Paradoxically, from the point of view of the embassy, this made their Vietnamese counterparts into simultaneously better *and* worse collaborators than the Tanzanian partners some of them had previously worked with. If we were to have any chance of getting anywhere, the overall suggestion was, we, too, would need local partners.

This recommendation was corroborated by later conversations with Vietnamese research institutions as well as with Danish researchers who worked in Vietnam. Vietnamese and Danish economists, for example, worked together on macro-economic issues, and Danish visitors intermittently set up shop in Hanoi to teach economics courses to Vietnamese students. Anthropologists who had worked in Vietnam had been able to do so effectively by hiring several university students as Ph.D. field workers. In a conversation with a Danish biologist with long experience from the Danish Development Research Council, we were told that not engaging in partnership would be unethical. In a way, of course, we could only agree. Thus we found ourselves increasingly encompassed by the context of the partnership that we meant to study externally, as it were. It could be argued that while we had *hoped* to adopt an 'external, critical' position akin to that of James Ferguson, we had *ended up* in a position more similar to the involved stance recommended by David Mosse.

But this change in approach was neither of our volition, nor due to an analytical or political predisposition. Rather it was a practical circumstance relating to an ethnographic absence of control in the context of partnerships. If we wanted to study the infrastructures of accountability that tied together development partners, then, we too would have to become partners. Eventually, we got into contact with a high-ranked researcher from a Vietnamese institution who studied science and technology policy and strategy, and who was keen to collaborate. While emphasizing that he knew everyone – desk officers at the ministries, officials in the provinces and relevant NGOs – our contact did not volunteer any specific information. Instead he encouraged us to turn our conversation into a proper, formalized collaboration with specified resources. Thus, our efforts at enacting partnerships began.

Back in Denmark we wrote an application for the Development Research Council. Applications enforce their own form of partnership, literally speaking, as they require detailed information on partnering institutions, modes of collaboration, efforts at capacity building and percentages of budgets spent. Development research proposals are scanned and sent to the embassies, where they are evaluated once again according to criteria relating to relevance for the implementation of Danish development policy, and with an eye to not unduly bothering Vietnamese partners. From national partnerships to institutional partnerships to individual partnerships and back again: the recursivity of partnerships is elicited in this cross-scalar process. The question of how research opportunities, legible questions and feasible answers are constructed in these processes merits consideration, in both practical and theoretical terms.

Recursive Partnerships

We view the emphasis on partnership that currently informs development programmes and projects as a specific differentiating feature of development practice and research. On the one hand, partnership has been enterprised-up. Thus, development partnership is currently ubiquitous and cross-scalar: this is one feature that differentiates current development practices. On the other hand, we propose that an analytical focus on partnership formation inspired by STS and social anthropology provides an opportunity for exploring new avenues of analytical and practical engagement with development. Central to this approach is the insistence that whatever development partnerships are, however they are performed, they involve new 'geological' entanglements of discourse and materiality, vision, practice and infrastructure.

Critical analysis might conclude that partnership has had no significant transformative effect since the Paris declaration. Yet this is to assign to it both too much and too little power. By believing too much in the powers of discourse, one is disabled from tracing all those minor infrastructural and interactional transformations that partnership brings about in multiple settings. In our examples, these include new indicators, database systems and monitoring and evaluation tools, and this list is by no means exclusive. Tracing the complex and unpredictable relationship between causes and effects in policy making and implementation of development policy (Fforde 2009), however, has precisely been our interest. It is for this reason that we have aimed to show how development actors perform different versions of partnership in ways that make them real for specific practices. This 'a-critical' approach differentiates development by keeping policy making and policy implementation at the same analytical 'level': it allows us to see partnership as simultaneously encompassing and multiply differentiated.

An attention to the geologies through which *partnership as form* sediments is helpful in coming to terms with why development activities are so hard to implement and control, their effects so uncertain. The Paris declaration is but one event in a complex unfolding process through which partnership has transformed development practice. As our examples suggest, this occurs, among other ways, through bureaucratic meetings, the building of platforms and the formulation of action plans and recommendations. All of these efforts are tied into technical systems facilitating measurement, tracking, monitoring and evaluation of outcomes and effects.

Partnerships are at one and the same time immediate (as when auditors at the National Audit Office struggle to walk the delicate line between acting as controllers and counsellors) and symptomatic of dynamic but much more gradual processes of changing development practices and infrastructures. There is a distinct loop-like quality to these processes. Partnerships seem to spread and generate partnerships, from international declarations to national and local government and business, NGOs or researchers. In turn these multiple collaborations flow back and feed into global partnership discourses and practices as propagated at high-level meetings in Paris or Accra.

We have pointed to three situations in order to elicit the recursivity of partnership. We view this recursivity as indicative of how partnership as form is differentially reproduced *across* the scales of what development researchers think of as the local-global continuum. Loops of partnership render the aspiration to locate partnership anywhere in particular (either at a given 'level' or pertaining primarily to specific types of practice) suspect. Indeed, we have argued, partnership has been enterprised-up in such a way that it encompasses all relevant levels of development engagement.

For this reason, partnership also has a particular bearing on the aspiration to conduct ethnographies of it. As a ubiquitous form, partnership *envelops* those who study its modes of operation. It engages the researcher in empirical as well as analytical loops of interaction, whereby he or she comes to participate in the same form of conduct (appropriate to partnerships) as his or her informants. In turn, this recursivity calls into question the distinction between what counts as 'analytical/

theoretical' or 'empirical' knowledge. This blurring may be one central 'differentiating' feature of development as partnership: partnerships, besides crossing scales, also *make* scales of knowledge and action.

As in Annelise Riles's evocative phrase, what we have been describing may be partnership 'seen twice': as both practical accomplishment and analytical focus. Both are necessary, and neither can be suspended: recursively and interactively, partnership encompasses our research, even as our research attempts to encompass it. Perhaps, seen thrice, partnership is elicited as a contemporary scale of no-scale in development. Partnership, it might be ventured, has become the sine qua non of contemporary knowledge making about development.

NOTES

1. Tsing (2005), for example, compares global development processes to changing riverine landscapes.
2. A performance review comprises a pre-study, the audit, an initial report and a public report with recommendations for change.
3. A recent case concerns a report criticizing the liberal government for paying very expensive fees to private hospitals. Politicians interpreted the report as critique of the ideological choices that led to determining the level of the fees. It was thus considered 'political'.
4. The Overseas Development Institute is an independent consultancy and research institute on development issues located in London.

BIBLIOGRAPHY

Anders, G. 2005. 'Good Governance as Technology: Towards an Ethnography of the Bretton Woods Institutions', in David Mosse and David Lewis (eds), *The Aid Effect: Giving and Governing in International Development*. London and Ann Arbor: Pluto Press, pp. 37–61.

Bornstein, E. 2005. *The Spirit of Development: Protestant NGOs, Morality and Economics in Zimbabwe*. Stanford: Stanford University Press.

Cooke, B. and U. Kothari. 2001. *Participation: The New Tyranny?* London: Zed.

Corbridge, S. 1998. '"Beneath the Pavement Only Soil": The Poverty of Post Development', *Journal of Development Studies* 34(6): 138–148.

Crush, J. 1995. *The Power of Development*. London and New York: Routledge.

de Laet, M and A. Mol. 2000. 'The Zimbabwe Bush Pump: Mechanics of a Fluid Technology', *Social Studies of Science* 30(2): 225–63.

Deleuze, G. and F. Guattari. 1987. *A Thousand Plateaus: Capitalism and Schizophrenia*. Minneapolis and London: University of Minnesota Press.

Escobar, A. 1995. *Encountering Development: The Making and Unmaking of the Third World*. Princeton: Princeton University Press.

Ferguson, J. 1990. *The Anti-Politics Machine: 'Development', Depoliticization, and Bureaucratic Power in Lesotho*. Cambridge: Cambridge University Press.

Fforde, A. 2009. *Coping with Facts: A Sceptic's Guide to the Problem of Development*. West Hartford: Kumarian Press.

Foucault, M. 2001. *Power*. New York: The New Press.

Goldman, M. 2005. *Imperial Nature: The World Bank and Struggles for Social Justice in the Age of Globalization*. New Haven: Yale University Press.

Gould, J. 2005. 'Timing, Scale and Style: Capacity as Govenmentality in Tanzania', in David Mosse and David Lewis (eds), *The Aid Effect: Giving and Governing in International Development*. London and Ann Arbor: Pluto Press, pp. 61–84.

Grillo, R. D. and R. L. Stirrat. 1997. *Discourses of Development: Anthropological Perspectives*. Oxford: Berg.

Jensen, C. B. 2007. 'Infrastructural Fractals: Revisiting the Micro-Macro Distinction in Social Theory', *Environment and Planning D: Society and Space* 25(5): 832–850.

———. 2008. 'Power, Technology and Social Studies of Health Care: An Infrastructural Inversion', *Health Care Analysis* 16(4): 355–374.

Jensen, C. B. and P. Lauritsen. 2005. 'Reading Digital Denmark: IT-reports as Material-Semiotic Actors', *Science, Technology and Human Values* 30(3): 352–373.

Latour, B. 1986. 'The Powers of Association', in John Law (ed.), *Power, Action and Belief*. London: Routledge and Kegan Paul, pp. 264–280.

———. 2004. 'Why Has Critique Run Out of Steam? From Matters of Fact to Matters of Concern', *Critical Inquiry* 30: 225–248.

———. 2005. *Reassembling the Social: An Introduction to Actor-Network-Theory*. Oxford: University Press.

Lewis, D. 1998. 'Partnership as Process: Building an Institutional Ethnography of an Inter-Agency Aquaculture Project in Bangladesh', in David Mosse, John Farrington and Alan Rew (eds), *Development as Process: Concepts and Methods for Working With Complexity*. London and New York: Routledge, pp. 99–117.

Mehta, L. 1999. 'From Darkness to Light? Critical Reflections on the World Development Report 1998/1999', *Journal of Development Studies* 36(1): 151–161.

Mosse, D. 2004. 'Is Good Policy Unimplementable? Reflections on the Ethnography of Aid Policy and Practice', *Development and Change* 35(4): 639–671.

Mosse, D. and D. Lewis. 2005. *The Aid Effect: Giving and Governing in International Development*. London and Ann Arbor: Pluto Press.

Power, M. 2003. *Rethinking Development Geographies*. London: Routledge.

Riles, A. 2000. *The Network Inside Out*. Ann Arbor: University of Michigan Press.

———. 2005. 'The Network Inside Out', in Marc Edelman and Angelique Haugerud (eds), *The Anthropology of Development and Globalization: From Classical Political Economy to Contemporary Neoliberalism*. Malden, MA: Blackwell, pp. 262–267.

Sachs, W. 1992. *The Development Dictionary: A Guide to Knowledge as Power*. London: Zed Books.

Strathern, M. 1992. *Reproducing the Future*. New York: Routledge.

Thévenot, L. 1984. 'Rules and Implements: Investment in Forms', 23(1): 1–45.

Tsing, A. L. 2005. *Friction: An Ethnography of Global Connection*. Princeton: Princeton University Press.

Yarrow, T. 2011. *Development Beyond Politics: Aid, Activism and NGOs in Ghana*. London: Palgrave MacMillan.

CHAPTER **6**

Intersection
A Gift Back – The Village and Research

Annemarie Mol

The effects of science do not come after the facts. That something is altered (organized, staged, manipulated, experimented with) is a precondition for finding facts in the first place. Both preceding chapters bring this out very clearly. Science in action always also implies transactions, says Kelly. But which transactions? Studying a subject like 'partnership' may appear to depend on engaging in 'partnership', say Jensen and Winthereik. But what is 'partnership'? Answering such questions is partly a descriptive task. The ethnographer tells about the transactions or partnerships that, say, biomedical malaria researchers, or Danish development professionals, engage in. What do they promise, and do they keep their promises? What do they negotiate over, and what do they care about? And then there is self-description, flowing over into design. What transactions and partnerships has 'the ethnographer' engaged in – and where to go from there? What to single out as an object, which questions to ask, what to negotiate over, what to care about?[1]

Research does not stay outside its fields of study but interferes with them. However much we use the term 'observation', our work is not done by our eyes only. There is talking, travelling, trading. Things take time – not just *our* time, but also that of technicians, translators, research assistants, experimental subjects and our so-called informants. 'Truth' depends on collaborative work. As these things go, researchers tend to earn far better salaries for their part of this work than most of the others involved. The experimental subjects and informants are likely to earn least. But is that the crucial problem? There is something *thin* about turning 'being the object of research' into a mere economic claim, a claim that can be settled by a financial transaction or a gift. Not so long ago, I came across nutrition science research that proudly proclaimed itself to be 'ethical' because the people (in the global South) who provided the necessarily body materials had been promised a share in the profits that were expected from selling (in the global North) the 'nutriceuticals' that the researchers sought to design.[2] But which research questions are being asked and which others never considered? Which parameters come to represent the reality of people's physicalities and lives? Which interventions are designed that interfere with a reality always only partially known and necessarily surprising? The surprises may be bad. Who cares for the always unexpected 'side effects'?

These are questions that the two preceding chapters bring out in slightly different and yet related ways. Here, by way of comment, I would like to add another question, one that they do not ask but that arises from them. The question (by now classic in anthropology) is where the results of 'our' studies may go. Nutriceuticals designed using data from poor places may be marketed in sites that are affluent. What about the social sciences: whom might they/we seek to serve, and – and this is a different question – whom to write for? There are various tensions here. This struck me when I recently gave a 'methods and theory' class to an international group of social science Ph.D. students who were all linked up with development projects. When I asked the obligatory method question 'For whom do you write?' quite a few of these students said that they wrote for the villagers targeted by the development project they were linked up with. *'These are the people I worked with. I want to give something back to them.'*

No doubt the villagers in question can do with a gift. But what kind of gift? First, there is an obvious practical problem here: even if they are literate, and even if they understand English, most people targeted by development projects are not necessarily interested in the kind of texts that Ph.D.'s may hope to earn a degree with, let alone publish in peer-reviewed journals. But (if only there were time and money) this problem might yet be solved by drafting a 'popularized version' – or by making an enticing film. There is a second problem, however, that is more difficult to handle. As it is, social scientists joining development projects are likely to be asked to provide 'the project' with the perspective of the villagers (or city dwellers) that the project hopes to target. The situation in which Kelly found herself is a case in point. In many ways this is an achievement. For a long time, technical solutions were designed as if techniques work all by themselves. These days most researchers and policymakers know all too well that a disease like malaria will only ever be eradicated if the people in the targeted areas will help to implement – will support – the techniques and plans designed to eradicate it. Techniques do not work by themselves.³ But this implies that what 'villagers' (or city dwellers) are able and willing to do should be taken into account from the start. This makes it crucial to know what is relevant to them, what moves them. Their 'perspectives' are called for. Articulating these is not easy. Kelly brings out very clearly that it is difficult, and sometimes even impossible, to learn about a group of villagers' 'own perspective' on malaria so as to carry those insights to the centre where the designing is done. But centres (be they inhabited by biomedical researchers, policymakers or others) would do much better if they had access to the perspectives of 'villagers'.

If social scientists are to craft knowledge about the village that is relevant to designing development projects, their audience, by implication, consists of those who design development projects: scientists, technicians, policymakers of all kinds. After all, why would one write for villagers about the village? Whatever their needs may be, villagers do not lack knowledge of their own perspectives. What, then, might social scientists 'give back' to those among whom they do their fieldwork? If we want to directly address the 'villagers', if we want to write for them, we might consider engaging in different research altogether. Maybe social scientists would do well to engage in studies of centres of all kinds (biomedical research projects, government practices, policy offices, funding bodies) to then present the results in interesting and compelling formats to audiences in 'the village'. It is not obvious how this might be done.⁴ Kelly points out that the biomedical 'facts' about malaria, as currently presented to villagers in The Gambia, do not travel especially well. Bare social science 'facts' are unlikely to do much better. So there is something to invent there. Will writing do, or should the results be formatted as films, or as theatre, or in some other way? Finding money may not be easy either: who is going to pay for research into powerful places meant to inform and inspire those in the margins? These are open questions. But some experimentation seems to be called for.

Jensen and Winthereik's case adds another dimension to questions to do with giving appropriate return gifts. The partnerships that they are setting up in Vietnam in order to study partnerships, are not with 'villagers', but with local researchers. Most of these researchers will be able to read whatever it is that Jensen and Winthereik may write in the course of their collaboration. Reading is not their problem. But writing is. What they are likely to want is to get published in peer-reviewed, international, English-language journals. They want to reach audiences in 'the centre' and audiences in other dispersed sites. This is not easy. Partly this is a matter of language.⁵ Partly it is a matter of presentation, plot, tone, ordering – of all kinds of hardly articulated skills, difficult to transport. Thus, Jensen and Winthereik might consider co-authoring with their local partners and supporting them as they seek to publish. And what about the rest of us? Here is my proposition: all scholars who are native speakers of English engage in some form of partnership with a few colleagues who are not, and caringly edit their articles.[6] They may get comments on their own work, advice about interesting reads, the names of friends or other gifts in return. And even those of us who are not native speakers of English may experiment with long-distance collaborations, mentorships and yet-to-be-invented forms of intellectual gift-exchange.

Writing *about* the village for researchers and policy makers, *for* the village about research practices or policy techniques, *with* local research partners for peer-reviewed journals: these are ever so many things to do. For whom? For *you*. Implied in its ways of framing questions and making suggestions, this particular piece is written for an audience of ethnographers concerned with development projects. It is my wilful attempt to give a small gift back in return for what, by reading around in your work, I have learned from you.

NOTES

1. Anthropology has a serious tradition of asking itself (all but endless) self-reflexive questions. I will not attempt to list all relevant titles here, but just evoke the essays in Meneley and Young (2005), whose authors dare to ethnographically study their own academic settings; and the work of Marilyn Strathern (in this context, e.g., Strathern 1999), who tends to simultaneously present *and* question her own empirical stories and theoretical repertoires.
2. I have analysed an exemplary article in detail but have not yet found a way of writing about it. To be continued. For a study that manages to sharply articulate the practices involved, see Petryna 2009.
3. Many technologies were designed, built and sold, but never put to use, as their 'inbuilt user' did not match with the users 'on the ground'. Water pumps for Africa made to be used by men are the classic case in point. The literatures about this are extensive – for a classic see Akrich (1995).
4. That centres deserve to be studied ethnographically is one of the drives behind STS studies of labs, hospitals, banks, etc. See Latour 1993 for this argument; and Mol 2002 and M'Charek 2005 for examples. How to present such work to 'the village' is as yet an open question. For issues of travel and situatedness relevant in this context see, e.g., Marques (2004).
5. But language is always also content. For a beautiful and clear analysis of this, comparing English and Akan, see Wiredu 1996.
6. As a non-native speaker I have always needed such care, even though Dutch, my mother tongue, is very close to English. For those who speak more distant tongues, things are worse. At the same time, many centres may be reached much more easily by texts in languages other than English – Mandarin,

Spanish or even French. There are questions here to do with what 'international' means. See also De Swaan (2001).

BIBLIOGRAPHY

Akrich, M. 1995. 'User Representations: Practices, Methods and Sociology', in A. Rip, T. J. Misa and J. Schot (eds), *Managing Technology in Society: The Approach of Constructive Technology Assessment*. Pinter Publishers: London, 167–184.

de Swaan, A. 2001. *Words and the World: The Global Language System*. Cambridge and Malden, MA: Polity Press.

Marques, I. da Costa. 2004. 'Mathematical Metaphors and Politics of Presence/ Absence', *Environment and Planning D: Society and Space* 22(1): 71–81.

Latour, B. 1993. *We Have Never Been Modern*, trans C. Porter. London: Harvester Wheatsheaf.

M'Charek, A. 2005. *The Human Genome Diversity Project: An Ethnography of Scientific Practice*. Cambridge: Cambridge University Press.

Meneley, A. and D. Young (eds). 2005. *Auto-ethnographies: The Anthropology of Academic Practices*. Toronto: Broadview Press.

Mol, A. 2002. *The Body Multiple: Ontology in Medical Practice*. Durham, NC, and London: Duke University Press.

Petryna, A. 2009. *When Experiments Travel: Clinical Trials and the Global Search for Human Subjects*. Princeton: Princeton University Press.

Strathern, M. 1999. *Property, Substance and Effect: Anthropological Essays on Persons and Things*. London: Athlone Press.

Wiredu, K. 1996. *Cultural Universals and Particulars: An African Perspective*. Bloomington: Indiana University Press.

PART III

Doing and Knowing

CHAPTER 7

Beyond an Anthropology of 'the Urban Poor'

Rethinking Peripheral Urban Social Situations in Brazil

John Gledhill and Maria Gabriela Hita

The ethnographic study of the 'urban poor' has been intimately connected to public policy interventions. Although their nature has changed over time, in accordance with shifting state and international donor policies and the growing importance of NGOs, the practical 'relevance' of ethnographic enquiry provides a major justification for its funding. In some cases the 'pitch' is direct: ethnographic research (as distinct from surveys) can provide more nuanced accounts of the social reproduction of poor families, their demographics, health, modes of livelihood and other matters directly relevant to the scrutiny of individual family circumstances necessary in targeted conditional cash transfer programmes. But in recent years, as a focus on service provision and poverty alleviation has been complemented by broader perspectives on social development, anthropologists have also participated critically in debates about 'capacity building' and 'the thickening of social capital' through studies of grass-roots social organization, networks and forms of association, within a framework in which 'empowerment' and 'participation' are watchwords guiding general policy statements. Although much that is done in the name of these keywords reflects neo-liberal ideologies of 'helping the poor to help themselves', we will suggest that social research critiquing the underlying logic of policies and public representations of social problems can be combined with academic engagement that supports the aspirations of grass-roots organizations to make their voices more effective in the public sphere.

As Charles Hale argues, such engagement is unlikely to escape contradictions, but it does force us to produce 'theory grounded in the contradictions that the actors themselves confront' as we strive to generate 'the kinds of knowledge that they need us to produce' (2006: 115). Hale contrasts 'activist research' of the kind in which he has been engaged in contributing to territorial land rights claims brought to the Inter-American Human Rights Court by indigenous communities in Central America with 'cultural critique' that 'speaks truth to power' but also extends its critical gaze to the contradictions into which the less powerful are drawn in pursuing their struggles. These include possible deployment of 'essentialist' constructions of indigeneity and the fact that those struggling for recognition of their rights will generally be obliged to use 'the language, the legal and political tools, and even the funding of their oppressors', in this particular case funding provided by the World Bank (2006: 111). Although Hale illustrates ways in which indigenous political actors subvert some of these constraints, he fully recognizes the practical significance of maintaining a critical gaze. Yet his argument, which parallels those made elsewhere in this volume against the critical anthropology of development offered by scholars such as Arturo Escobar and James Ferguson, is that critiques restricted to the academic field tend to foreclose on deeper engagement with movements and their advocates and allies, NGO workers, state officials and development agency personnel.

From this perspective, critical academic work may be politically positioned in its own academic space but erases much of the contentious politics taking place beyond that space within the complex, multi-scalar fields of social relations established by 'the development apparatus' (Mosse 2005: 6). By refusing to engage that other political space directly, 'cultural critique' fails to foster change in established anthropological research methods and practice (Hale 2006: 104). Hale applies this argument even to the work of Anna Tsing (2005), whose critical analysis of the utopias of middle-class environmental activists he applauds for its unusual expression of solidarity, call for anthropological 'openness' towards actors lacking the scope for analytical reflection on their actions enjoyed by researchers, and recognition that activist 'romanticism' has actually made a difference in a place that 'experts' abandoned.

In this chapter we describe how we were drawn into a different kind of engagement with our research subjects as a result of their reflection on ways in which academics might be useful to them. We begin with an argument against the political pessimism that some analyses of contemporary urban situations seem to be inducing. This leads us to explore specific historical and structural reasons why our case study provides grounds for retaining the Gramscian 'optimism of the will' that Tsing advocates. By looking for explanations of the heterogeneity that still exists in 'peripheral urban situations' in Brazil, we seek to deconstruct a framework that takes 'the urban poor' as an object of anthropological study, rather than the social and political processes that occur within spaces of poverty and between poor urban residents, government and members of other social classes. In this sense, we advocate a more classically holistic ethnographic approach to the changing lifeworlds of people whose limited economic means make them a target of state and NGO interventions. At the same time, however, we argue that academics can do that kind of research and play a significant role in supporting the construction of new kinds of community organizations that represent self-conscious grass-roots initiatives to transcend the contradictions that critical analysts highlight. It is through such engagement that our findings can challenge social stereotypes and the power traps that 'cultural critique' reveals to be of more immediate political significance beyond the academic field.

Peripheral Urban Social Situations: From Optimism to Pessimism

Today's work on the social organization of the poor repackages concerns with grass-roots self-organization dating back to the mass urbanization of the 1960s and 1970s in Latin America. In Brazil such research often had a politicized edge, seeking to dispel portrayals of the poor as 'dangerous classes' or a menace to public hygiene that justified policies of bulldozing slums. Furthermore, the now 'mainstreamed' international development rhetoric of 'participatory development' and 'pro-poor policies' draws on the politics of this earlier era by, for example, invoking Paulo Freire's idea that 'experts' can learn from the poor. By showing that people who lived in irregular settlements were socially heterogeneous, self-organizing in ways that explained their ability to survive and in some cases achieve social mobility, and not uninterested in political rights, scholars such as Janice Perlman (1976) not only humanized the slums but also contributed to shifts in policy and practice.

Yet after neo-liberal economics pulverized the social fabric of Latin America in the 1980s, the limited impact of this body of academic knowledge on public perceptions became apparent. In the 1990s favelas became *more* rather than less socially stigmatized spaces in a context of mounting crime and violence, not simply in the eyes of the middle classes but amongst urban working-class people who lived in areas not classified as favelas (Caldeira 2000). Some Brazilian city governments responded with programmes designed to turn favelas into 'neighbour-hoods' equipped with better public spaces and infrastructure. Best known are the slum-upgrading programmes of Rio de Janeiro, devised by 'socially progressive' architects and planners (Soares and Soares 2005). Public housing projects favoured the construction of low-cost apartment blocks to replace self-built houses. Yet many poor families remained unenthusiastic about this kind of solution. Housing that is not adapted to the dynamic practices of family and household development, and to the informal social networking that is integral to the everyday lives of the poor, can foster a decline in levels of sociability even if it is low-cost and levels of public service provision are above average, as illus-trated by the Cidade Tiradentes housing complex on the edge of São Paulo (De Almeida, D'Andrea and De Lucca 2008). Furthermore, lack of affordable housing even for those lower-income people who had reg-ular work ensured that 'irregular' settlements would continue to grow.

The 'social problems' that made such settlements targets of interven-tion also multiplied, in part because of the growth of drug trafficking and consumption, but also because of new sensitivities, from above but also from below, about issues such as domestic violence. Not all inter-ventions from above were welcome, let alone effective: those focused on the rights of children and what middle class people defined as 'the problem' of child labour, for example, have proved contentious, despite a desire on the part of parents to improve their children's access to edu-cation (and keep them away from gangs, an objective to which engage-ment in work is seen as making an important contribution). Multiplying state and NGO interventions have added to the perceived value of eth-nographic research. Yet the environment in which such research is con-ducted often seems bleak.

Questions of 'poverty' are increasingly linked to questions of 'secu-rity' against crime and violence. The resources dedicated to anti-poverty programmes in Brazil increased significantly from 2002 under the PT (Workers Party) governments headed by Luiz Inácio 'Lula' da Silva, but despite some efforts at reform, the deployment in the favelas of milita-rized police forces with a deserved reputation for extrajudicial violence has remained the other side of the coin of state strategies. Another chal-lenge is the cumulative impact of neo-liberal capitalism on the economic opportunities of poorer citizens. Both have provoked more pessimistic diagnoses about the future of the urban poor than were found in the literature before the 1990s.

A self-critical reflection on that earlier optimism came from Susan Eckstein (1990), comparing the fortunes of an inner-city slum with a shantytown located on the edge of Mexico City at the end of the 1980s. It had been assumed that 'degraded' inner-city areas were mainly occupied by a transient population and would be eliminated by redevelopment and gentrification. Eckstein showed that some of these areas had avoided that fate because they possessed a high capacity for collective self-organization based on strong 'popular' cultural traditions and a flourishing informal economy benefiting from a central urban location and accessibility to members of other social classes. In contrast, with falling incomes and employment organization seemed to have atrophied, even in those more peripherally located squatter settlements that had received substantial public investment. Crime and violence had increased, and there was a widening economic gap between homeowners and the increasing proportion of renters in a neighbourhood whose original attraction had been cheap housing.

Eckstein's analysis of the impacts of growing economic precariousness is taken much further by Loïc Wacquant (2007), who frequently invokes Brazil as a parallel case, although his main focus is on the 'new poverty' in the United States and France. Wacquant's subproletarian 'precariat' is consigned to urban 'spaces of relegation' stripped of the possibility of being socially meaningful 'places' for their residents by a territorial stigmatization added to those of poverty, ethnicity and race, justifying strategies of containment effected through the police and prison systems. Sociability is weakened by the way that people assuage their sense of social indignity by stigmatizing other residents for bringing the neighbourhood down through their criminal or antisocial activities. This phenomenon is certainly common in Brazilian slums, often aggravated by social differences between successive waves of settlers entering the neighbourhood. As far as Wacquant is concerned, a fissiparous 'precariat' cannot be a political actor. It inhabits a social world in which the only hope is escape.

Social Relations, Culture, Politics:
The Need to Recognize Diversity

Wacquant's ideas are relevant to *some* 'peripheral urban social situations' in Brazil. We agree with him about the self-defeating nature of 'punitive containment' of populations that neo-liberal capitalism has consigned to economic insecurity. But we contest the bleakness of the political analysis that he offers, and like Perlman (2004) resist reduction of Brazil's favelas to 'spaces of relegation'. To the extent to which he is interested in culture at all, Wacquant focuses on the past and what has been lost – the U.S. 'communal' ghetto is contrasted with today's deindustrialized 'hyperghetto', the French *banlieue* with the old 'Red Belt' of a working class proud of its identity and organization. Yet in the case of Brazil, there continue to emerge *new* political projects that are difficult to dismiss as insignificant in terms of advancing democracy, ending racial discrimination and demanding rights for the poor in the capitalist city. They are in part stimulated by NGO interventions, in part responding to neo-liberal governmentality strategies (Gledhill 2005), and in part reflecting the fact that some state policies do advance social justice. Yet the main reason seems to be that slums are not always spaces where all hope dies and no project of constructing place is conceivable, even when they suffer from high levels of stigmatization. Established, resignified and new, sometimes transnationally inspired, forms of 'popular culture' can animate new forms of organization and political projects within poor urban communities. Non-criminal 'informal' economic activity may bring better economic returns, security and a greater sense of social dignity than low-paid 'regular jobs'. Sociality does not always collapse to the extent assumed by the most pessimistic visions of the 'new poverty', as the lively religious and secular associational life of our own study community shows.[1]

It is one thing to avoid romanticizing the 'agency' of poor people, but another to deny them any agency at all. As ethnographies of development practice show, projects both shape and are shaped by the responses of the socially differentiated groups of beneficiaries that engage with local and international 'experts' (Mosse 2005). Concepts such as 'advanced marginality' also obscure the fact that poor people live lives that transcend their condition of poverty at least part of the time. Our research in Bairro da Paz,[2] a poor neighbourhood with a population of 60,000 in Brazil's third city, Salvador, Bahia, a metropolis with more than three million residents, suggests that the subjective experience of being poor is not identical across the city's slums. We need to consider why that is so. We also need a better understanding of how differences in social conditions and organization, along with different histories of slum formation and settlement, affect the capacity of internally contentious communities to come together sufficiently to engage in contentious politics with NGO patrons, state agencies and politicians.

In Bairro da Paz, our academic team conducted ethnographic research on families, their social networks and religious and secular associations, while supporting the development of a new community representative body established in 2007, the (Permanent) Forum of Social Entities of Bairro da Paz. The emergence of the Forum reflected a grass-roots desire to put the shattered fragments of community organization back together again to achieve greater leverage in presenting demands to public authorities. The Residents' Council – the most powerful existing organization because it mediates much of the flow of public and private-sector resources into the community – is a leading participant, along with community leaderships linked to Catholic NGOs running projects in the *bairro* and investing in its infrastructure. This new institution has also stimulated the active participation of members of youth groups orientated to Afro-Brazilian cultural projects such as musical and dance performance. These groups have been highly critical of traditional ways of doing politics and the conduct of community affairs by the Residents' Council. Their distinct goals range from development of 'affirmative action' policies to a politics of restitution in which past injustice entitles the descendants of slaves to the urban equivalent of the *quilombo* communities founded by escaped slaves. From these perspectives, Bairro da Paz is not a 'space' but a *place* to be built through new struggles for social justice (Hita 2012).

We as researchers and the community actors themselves are conscious of the limitations of the 'participation' currently on offer from government, and of the neo-liberal premises of much current intervention, with its strong focus on public-private partnerships. Although the purpose of the Forum is to negotiate, Bairro da Paz's history, described briefly in the next section, has generated a combative political culture, suspicious of 'impositions' and focused on demands (Hita 2012). People operate with few illusions about how politics works and cannot be regarded as simply reproducing clientelistic forms of politics, although the Forum has also attracted older male and female leaders who felt perfectly comfortable with that model of what engagement with public power was about. At the same time, however, there are ambiguities in the positions adopted. Young men manifesting sympathy with U.S.-style 'black' politics are attracted by neo-liberal models of constructing the self through consumption, and by prospects of gaining social mobility through training courses created under private-public partnerships. At the same time they express sharp critiques of capitalist globalization and the self-serving nature of politicians.

As academic advisors reflecting on the organizational process itself as well as providing data for the Forum's grass-roots diagnoses of community problems and proposed solutions, we do not wish to minimize the contradictions that persist in this new framework. Although all Forum participants believe that it needs to be inclusive to be effective, we worry about issues such as the tendency for members of Catholic organizations to dominate, and the underrepresentation of the neighbourhood's many

Evangelicals. The extent to which the Forum is able to speak for residents living in the areas more distant from the more urbanized central zone is also an issue, although large turnouts and lively debates at public meetings attended by representatives of government agencies have been encouraging. The original context of the research project was evaluation of the Lula government's social programmes (in particular the *bolsa familia*, family stipend, programme) through qualitative, ethnographic methods. But the support that we are giving to the Forum emerged out of community actors' own perspectives on how the expertise of an academic research team could be useful to them. Even at their most ambiguous, the new identities and projects appearing in Bairro da Paz take us away from the 'precariat' model.

The Shaping of a Place and Its People

Even peripheral spaces have histories that can turn them into places. An important, but not unique, irony in the history of Bairro da Paz is that the poor inhabitants of what was initially a peripheral space beyond the limits of urban settlement ended up being encircled by the rich.

The squatters who established the neighbourhood in the 1980s defied government attempts to relocate them by force, supported by politicians of the Left, the Movement for the Defence of Slum Dwellers (Movimento de Defesa dos Favelados) and Catholic organizations. The most important of the latter was CEAS (Centre of Studies and Social Action), a Liberation Theology–inspired Jesuit NGO created in 1967 to engage in politico-educative activity throughout the Brazilian Northeast. In the early years the community was known as 'the Malvinas', a reference to the Falklands War. This sobriquet reflected its militant resistance prior to receiving limited guarantees and promises of infrastructure investment from state and city governments in 1987, after military rule ended and left-leaning political forces had an opportunity to enter office (Hita and Duccini 2008). Although the change of name reflected willingness to collaborate with the authorities, the foundational myth of a community built on struggle remains central to the political culture of Bairro da Paz (Hita 2012). Furthermore, the change of political environment proved only a brief interruption to the domination of Bahian politics until the recent past by the political machine of Antônio Carlos Magalhães (hereafter ACM). ACM was appointed city prefect in 1967 as a reward for his support for the military 'revolution'. He was subsequently made state governor and held this post for three terms, along with offices in federal government.

ACM's administrations were determined to prevent favelas from blighting the development of new commercial, administrative and higher-income residential areas along the coastal strip and subsequently along the Avenida Paralela, the main road to the airport along which the Malvinas invasion occurred, a few kilometres beyond a new state government administrative centre inaugurated at the start of the 1980s. From the beginning ACM dedicated his efforts to the reinvention of Salvador as a modern business, service and international tourist hub. A Law of Urban Reform paved the way by authorizing the alienation of all public land that was leased, rented or occupied without contract. Although ACM claimed that it would be beneficial to the poor by allowing them to acquire full property rights over their dwellings, the legislation brought much clearer benefits to property developers, allowing many poor families to be cleared from central areas, which added impetus to land invasions elsewhere (Dantas Neto 2006: 336).

Eviction of the Malvinas squatters was supported by conservationists who argued that human settlement should be prohibited in this zone in order to preserve the Atlantic forest. The invaders' determination to defy the settlement ban therefore also served the interests of property developers, who subsequently installed high-income condominiums in the surrounding area. The context was one in which Salvador's poorer sectors could not obtain housing via the market, while limited public housing schemes were aimed at working families with higher incomes (Gordilho 2000; Valença 2007). Salaries remained low and employment precarious in a process of economic modernization based initially on oil, petrochemicals and capital-intensive industrialization whose centres of accumulation remained outside Bahia. Salvador's development as a global tourist destination augmented service employment and had other significant social and cultural effects. But it did not resolve the basic labour market problems facing an urban population that continued to expand due to both rural-urban migration and natural increase.

Employment opportunities in Bairro da Paz remain precarious, but the settlement has gained some advantages from the proximity of higher-income residents, offices and a private university, offering construction work and seeking suppliers of low-cost services. Yet the image of the slum suffers from the media's linking it with the growth of armed violence associated with drug trafficking, and the military police classify it as one of the thirteen most dangerous neighbourhoods in the metropolitan region. The 1987 political settlement ended the immediate threat of eviction, but offered guarantees only to residents living in a central polygon. Nevertheless, there has been slow improvement in infrastructure and access to services. The relative stabilization of the situation reflects changes in public policies on popular housing and settlement, combined with increasing emphasis on 'popular participation' in urban planning that recognizes poor people's capacity to exercise the rights and responsibilities of citizenship. The latter change is one to which the mobilization of communities such as Bairro da Paz made an important contribution through pressure from below (Caldeira and Holston 2004; Texeira 2001).

There have, however, been many internal conflicts and crises of leadership. These reflect the impacts of political clientelism, NGO interventions and the socio-economic differentiation that exists in all slum communities, which their residents may see as very important even when it seems distinctly relative to outsiders. The conflicts also reflect religious differences – of particular importance in Brazil, given the continuing growth of Evangelical churches, of which there are forty in Bairro da Paz alone. Accused of self-serving and undemocratic behaviour, an earlier Residents' Association collapsed, but the more transparent Residents' Council that replaced it also has its critics. Catholic NGOs play a prominent part in community life, but the political positions of different Catholic community actors range from a conservative 'assistentialist' posture to radical, Liberation Theology–inspired projects.[3] The Catholic groups can coexist relatively comfortably with groups associated with the *bairro*'s fifteen Candomblé temples, one of which also runs a comparatively underfunded community crèche. But Candomblé adherents have complained of aggression from members of the Universal Church of the Kingdom of God, a powerful neo-Pentecostalist church.

Baptists have recently been led by a socially activist pastor whose role has reflected his own church-building agenda and his connections with a municipal administration that defeated ACM's machine in 2005 and won a second term in 2008, headed by a prefect who is also Evangelical. Yet it is because these divisions are so significant that countervailing community efforts to transcend them have emerged. The Forum of Social Entities has enhanced the 'political voice' of this particular favela under city and state administrations, the latter since 2007 in the hands of a governor from Lula's PT. The development of activist youth groups promoting aspects of Afro-Brazilian culture that now receive positive public recognition has also aided the residents' struggle to combat a form of symbolic violence prevalent in the wider society, one that explains persistent inequality in terms of racialized models of the incapacities of poor people. This is one significant sense in which we can speak of changes in the meaning of being 'peripheral' relative to the established socio-cultural and political 'centres' of a white elite–dominated Bahian society. It is one that offers a revival of 'hope' and orientation towards securing a better future in the political projects of people who live in precarious conditions.

Rethinking Spatial Segregation

Salvador has also become more spatially 'polycentric' over time. Bairro da Paz's location is no longer economically peripheral. Sited on the main road linking existing commercial and administrative centres with the airport and northern coastal beaches, real estate values in the area have increased substantially. The favela is now surrounded not only by closed condominiums but also by 'new economy' projects currently being extended through the construction of a technology park. Relations between rich and poor in this locality have been influenced positively by private-sector financing of social projects for the slum but are still principally coloured by fear of crime on the part of the affluent and fear of eviction on the part of slum-dwellers. The opening of a new upscale shopping centre close to the *bairro* in 2009 awakened new fears that developers would try to buy out the residents of the humbler homes beyond the centre of the neighbourhood. Further fears of eviction were prompted by city government plans for redevelopment linked to the 2014 World Cup, which provoked a protest campaign of highway blockages in the best militant traditions of the neighbourhood. The 'engagement' of the *bairro*'s political actors with external agencies is often sceptical and wary of criticism for cooptation. Yet the variety of forms of engagement and plurality of social actors involved invites reflection on whether undertaking research on 'urban poverty' produces initial definitions of the social situation that blinker our vision until they are replaced by the more rounded understanding of social realities that ethnography provides.

It therefore seems important to compare Bairro da Paz with other slum settlements. These are to be found in a wide variety of locations in the city, whose geographical structure is peculiar as a result of its interrupted topography. The elite originally lived together with slave and free blacks in multi-storied housing located on the plateau overlooking All Saints Bay, an 'upper city' whose decaying historic centre was gentrified in the 1990s after being declared a World Heritage Site by UNESCO. This upper city overlooks the 'lower city' of the port and commercial area, although a good deal of the business sector had moved to the zone located at the beginning of the Avenida Paralela by the end of ACM's second period as governor in 1983 (Almeida 2006: 39). Working-class areas also developed in the nineteenth century along the railway line

connecting the port to the agro-export hinterland known as the Recôn-
cavo, following the line of All Saints Bay into the interior of Bahia. As
the few industries located in this zone declined, it became the area of
slums known as the Subúrbio Ferroviário. Another major working-class
area developed in the inland zone known as the Miolo, beyond the old
upper city. The Atlantic coastal strip (the Orla), originally occupied by
fishing communities, was colonized by elite and middle-class residents
between 1940 and 1960, although some large irregular settlements were
also established there, producing another context in which rich and poor
lived in close proximity (Gordilho 2000: 145–146). Bairro da Paz was
established at the time when the remaining free spaces within the urban
landscape were being filled in wherever they could be found, but ended
up being located on the most important future vector of expansion of
the capitalist city.

Different spaces offered different opportunities, advantages and dis-
advantages, not simply in terms of employment opportunities and travel
distances to work but also in terms of the density and precariousness
of housing. The self-built environment of the poor is both a product
of their social practices – particularly the dynamics of extended family structures that are often built around women/mothers in the senior
generation (with circulating male members) – and also a factor shaping
the evolution of those practices and the kinds of choices that people
can make about the lives they wish to lead. As a result of agreements
reached between the representatives of the invaders and public authorities to restrict future growth of the settlement in return for public
investment, Bairro da Paz is less densely settled than many other Salvador slums (Gordilho 2000: 148). Since individuals can move between
different spaces in ways that reflect the nature of property relations as
well as systems of kinship, affinity and alternative models for residential groups, what emerges from this wider comparative picture is not a
homogeneous 'peripheral urban situation' but a series of distinct ways
of being poor, building families and earning a livelihood, in a complex
of situations that are in part determined by the relations between slum-
dwellers and the non-slum areas that surround them.

An ethnographic example will be helpful to illustrate the complexities that emerge when we focus on individual family strategies for occupying urban space and their social meanings.[4] Edileusa was a Candomblé
priestess (*mãe de santo*) who ran the crèche in Bairro da Paz associated
with a temple (*terreiro*) that she founded early in the history of the invasion in pursuit of the preferred strategy of separating the temple from
the family home. Her original home was located some distance away in
the lower-class part of the Boca do Rio neighbourhood, on the coastal

strip. The Boca do Rio beach was much enjoyed by Salvador's liberal artistic community in the 1970s, and more recently has seen new developments for wealthier people such as a shopping mall and convention centre. Mãe Edileusa not only retained her original house in Boca do Rio, where two of her daughters and three grandchildren formed part of a co-residential unit, but also seized the opportunity provided by city government efforts to end the Malvinas invasion to acquire a third house in 1983, when the prefecture offered public housing in the distant Subúrbio Ferroviário to those willing to leave. Brought up by her grandparents, whose deaths forced her to begin work in domestic service at the age of eleven, Mãe Edileusa not only managed to found a *terreiro* but also trained as a nursing assistant and left her children three pieces of property. By seizing all the opportunities available within the urban spaces in which she could operate, including those created by land invasions, Mãe Edileusa maximized the prospects for the next generation. Yet the fact that family reproduction takes place across this extensive and diversified urban environment also means that whether kin stay together or separate residentially in the next generation in part depends on the resources that can be mobilized and on relations between parents and children – especially, in the social and cultural worlds of the Afro-Brazilian poor of Salvador, those between mothers and daughters.

Processes of social segregation are evident in the city, most obviously on the part of the upper classes. But it is important not to lose sight of the implications of the mobility of poor people in urban space and the pervasive physical proximity of the residences of rich and poor, if we are to understand how segregation is produced and its terms contested. For example, one of Bairro de Paz's Candomblé temples is frequented by the rich and famous and is representative of the kind of *terreiros* that have become objects of an official politics of patronage of Afro-Brazilian culture and heritage. Yet this *terreiro* is 'in' but not 'of' the *bairro*, as far as the residents are concerned. The Candomblé temples 'of' the *bairro* are quite different in terms of both ritual practice and financial resources, and play a significant role in community politics. A considerable amount of symbolic work is still done by other sectors of Bahian society – including some that are themselves far from affluent – seeking to draw boundaries, segregate and peripheralize. Many people may hide a stigmatized place of residence as they navigate job interviews or other social encounters in the city. However, a good deal of community politics in Bairro da Paz, and in zones such as the Subúrbio Ferroviário, now focuses on contesting territorial stigmatization and projecting a 'positive' public image, although this is no longer necessarily a 'mainstream' or 'whitened' image. Analytically, social segregation as a concept may obscure more than it reveals, not least because interactions across social boundaries affect the way different low-income neighbourhoods develop.

Our analysis indicates the importance of particular political histories and socio-economic contexts in shaping individual slums' capacity to 'act' collectively. Given that, we are drawn to the conclusion that a more sociologically neutral focus on the way people live their lives and relate to each other when they construct places in which to dwell in the city – a more classically 'holistic' ethnographic vision – often better aids us to understand how 'peripheral urban situations' differ in ways that are important both for the people who live in them and for developing public policies that might give better results for those people as well. If we allow frames such as 'slum-dwellers' and 'poverty' to foreclose on the possibilities of such analysis before we undertake it, we will never understand why some people seem more willing than others to buy into some aspects of the 'package' of social development and constructively engage public powers in order to obtain its benefits.

There is, of course, no unitary collective actor in Bairro da Paz, even if the Forum is a more inclusive voice of 'the community'. Yet to understand how fragile balances of counter-hegemonic force can be fostered by the contributions of academics and practitioners from outside poor communities, we need the kind of holism that can see the politics in the everyday and apparently apolitical aspects of the flow of life. Framing people as poor, even as a point of departure (as if this were their transcendent subject position), puts us in danger of forgetting the need to discover, ethnographically, what their lives are mainly about and the sources of hope that may still animate their politics.

At the same time, however, our experience in Bairro da Paz suggests that the way academics engage with the people we study today will be increasingly determined by those people, if we wish to secure their collaboration for intensive and often intrusive fieldwork. In this respect, to return to our starting point, it is difficult to maintain any kind of insulation between studying the social lives of poor people and the interventions of NGOs and the state in those lives, because the latter are central to the preoccupations of the poor, the field is already politicized from below, and all parties call upon academic researchers to make a contribution. In the Forum of Social Entities, the academics work with representatives of the NGOs and state-funded agencies that operate in the community. When it comes to drawing up demands and negotiating with higher public authorities, we are part of the collective process that also involves other entities from outside the *bairro*, which demands prior consensus building. Exchanges in the Forum often highlight contradictions of the kind that are at the forefront of academic critiques. These include the tensions between the way some of the NGO personnel invoke a morality of charitable giving and the community's responsibility to show its gratitude, and community members' concurrent desire to talk about social rights and entitlements. Yet community leaders themselves raise these kinds of issues without any prompting from the academics present. As a deliberative body the Forum provides a space in which everyone feels able to speak freely, since it was created to transcend recognized differences of interest and ideology. It has therefore promoted a consensus amongst all the participants on the need to go beyond a city government discourse of 'popular participation', which often seems little more than a strategy for identifying and co-opting local leaderships with strong popular bases who are likely to press demands with particular vigour.

Because the Catholic NGOs command the greatest resources, the Forum of Social Entities is not an organization of true equals, and it is still struggling to be truly inclusive of all the *bairro*'s organizations, an issue which has been one of the chief concerns of our interventions as an academic team. But it does represent a conceptual step beyond the kind of 'participatory development' practice so frequently criticized in the anthropological literature for its selective empowerment of particular community interests (Green 2000; Mosse 2005). It has also proved possible in this case for the academics to avoid the problems associated with the speed and superficiality of techniques such as participatory appraisal by embedding their engagement in a long-term research programme that has also enabled deeper relationships to be built with a diversity of local actors in and of the neighbourhood (Pottier 1997). This kind of engagement makes the anthropologist's 'broker' role as a mediator between external organizations and members of study communities into an increasingly complex balancing act. Yet the Forum also enables us to put what we 'know' about community social life and politics at the direct service of community organizations in their struggles to improve things. It therefore resolves part of the tension between 'doing' and 'knowing' for us, whilst inevitably leaving the question of 'what to do' to be resolved in the light of experience and through collective consensus building, with the usual lack of guarantees of universally happy and uncontested outcomes.

NOTES

1. A survey conducted in 2006 by the Centre for Metropolitan Studies of CEBRAP, the Brazilian Centre for Analysis and Planning, showed that more than half the residents had participated in some kind of association during

their lives. Although churches were the main form of association, 20 per cent of those interviewed had been active in social movements.

2. The research is part of a comparative study that includes similar projects in Rio de Janeiro and São Paulo, funded by CEBRAP. The work with the Forum has been supported by FAPESB, the Bahian State Foundation for Research Support.

3. The Santa Casa de Misericordia (founded in 1549) and Dom Avelar Foundation, led by an Italian nun, run the six biggest community crèches and provide educational and artistic courses to young people, in partnership with the Cidade Mãe (Mother City) Foundation, launched in 1993 under the left-leaning Prefect Lídice da Mata, with UNICEF funding. But figures associated with the Santa Casa do not have homogeneous views. The radical CEAS, mentioned earlier, continues to be active in the Bairro but has disengaged from the Residents' Council, whose replacement of the original Association the CEAS helped to engineer. The CEAS now focuses on supporting Afro-Brazilian youth groups.

4. For additional case studies of the social networks of residents, see Hita and Duccini 2008.

BIBLIOGRAPHY

Almeida, P. H. 2006. 'A economia de Salvador e a formação de sua região metropolitana', in I. M. Moreira de Carvalho and G. Corso Pereira (eds), *Como Anda Salvador e sua Região Metropolitana*. Salvador: Editora da UFBA, pp.11–53.

Caldeira, T. P. R. 2000. *City of Walls: Crime, Segregation and Citizenship in São Paulo*. Berkeley: University of California Press.

Caldeira, T. P. R and J. Holston. 2004. 'State and Urban Space in Brazil: From Modernist Planning to Democratic Intervention', in A. Ong and S. J. Collier (eds), *Global Assemblages: Technology, Politics and Ethics as an Anthropological Problem*. Malden, MA: Blackwell, pp. 393–416.

Dantas Neto, Paulo Fábio. 2006. *Tradição, Autocracia e Carisma: A Política de Antonio Carlos Magalhães na Modernizacão da Bahia (1954–1974)*. Belo Horizonte: Universidade Federal de Minas Gerais.

De Almeida, R., T. D'Andrea and D. De Lucca. 2008. 'Situações periféricas: etnografia comparada de pobrezas urbanas', *Novos Estudos* 82(November): 109–130.

Eckstein, S. 1990. 'Urbanization Revisited: Inner-city Slum of Hope and Squatter Settlement of Despair', *World Development* 18(2): 165–181.

Gledhill, J. 2005. 'Citizenship and the Social Geography of Deep Neoliberalization', *Anthropologica* 47(1): 81–100.

Gordilho Souza, A. 2000. *Limites do Habitar: Segregação e Exclusão na Configuração Urbana Contemporânea de Salvador e Perspectivas no Final do Século XX*. Salvador: Edufba.

Green, M. 2000. 'Participatory Development and the Appropriation of Agency in Southern Tanzania', *Critique of Anthropology* 20(1): 67–86.

Hale, C. R. 2006. 'Activist Research v. Cultural Critique: Indigenous Land Rights and the Contradictions of Politically Engaged Anthropology', *Cultural Anthropology* 21(1): 96–120.

Hita, M. G. 2012. 'From Resistance Avenue to the Plaza of Decisions: New Urban Actors in Salvador, Bahia', in J. Gledhill and P. Schell (eds), *New Approaches to Resistance in Brazil and Mexico*. Durham: Duke University Press, pp. 269–288.

Hita, M. G. and L. Duccini. 2008. 'Exclusão social, desafiliacão e inclusão social no estudo de redes sociais de famílias pobres soteropolitanas', in A. Ziccardi (ed.), *Procesos de urbanización de la pobreza y nuevas formas de exclusión social: los retos de las políticas sociales de las ciudades latinoamericanas del siglo XXI*. Bogotá: Siglo del Hombre Editores, Clacso-Crop, pp. 181–212.

Mosse, D. 2005. *Cultivating Development: An Ethnography of Aid Policy and Practice*. Pluto Press: London.

Perlman, J. 1976. *The Myth of Marginality: Urban Poverty and Politics in Rio de Janeiro*. Berkeley: University of California Press.

———. 2004. 'The Metamorphosis of Marginality in Rio de Janeiro', *Latin American Research Review* 39(1): 189–192.

Pottier, J. 1997. 'Towards an Ethnography of Participatory Appraisal and Research', in R. Grillo and R. Stirrat (eds), *Discourses of Development*. Oxford: Berg Publishers, pp. 203–227.

Soares, F. and Y. Soares. 2005. 'The Socio-economic Impact of *favela-bairro*: What Do the Data Say?' Working Paper OVE/WP-08. Washington, D.C.: Inter-American Development Bank. Retrieved 12 September 2008 from http://www.iadb.org/ove/GetDocument.aspx?DOCNUM=600835&Cache=True

Texeira, E. 2001. *O Local e o Global: Limites e Desafios da Participação Cidadã*. São Paulo: Ed. Cortez.

Tsing, A. 2005. *Friction: An Ethnography of Global Connection*. Princeton: Princeton University Press.

Valença, M. M. 2007. 'Poor Politics, Poor Housing: Policy under the Collor Government in Brazil (1990–92)', *Environment and Urbanization* 19(2): 391–408.

Wacquant, L. 2007. 'Territorial Stigmatization in the Age of Advanced Marginality', *Thesis Eleven* 91: 66–77.

CHAPTER 8

Extraordinary Violence and Everyday Welfare

The State and Development in Rural and Urban India

Amita Baviskar

Introduction

The notion of anthropology as cultural critique (Ferguson 1997; Marcus and Fischer 1986) is exemplified in the field of the anthropology of development, which over the last two decades has provided trenchant analyses of how power relations permeate projects of welfare. Critical ethnographies of development (e.g., Ferguson 1990; Mosse 2005) have examined particular projects in order to reveal how the workings of these initiatives draw upon institutional and political logics that often run counter to the official discourse of welfare. Some studies have focused on the discursive work performed by 'development' (Escobar 1995; Pigg 1992) and its role in legitimizing interventions by Northern 'experts' in the lives of subalterns. Subsequent research has extended its critique beyond the trope of 'development as domination' to examine the multiple meanings at work in practices of development, especially for development workers and others for whom the universalizing vocabulary of the discourse may be a mode of articulating ethical and other concerns. By focusing on how the discourse of development may be appropriated and re-signified by its designated targets, recent ethnographies (including those in this volume) delineate the complexities of differentiated development, showing the formidable challenges that it presents as well as the possibilities for its transformation.

This chapter supplements the 'anthropology of development' as described above by locating it within a wider sphere of cultural politics. Instead of concentrating on the official world of Development – i.e., projects of welfare initiated by the state or NGOs and often funded by international agencies – it focuses on development with a small *d*: a historical process of capitalist accumulation and legitimation where Development is embedded in a larger cultural politics that includes resource extraction, dispossession and displacement. This wider set of meanings is critical for illuminating how Development is understood and acted upon by 'development workers', who include not only professionals employed by the state or NGOs, but also subaltern citizens engaged in the contentious business of staying alive in the face of entrenched inequalities underwritten by the state.

This essay examines experiences of development among two social groups: (1) Bhilala *adivasis*[1] displaced by a dam in the Narmada Valley in central India; and (2) slum-dwellers and squatters evicted from their homes in Delhi. Both these groups are poor in absolute and relative terms, and their lives have been made infinitely harder by the displacements that they have suffered at the hands of the state. Through their experiences, I trace the state practices that they encounter, where extraordinary violence exists alongside everyday welfare functions. Such an analysis is important for understanding the relations between claiming citizenship and cultural identity for different subaltern groups, and how these have changed with economic development and liberalization. I describe how state action in relation to these two groups has been contingent on how they have mobilized collective symbolic capital, and on their embedded histories of opposition, collaboration and negotiation.

This analysis of citizenship, place and the politics of recognition is based on critical engagement with subaltern experience in the hope that such an analysis will provide some insights into the processes producing and perpetuating poverty and inequality, and how they might be challenged. Such a stance addresses the field of development in the wider sense and foregrounds the operations of power in ways both discursive and material. It is based on the notion of critique as writ large in the lifeworld of subalterns. Such an account of development must be placed alongside other accounts that address Development, in order to understand how they relate to each other and to examine how and why the political economy of academic production in anthropology across different locations privileges one set of issues (around Development) over another (development).

Narmada and Delhi

August 2004 witnessed the flooding of Anjanvara, the Bhilala adivasi village where I first lived in 1990 when starting research in the Narmada Valley in Madhya Pradesh (Baviskar 1995). It was in Delhi that I first heard about the flooding from Khajan, the adivasi activist in whose home I stayed in Anjanvara:

> Khajan telephoned from Sondwa on the night of August 14. He had come to the town from his village Anjanvara to collect 'relief' at the Block headquarters. For the first time ever, his village and others adjoining it on the banks of the Narmada saw their fields submerge in the rising waters of the reservoir of the Sardar Sarovar dam. Their standing crops disappeared under water. With the land was lost their supply of food and income for this year and for the years to come.
>
> By now, this has become a familiar story. We knew of the tragedy of the Narmada dams. I knew that Anjanvara would be submerged during this year's monsoons. Since the Supreme Court order of 2000 permitting dam construction in the 'national interest', we had seen the river rise slowly, irreversibly altering the landscape. We knew this was imminent. But when it finally happened, it was still awful beyond words.
>
> On the phone, Khajan's voice is hesitant, blurred with tears. He manages a couple of halting sentences: '*Amita, maari zingi doob gayi . . . Maara kheton ma boot phirtali*' [My life has drowned . . . a boat now sails over my fields]. Binda, his wife, has been crying ever since. They are farmers, this land was their life. They haven't received any land or equivalent monetary compensation from the government, their legal entitlement. Last year, they had rebuilt their house further up the hillside, so they were at least spared the additional trauma of losing everything they owned. But next year, they will have to move out of the area and they will have nowhere to go. Their struggle for survival – fighting hunger, disease and exploitation, trying to secure a better life for themselves and for their children, has just become immeasurably harder.
>
> Khajan was the *sarpanch* (elected head of local government) of the Sakarja *panchayat*. He had come to Sondwa, the Block HQ, to collect the wheat and rice sanctioned by the District Collector as 'relief'. The meagre amounts allotted per household will barely last them a

couple of months. Beyond that, if the government thinks of them at all, it probably expects them to fight starvation in the time-honoured way – through migration.

Khajan says that government officials and shopkeepers in Sondwa regard him as a figure of fun. '*Maadarchod mere upar hanste hain*' [The motherfuckers laugh at me]. The *bazaarias* (people of the town) have always despised and feared adivasis like Khajan who were key members of the Andolan and Sangath, and whose collective mobilization over a twenty-year period forced them to change their practices – offer respect and fairer treatment, better prices and wages. These adivasis are now once again at the bazaarias' mercy. There is ignominy in pleading for a few quintals of grain from a state you once challenged and officials lose no opportunity to make the experience as humiliating as they can.

Further into the conversation, as he repeats the same disjointed sentences, it occurs to me that Khajan is drunk. But the comforting numbness that liquor should bring is denied to him. The pain pierces through and he returns again and again to the immense grief of a living death: *maari zingi doob gayi* [my life has drowned].

(Diary, 14 August 2004)

Submergence and displacement have been the most extreme forms of state intervention suffered by Bhilala and Bhil adivasis in the hills of the Narmada Valley. However, prior forms of state action have not been altogether benevolent either. In a hilly, forested area where the process of land settlement was sketchily conducted, the fluidity and continuity between fields and forests that marked adivasi land use practices was never recognized. For decades, adivasis who supplemented their tiny legal holdings of agricultural land with *nevad* (literally, new field) clearings in areas owned by the Forest Department, had been at the mercy of the forest bureaucracy (Baviskar 1995). Nevad is illegal: officially, it is an encroachment on forest land. As encroachers in the eyes of the state, all adivasis are automatically treated as criminals. They have paid fines and bribes and been beaten up and jailed, they have had their bullocks and ploughs confiscated, they have watched as Forest Department staff destroyed their standing crops of maize and sorghum. Adivasi use of the forest, crucial for survival yet forbidden by law, has been the chief conflict shaping their relationship with the state. This conflict became muted in the late 1980s, when adivasis in this area collectively mobilized as a trade union of peasants and labourers (Khedut Mazdoor Chetna Sangath) and, after years of agitation, wrested an uneasy stand-off with the state. While they have not succeeded in getting legal title to their nevad fields, they have managed to ensure that forest officials no longer harass them.[2] Even this fragile victory means a lot: in other parts of Madhya Pradesh, adivasis still routinely face state violence, including torture and killing, over the issue of nevad (Baviskar 2001).

Poverty for adivasis in Madhya Pradesh, then, is predicated not only upon the vagaries of weather that define smallholder dryland agriculture, but also upon the uncertainty and insecurity that derives from their relationship with the state and its legal classification of land. Added to this is the stigma of being adivasi, a social category that is still viewed as savage and backward, not amenable to state projects of Improvement. It is another matter that such state projects languish by the roadside well before they reach adivasi villages. Like most adivasi villages in the Narmada Valley, Anjanvara had no school, health centre, handpump, electricity or any of the basic provisions supposed to be provided by the government. Even universal programmes such as immunization founder when faced with the physical difficulties of reaching villages nestled in the fastness of the hills. It is thus a cruel irony that the only time many adivasis encounter state welfare is when they have been displaced and are eligible to be given 'relief'.

The drowning of Anjanvara is one reality. A parallel world is to be found in Delhi, where poor slum-dwellers, squatters on public land along the river Yamuna, have been evicted in punctuated bursts of brutality since 2004. On a blazing day in July 2006, I visited Savda Ghevra, a 'transit camp' for squatters who had been evicted from Lakshmi Nagar and Geeta Colony on the east bank of the river Yamuna in central Delhi. The camp was located 35 km from their former homes, on the north-western edge of the city at the end of a rutted dirt track. Elaborate signage announced the camp: freshly painted metal boards, white-on-black, were posted every fifteen feet indicating block and plot numbers. Larger boards indicated the 'public conveniences' and the water source, a handpump. The signs suggested order and permanence, thoughtful planning and effective implementation. And yet the physical structures they pointed to were either missing or so modest as to be pathetically out of sync with the assured confidence of the signs. The blocks and plots were numbered, but the houses that stood there were flimsy bamboo sheds with mud floors – a far cry from the brick and cement homes that people had built in Lakshmi Nagar. There was nothing else: no schools, health clinics, shops, public transport. In the unrelenting grimness of this place, the signs seemed more tragic than ironic, their presence a reminder of the state's failure to live up to its promise of resettlement. On talking to people, we learnt that they had been put up the previous week for a visit by the chief minister of Delhi.

The people at Savda Ghevra are mainly poor Muslim migrants from eastern India. A month after the evictions, the trauma was still fresh in their minds. '*Shukravar aag jalayi, Somvar jhuggi todi*' [Friday they set fire to the *jhuggis* (shanty houses), Monday they demolished them], said Amir from Lakshmi Nagar *thokar* [milestone] number 8, who had come to Delhi in 1984 from Bijnor, in western Uttar Pradesh: 'Everyone was away at work; only the children were home. We lost everything.' The fire destroyed documents as well – the voter ID, ration card and receipts for fines paid that are crucial for establishing claims to residence and resettlement. Manju Devi, the wife of a mason, said, '*Eko samaan nahin bacha. Machine chalaya, tod diya*' [Not one article was left. They ran the machine, broke everything]. After bulldozers razed her home to the ground, Manju is left with one aluminium pot. 'I cut vegetables in it, I cook dal in it. That's when I *can* cook. Most days I give the children puffed rice to eat and put them to sleep. There's no money for *mitti ka tel* [kerosene] and it's hard to find fuel wood here. When it rains, there's knee-deep water, so where am I to cook?'

The people at Savda Ghevra believe that the fire that preceded the bulldozers was no accident but was deliberately set by the government. The bulldozers that followed only sealed their fate. The dislocation deprived them of water, sanitation, education, health care and access to shops. But their biggest problem with the site is its location. Lakshmi Nagar and Geeta Colony had been next to the dense, small-scale industrial belt of Gandhi Nagar, where there was plenty of work available for earning a livelihood. Women worked at a variety of jobs – at a thread factory, wrapping toffees, making dried mango, or as domestic help. None of this is now possible. Little work is available for either women or men near Savda Ghevra. They go to the Delhi-Haryana border nearby in search of employment, but cannot find anything.

The experience of a sudden and sharp decline in family assets and incomes, and of hardship and uncertainty, has been exacerbated by the knowledge that people will not get title to the plots of land where they are housed. Even with their diminished means, owning land or having secure long-term access to it would greatly ease the task of once again mobilizing resources to build permanent dwellings. For more than twenty years in Lakshmi Nagar, people had borne the hazards of insecure tenure, periodic demolition and constant harassment by municipal officials, to gradually build *pukka* houses in the hope that eventually they would be 'regularized' (legalized with retrospective effect). However modest these homes, and however squalid the settlement in Lakshmi Nagar, their present circumstances make people look back with regret at what they lost. Said Shankar Rai, who used to run a tea shop, *'Jo bhi tha, hum logon ke liye kaafi tha'* [Whatever it was, it was enough for us].

Eviction and relocation have extinguished that hope of permanence. The status of people at Savda Ghevra is contested because the land that they had occupied along the Yamuna is owned by the Uttar Pradesh (UP) Flood and Irrigation Department. According to the Delhi government, the costs of resettlement must be borne by the UP government. Since the latter has refused to do so, the Savda Ghevra people are only being temporarily sheltered in a 'transit camp' and cannot claim any long-term shelter. The evictions in Delhi are the result of the resumption of government control over land in order to facilitate new private-public real estate development that cashes in on the booming value of landed property, whereas the displaced are not legally entitled to any compensation because they are encroachers. Should some of them get resettled, it is thanks to the 'generosity' of the government – it is not their right (see Tarlo 2003). The lack of legal property is the crucial condition underlying poverty and powerlessness in the face of evictions in Delhi. What is usually overlooked in the public discourse on evictions is the fact that the poor are compelled to be squatters, and therefore forced to inhabit a criminalized status, because the government has provided hardly any legal affordable housing for the working poor whose labour is critical for running the city (Baviskar 2003; Ramanathan 2006).

Poverty, Development and Liberalization

It might be argued that the displacements in the Narmada Valley and in Delhi represent two different moments in the trajectory of development and growth in independent India. The Narmada case is a classic instance of land alienation as a part of the state-led project of national development (Dwivedi 2006). The Sardar Sarovar dam is iconic of the Nehruvian era and its celebration of the 'temples of modern India', large public-sector investments aimed equally at increasing agricultural productivity and announcing state capacity and authority (Klingensmith 2007). The predicament facing Anjanvara is not an anomaly: it is estimated that 30 million people, more than the entire population of Canada, have been displaced since India became independent in 1947 (Fernandes 1991). Of these, almost 75 per cent are, by the government's own admission, 'still awaiting rehabilitation'.[3]

The evictions in Delhi illustrate what is now an all-too-common phenomenon across the country since the adoption of economic liberalization policies since the 1990s: land acquisition by the government followed by its transfer to private firms. In this period, government policies have been geared to divesting the state of its welfare functions, enabling foreign investment, easing imports, privatizing public-sector assets, and dismantling the institutions regulating private firms. Economic policy has been reoriented to maximize foreign exchange earnings, with concessions and subsidies given to Indian and foreign firms to encourage them to invest in production for export. While conflicts over some land transfers have generated media attention and wider mobilization that has aided resistance (Baviskar and Sundar 2008), in the majority of cases, affected farmers and labourers have not been able to garner support beyond their limited resources.

Yet from the point of view of those facing displacement, the difference between a public-sector and private-sector project is moot. Both sets of displacement involve the same legal instrument: the Land Acquisition Act. Both derive their legitimacy from the assertion that such land acquisition is desirable in the public interest. Since public and private projects continually intersect (many of the tasks in any public-sector project are outsourced and contracted to private firms), it would be more accurate to describe the two moments of developmentalism and liberalization as existing simultaneously on the spatio-temporal map of contemporary India. The difference between the 'older' development project and the postliberalization one is that the transfer of resources from small peasants to powerful capitalist firms has now been accelerated by the accompanying transformation of the legal framework within which such transfers take place. The Land Acquisition Act, for instance, is being amended to facilitate faster takeover, leaving less time for affected people to intervene in the process.

The logic of liberalization is exemplified in the establishment of new Special Economic Zones (SEZs), a major state initiative started in 2000 that has met with widespread resistance across the country. An SEZ 'is a specially demarcated area of land, owned and operated by a private developer . . . [w]ith the intent of increasing exports . . . utilising a large number of concessions – tax exemptions, guaranteed infrastructure and the relaxation of labour and environmental standards' (Srivastava 2007a, also see Srivastava 2007b). Real estate developers and builders from India and abroad rushed to invest in SEZs, leading to skyrocketing land prices even as small-scale agriculture became more unviable than ever. The alarming numbers of farmer suicides and the phenomenal growth in rural out-migration across India point to a deep divide that splits the country into two: the affluence created by India's economic boom is accompanied by distress and dispossession for subaltern groups. Just when the consumerist promises of liberalization are being beamed nationwide, creating a rising tide of aspirations and expectations, large sections of the Indian population find themselves worse off than before.

Those who make it to urban India find that, while there is employment and some opportunity for upward mobility, it is contingent on the cultural capital with which one migrates. Without the qualifications and connections essential for securing jobs and shelter or starting a small business, most migrants can at best only eke out a precarious and constantly threatened living. The relationship between the city and its residents is also being recast by programmes like the Jawaharlal Nehru National Urban Renewal Mission (JNNURM) of 2005 that aim to invest in urban infrastructure while making city government more corporatized and financially self-sufficient.[4] As with the present policy of divesting some governance functions to Resident Welfare Associations (RWAs), the creation of urban local bodies under the JNNURM excludes the majority of the urban poor who cannot establish the legality of their residence in the city.

Citizenship, Place and the Politics of Recognition

Given the continuities in how economic policies affect the poor, the current phase of economic liberalization is better understood in terms of a shift in the notion of the nation. Among the elite, the idea of India as a democratic society where the state is charged by the Constitution to safeguard and promote the rights of the poorest citizens first, is gradually giving way to an impatience with the 'old' problems of being a third world country and an ambition to achieve 'world power' status (see Baviskar et al. 2006). The promise of development for all citizens, however ineffectively rendered, was at least an acknowledgement of the state's role in bringing about social justice and economic betterment. This commitment is being jettisoned in favour of a vision where economic growth is paramount and inequalities in the distribution of assets and opportunities are no longer a matter of serious state concern. The transformation in the state's idea of India is reflected in the shrinking of the public sphere and the increasing exclusion of subaltern groups from public discourse. Denied full membership in civil society because they lack landed property and other forms of symbolic capital from which social legitimacy flows, disadvantaged groups are condemned to strive for recognition as members of 'political society', invoking the fictive ideal of 'community' with moral claims upon the nation-state (Chatterjee 2004: 57). This is the discourse that many social movements, including the Narmada Bachao Andolan (Save Narmada Campaign), have had to adopt as a part of their strategy of resistance.

In the Andolan's struggle against the Sardar Sarovar dam, the grounded histories of struggles against displacement have shaped the objects and subjects of social action in particular ways. For instance, a specific development project such as this has been easier to mobilize against, offering geographically concentrated affected populations and particular government agencies against whom to direct protest.[5] In addition, the presence of international NGOs engaged in conducting worldwide campaigns focused on issues such as the environmental impacts of large dams, also helped to provide access to a wider network of support, especially useful for targeting the multilateral financiers of the project. The gradual growth in public concern about the environmental impacts of large-scale infrastructure development projects offers a more receptive audience for some campaigns than others. That is, the formation of collective identities and interests within the anti-dam movement has been an iterative process of 'making history under conditions not of one's choosing' (Marx 1963 [1852]: 15).

This process has generated distinctive ideas of social justice reflected in how particular groups and concerns have come to be regarded as legitimate. Notably, the anti-displacement campaigners have succeeded in turning the spotlight on the claims of people threatened with the loss of land-based livelihoods. Their critique points to the difficulty, if not impossibility, of compensating for the farmlands, forests, pastures and rivers that sustain material and symbolic collective being. Those struggling against displacement focus on the multiple meanings of *place* – the cultural attachments embodied in the practices of everyday life, and the injustice of severing these ties through the process of 'involuntary resettlement'. Notions of place, invoking genealogies of settlement (clans that cleared fields and planted trees), histories of establishing property rights vis-à-vis the state, cosmologies and creation myths, and the bountiful properties of localized Nature, are used to protest against the meagre monetary valuation that the government attaches to land.

This complex notion of place, conveyed through the political action of anti-displacement struggles, has gradually (and grudgingly) been granted some recognition within policy circles, so the plight of poor adivasis now summons supportive (though still paternalistic) statements from officials. But even this recognition is carefully circumscribed. As government officials are quick to point out, only those adivasis who practice their 'traditional livelihood' should qualify for compensation. Only those people who have legal rights to private property can receive redress, not 'illegal encroachers'. By using these parameters of judging legitimacy – 'traditional livelihood' and 'legal ownership', the government paradoxically assigns adivasis to an unchanging existence (imagined as outside modernity) while giving primacy to state-induced changes in property regimes that render most adivasi agricultural practices illegal.[6] This catch-22 of being expected to uphold the fiction of 'tradition' when survival depends on improvising ever-newer livelihood strategies combining land encroachment, illicit harvesting of forest produce, and migrant labour, means that many adivasis fail to qualify as legitimate subjects of state support.

The predicament of poor 'encroachers', undeserving of compensation in the case of displacement, is shared by the other set of people who are not recognized as legitimate subjects for social action: poor migrants. The same poor adivasis whose tiny landholdings gave their claims to place some legitimacy when they lived in the Narmada Valley, lost even that precarious bargaining power when they became dispossessed migrants into Indian cities. With migration comes increased vulnerability, as people who are compelled to inhabit illegal spaces labour under the burden of being stigmatized as 'outsiders', perceived by middle-class populations and the authorities as sources of contagion and crime. Even among social activists the consensus seems to be that migrants are a lost cause, and that there is little that public action can do to address their conditions of being.

Both adivasi 'encroachers' and urban 'squatters' find it hard to be recognized as the 'deserving poor'. The fact that 'crime' is the only avenue open to adivasi encroachers and urban squatters is not acknowledged in the current discourse on rights and entitlements. Acts of agency such as encroaching and squatting invite judicial wrath and punitive orders. Even though they are the only recourse available to the poor for securing basic subsistence and shelter, such transgressions are invariably seen as wilful and malicious.

Asserting a link between place and people in anti-displacement campaigns has been a powerful way of protesting against the injustice of forced eviction. Yet it has also had the obverse effect of disenfranchising the poorest, politically most vulnerable groups, which cannot claim long-standing ties to place. In Delhi, the Hindu nationalist Bharatiya Janata Party (BJP) proposed in 1996 that residents be issued identity cards so that migrants could be clearly identified.[7] Implicit in this move is the idea that the difference between migrants and long-time residents should be marked off in politically consequential ways. In discussions about planning for urban infrastructure in Delhi, planners and environmentalists constantly invoke the fearsome spectre of Delhi being overrun by hordes of migrants, its services choking and infrastructure collapsing under their weight. Behind this assumption that 'these people should go back to where they belong' is an unwillingness to recognize the political economy of migration, as well as a set of unequal relationships that in fact make the city possible by providing cheap labour.

Faced with the need to mobilize effective genealogies that entitle them to state support, many recent migrants, who may themselves be economic and ecological refugees, find themselves on the defensive, unable to muster ideological legitimacy. The disempowering effects of nativist narratives on migrants and even long-time residents who differ in terms of their linguistic, regional or religious identity are evident in cities like Bombay/Mumbai, where shifting communal cleavages have been marked by the violent scapegoating of minority 'others' (Hansen 2001). In Delhi, the demolition of slums has displaced tens of thousands of families. Only those who can prove long-standing residence (who have ration cards, voters' photo ID *and* municipal corporation 'tokens' dating before 1992) are entitled to receive a plot of 18 square metres on a five-year lease upon payment of Rs 8,000. Those without documentary evidence, which means the majority of slum-dwellers, are evicted with nowhere to go. At issue here is how place is claimed. The legitimacy of claims rests on temporal depth (length of residence) and property ownership, rather than on current dependence and relative needs. This exacerbates social inequality by further punishing people who are already impoverished.

The particular situation of poor 'placeless' migrants demands that we rethink the relation between property rights and claims to place. This would mean treating the idea of place not as a natural 'given' that people inhabit, but as a cultural artefact that is produced through material and symbolic labour – sweat, blood and dreams.[8] Such an idea of *place-making* allows us to recast questions of belonging, which have so far been framed in terms of legal property rights, ethnicity and ancestry, and uncritical localism, into a more inclusive frame of democratic rights. When deployed without attention to the dynamics of power and inequality, the concept that space and place are socially produced succumbs to a feeble relativism and buries the issues at stake even deeper. But when used as a tool for thinking through the cultural relations that create places, the concept helps highlight the hidden work performed by subaltern groups. This is most clearly evident in the urban context where migrants craft communities and create habitable places in the most inhospitable terrain – along railway tracks and storm drains, on low-lying and marshy ground, negotiating physical and legal challenges to slowly build homes. As bricks and mortar replace bamboo mats and plastic sheets, sewage and water systems are improved and electricity, toilets, taps and schools sought. This gradual accretion of value reflects the transformation of a place over time. It is impossible to encapsulate this collective effort, the sum of various complex political processes in which people engage, into a framework where recognition is based on legal ownership of private property. Attention to place-making that recognizes collective labour ('sweat equity') opens up the possibility of framing claims in a way that refuses to submit to the bureaucratic and legal logic of legitimacy. It also makes visible what is only too often denied and dismissed – the value of labour when performed by people who own little else.

The politics of recognition need to acknowledge the profound injustice in the allocation of urban space and services that forces working-class people to live in slums. Delhi's planners made hardly any provisions of housing space for the working class. While land was designated for industrial estates, middle-class residential colonies and commercial complexes, there was no thought of the large populations who would work in these establishments. The Delhi Development Authority (DDA), the body responsible for planned urban growth in the capital, has preferred to facilitate the building of middle-class homes rather than working-class ones. The growth of planned Delhi has thus been twinned with the growth of unplanned Delhi: as construction workers set up shacks near the places they were building and industrial workers' makeshift homes appeared next to the workshops and factories, an unauthorized city came into existence. When people compelled to live in this unauthorized city are penalized by eviction, the hard fact that legal affordable housing is hardly available is ignored. This criminalization of the working poor, a process similar to the criminalization of adivasis who are compelled to violate forest laws for their livelihood, makes scapegoats out of survivors.

The politics of recognition in commonsense understandings of displacement and migration, with their assumptions about which and whose claims matter, contain another structural fallacy. Displacement is generally understood to be an 'involuntary' process. The displaced as 'involuntary' refugees are contrasted with 'voluntary' migrants. Anthropologist Liisa Malkki notes that 'people have always moved – whether through desire or through violence' (Malkki 1992). Yet desire and violence are sometimes hard to disentangle. The line between coercion and consent is always blurred by the structural violence that implicitly shapes 'choice'. For instance, slum-dwellers who are promised titles to tiny plots of land on the outskirts of Delhi may, on the basis of that slender hope, dismantle the homes that they have painstakingly built over the years. When the decision to move is throughout informed by the paucity of affordable housing close to one's place of work, and by the overwhelming threat of state repression should slum-dwellers resist, can the process be termed 'voluntary' resettlement? This lack of meaningful choices places the displaced refugee and the poor migrant beside each other along a continuum of constraint, their 'unfreedom' created by class, caste, ethnicity and gender relations. As Ranabir Samaddar points out, the rational choice framework informing migration studies, which is able to clearly categorize reasons for migration into the binary of 'push' and 'pull' factors and thus distinguish between voluntary and forced migration, fails to do justice to the complex play of subjectivity that informs 'choice' (Samaddar 1997). When the lives of migrants, refugees, and the exiled overlap in terms of their predicament and the everyday social relations they encounter, their categorization into discrete slots may serve some exegetical purpose. However, the benefits from the analytical purchase thus obtained are offset by the costs of dealing with reified categories that do violence to people's lived predicament.

In the case of Delhi, much of the larger context of structural violence is provided by the process of economic liberalization. As state support for agriculture in the form of subsidized inputs and price guarantees has dwindled, agriculture has become more risky and less remunerative for small and medium-scale farmers. The terms of trade between the countryside and the city have drastically shifted, resulting in large-scale rural-urban migration of people in search of work. The displacement of these migrants from the centre of the city to its periphery is also linked to economic liberalization and urban restructuring. The project of making Delhi a 'world-class city' entails the reorganization of space, with prime locations reserved for capital-intensive commercial developments interspersed with green areas and approached on wide roads (Baviskar 2010, 2011). Such remodelling of the urban and rural landscapes marks a departure from previous moments of more populist politics, when the rural and urban working poor could expect a modicum of state welfare in the form of subsidized basic provisions. The new structural conditions are subjectively experienced as given and unyielding; they shape perceptions of opportunity and organize people's desires. Thus the sentiment often voiced by migrants, 'Ab to hamare liye gaon mein kuchh nahin rakha' [Now there's nothing left for us in the village], reflects an emptying out of the village that is not just a demographic move, but an ideological shift as well, as desire migrates elsewhere (Nandy 2006).

Disciplining the Poor: State Welfare and Collective Action

It is during the lived experience of displacement that the rural and urban poor encounter Development. However, welfare is not available to everyone who is displaced but only to the select who can demonstrate that they have previously been recognized by the state. When they seek to address this state-created predicament through various schemes for 'Resettlement and Rehabilitation', the displaced are confronted with the need to muster forms of official recognition that will entitle them to a stream of 'benefits' – land, housing, water and electricity, education and health care. In order to secure compensation, poor adivasis and urban squatters are compelled to represent themselves through the state's categories for determining eligibility. As discussed above, these categories can be cripplingly constraining, given the range of activities the poor engage in that do not easily fit into bureaucratic and legal straitjackets. For instance, the area of nevad land cultivated by an adivasi household, and the trees that they planted on it, were not eligible for compensation. In the case of urban squatters, three forms of official documentation were necessary (but not sufficient) to claim eligibility for a plot of land. In their absence, the majority of the displaced were disqualified from getting a legal foothold in the city.

These techniques of control, ostensibly set up to weed out the 'undeserving', have the effect of creating divisions among the affected people, such that those who stand to gain a modicum of compensation quickly part company with those who stand to lose everything.[9] In the case of dam-induced displacement as well as urban evictions, the principal instrument for differentiation is the 'cut-off date'. The first effect of the cut-off date, a bureaucratic device that determines eligibility on the basis of temporal advantage, is to set off a scramble as people strive to secure the documentary proof to show that they qualify for compensation. This often necessitates bribing officials and paying brokers to acquire official identification, forged if necessary. At the point of displacement, rather than being automatically recognized as persons entitled to compensation, the poor are treated as supplicants at the mercy of the state. The next, politically more insidious, effect of the cut-off date is to divide the poor, with one group being promised some benefits and the rest left in limbo. Among the poor, it is usually the least secure and most vulnerable who are denied recognition. In the case of those affected by the Sardar Sarovar dam, it was only the landed adivasis who were able to launch a prolonged campaign against the project; the landless in the Narmada Valley did not participate. In the Delhi evictions, migrants who could not produce proof of long-term residence quietly made other arrangements – moving to rented accommodation on the outskirts of the city, to other slums or, in desperate situations, going back to their rural homes.

This population, estimated to be far larger than that officially recognized as entitled to compensation, has never been enumerated; nor is the impact of displacement on its members' lives known to anyone but themselves. In place of assessing present circumstances and needs, deciding eligibility on the basis of an arbitrary temporal point is not only unjust but also serves to divide the affected population in a manner that undermines the possibility of collective action. Some long-term residents become quiescent, anxious to not jeopardize their tenuous chances of receiving some compensation and, without their support, recent migrants into the neighbourhood lack the means to sustain opposition to displacement. Thus, even at the point when people hope to be recognized as eligible recipients of welfare, state policies break up social solidarities and potential modes of mobilization.

Displacement and Welfare: The Anthropology of Development

Violence and welfare are often seen as opposite tendencies. In this essay, I have tried to argue that both are, in fact, inherent in the strategies of accumulation and legitimation orchestrated by the state. The epistemic violence of legal categories that are tied to property, place and temporal depth determines access to welfare. Within the larger politics of poverty and inequality produced by liberalization, Development – when encountered during the moment of displacement – often reproduces people's experience of powerlessness and vulnerability. The anthropology of development has not adequately examined the larger social and political context within which Development projects are embedded. This essay attempts to redress that lacuna by pointing out the continuities in development and Development, arguing that an appreciation of the former is crucial for understanding how Development is experienced and negotiated.

NOTES

1. Members of India's Scheduled Tribes, a category designated by the Indian Constitution, use the term *adivasi* to identify themselves in central India.
2. Evictions of forest-dwellers increased after 2002, when certain orders given by the Supreme Court in the Godavarman case were interpreted by the state forest bureaucracies as authorizing removal. Adivasi protests against evictions led, among other things, to the formation of the Campaign for Survival and Dignity (CSD), a coalition of tribal rights organizations from eleven states. The CSD took the lead in drafting and agitating for the Scheduled Tribes and Other Traditional Forest-Dwellers (Recognition of Forest Rights) Act of 2006, which provides forest-dwellers with some security of tenure.

3. See the draft National Rehabilitation Policy 2006 prepared by the Ministry of Rural Development, Government of India. Retrieved 28 September 2009 from: http://pmindia.nic.in/nac/concept%20papers/draft_national_rehab_policy.pdf
4. Retrieved 9 January 2008 from http://jnnurm.nic.in/jnnurm_hupa/index. html. Also see Mahadevia (2006).
5. For a comparative analysis of the political fortunes of two different campaigns, one concentrated against a dam and the other against more generalized state forest management practices, see Baviskar (2001).
6. The emphasis on 'traditional livelihoods' persists in the Forest Rights Act 2006 which does however legalize the rights of forest-dwellers to cultivate nevad lands.
7. The proposal was revived in early 2008 by the Delhi Lieutenant Governor, who had to quickly retract his statement after protests by the Congress state government and from other quarters (Ghosh 2008). While no details were provided about how such a policy would be operationalized, it would appear to be based on determining legal residents (i.e., those able to afford pukka housing or those able to prove their presence in the city prior to a stipulated cut-off date. It should be noted that such initiatives violate the fundamental right of free movement within the country guaranteed by the Indian Constitution.
8. Cf. Certeau (1984) and Massey (1995).
9. On the regulatory and discriminatory effects of welfare in the U.S., see Piven and Cloward (1993).

BIBLIOGRAPHY

Baviskar, A. 1995. *In the Belly of the River: Tribal Conflicts over Development in the Narmada Valley*. Delhi: Oxford University Press
———. 2001. 'Written on the Body, Written on the Land: Violence and Environmental Struggles in Central India' in Nancy Peluso and Michael Watts (eds) *Violent Environments*. Ithaca: Cornell University Press.
———. 2003. 'Between Violence and Desire: Space, Power and Identity in the Making of Metropolitan Delhi' in *International Social Science Journal*. 175: 89–98.
———. 2010. 'Spectacular Events, City Spaces and Citizenship: The Commonwealth Games in Delhi', in Jonathan Shapiro Anjaria and Colin McFarlane (eds) *Urban Navigations: Politics, Space and the City in South Asia*. New Delhi: Routledge.
———. 2011. 'Cows, Cars and Cycle-rickshaws: Bourgeois Environmentalists and the Battle for Delhi's Streets', in Amita Baviskar and Raka Ray (eds) *Elite and Everyman: The Cultural Politics of the Indian Middle Classes*. New Delhi: Routledge.
Baviskar, A., S. Sinha and K. Philip. 2006. 'Rethinking Indian Environmentalism: Industrial Pollution in Delhi and Fisheries in Kerala', in Joanne Bauer (ed.) *Forging Environmentalism: Justice, Livelihood and Contested Environments*. New York: ME Sharpe.
Baviskar, A. and N. Sundar. 2008. 'Democracy versus Economic Transformation?'. Comment on Partha Chatterjee's 'Democracy and Economic Transformation in India' in *Economic and Political Weekly* 43(46): 87–89.

Certeau, M. de 1984. *The Practice of Everyday Life*. Berkeley: University of California Press.

Chatterjee, P. 2004. *The Politics of the Governed: Reflections on Popular Politics in Most of the World*. New York: Columbia University Press.

Dwivedi, Ranjit. 2006. *Conflict and Collective Action: The Sardar Sarovar Project in India*. New Delhi: Routledge.

Escobar, A. 1995. *Encountering Development: The Making and Unmaking of the Third World*. Princeton: Princeton University Press.

Ferguson, J. 1990. *The Anti-Politics Machine: "Development", Depoliticization and Bureaucratic Power in Lesotho*. Cambridge: Cambridge University Press.

———. 1997. 'Anthropology and Its Evil Twin: "Development" in the Constitution of a Discipline', in F. Cooper and R. Packard (eds), *International Development and the Social Sciences: Essays on the History and Politics of Knowledge*. Berkeley: University of California Press.

Fernandes, W. 1991. 'Power and Powerlessness: Development Projects and Displacement of Tribals', *Social Action* 41: 243–270.

Ghosh, A. 2008. 'Delhi Citizens Ordered to Carry I-Cards', *The Times of India*, 5 January 2008. Retrieved 9 January 2008 from http://timesofindia.indiatimes.com/articleshow/2676075.cms.

Hansen, T. B. 2001. *Wages of Violence: Naming and Identity in Post-Colonial Bombay*. Princeton: Princeton University Press.

Klingensmith, D. 2007. *'One Valley and a Thousand': Dams, Nationalism and Development*. New Delhi: Oxford University Press.

Mahadevia, D. 2006. 'NURM and the Poor in Globalising Mega Cities', *Economic and Political Weekly* 41(31): 3399–3403.

Malkki, L. 1992. 'National Geographic: The Rooting of Peoples and the Territorialization of National Identity among Scholars and Refugees', *Cultural Anthropology* 7(1): 24–44.

Marcus, G. E. and M. M. J. Fischer. 1986. *Anthropology as Cultural Critique: An Experimental Moment in the Human Sciences*. Chicago: University of Chicago Press.

Marx, K. 1963 [1852]. *The Eighteenth Brumaire of Louis Bonaparte*. New York: International Publishers.

Massey, D. 1995 [1984]. *Spatial Divisions of Labour*. London: Routledge.

Mosse, D. 2005. *Cultivating Development: An Ethnography of Aid Policy and Practice*. London: Pluto Press.

Nandy, A. 2006. *An Ambiguous Journey to the City*. New Delhi: Oxford University Press.

Pigg, S. L. 1992. 'Constructing Social Categories through Place: Social Development and Representation in Nepal', *Comparative Studies in Society and History* 34(3): 491–513.

Piven, F. F. and R. A. Cloward. 1993. *Regulating the Poor: The Functions of Public Welfare*. New York: Vintage Books.

Ramanathan, Usha. 2006. 'Illegality and the Urban Poor', *Economic and Political Weekly* 41(29): 3193–3197.

Samaddar, R. 1997. 'Still They Come: Migrants in Post-Partition Bengal', in R. Samaddar (ed.) *Reflections on Partition in the East*. Delhi: Vikas.

Srivastava, A. 2007a. 'War Zones: The Present and Future of India's SEZs', *Himal* (July 2007). Retrieved 9 July 2007 from http://www.himalmag.com/2007/july/analysis_sez_india.htm.

————. 2007b. 'The Closing Circles: SEZs, Globalization and Shrinking Freedom in India', *Expanding Freedom: Social and Economic Transformation in a Globalizing World Conference, Delhi, April 2007*. Delhi: Institute of Economic Growth.

Tarlo, E. 2003. *Unsettling Memories: Narratives of the Emergency in Delhi*. Berkeley: University of California Press.

CHAPTER 9

Intersection

The Anthropology of Development and the Development of Anthropology

Harri Englund

'Development' with a small 'd', Amita Baviskar suggests, relates to the historical process of capitalist accumulation and, if subjected to social scientific analysis, 'critique as writ large in the lifeworld of sub-alterns'. Development with a big 'D', on the other hand, denotes the world of official programmes and projects to improve the lives of the poor. Baviskar's injunction is for anthropologists and other academic knowledge producers to pay more attention to 'the larger social and political context' of Development. What has given rise to the injunction?

To the extent that contextualization has long represented one of the most potent analytical tools at the anthropologist's disposal, the injunction may seem to state the obvious (see also Friedman this volume). Interrogating the obvious, however, offers an opportunity to consider how the anthropology of development has contributed to the development of anthropology. The issue here is not a gap between applied and pure anthropology. The issue is specialization gathering momentum at a pace that is not always congruent with the production of fresh insights.

Both chapters in this section resist specialization by offering detailed descriptions of specific social situations within policies and structures whose forms have global resonances. John Gledhill and Maria Gabriela Hita share a common concern with Baviskar in attempting to understand how squatters and slum-dwellers seek recognition of their interests within a policy framework that ostensibly promotes participation by the poor and enhanced liberalization in both political and economic arenas. Development with a big 'D' therefore looms large in these chapters, but it does so in two ways that provide refreshing distance from the anthropology of development. On the one hand, the authors are aware that Development has the capacity to set the agenda for everyday struggles. The politics of recognition that Development's current participatory predilections seem to elicit tends to impose a frame on the claims and grievances the poor can hope to make public. On the other hand, the chapters ingeniously subvert Development's agenda by attending, as good ethnographers have been expected to do since the times of Malinowski, to the intellectual and pragmatic contingencies of actual social situations.

The times of Malinowski are evoked in contemporary anthropology with a great risk of misunderstanding. An innocuous appeal to immersion and language learning in contemporary fieldwork (Englund and Leach 2000) resulted in the absurd charges of localism (Meyer et al. 2008: 1) and even nativism (Comaroff and Comaroff 2006: 82). Whether anthropological fieldwork no longer is what it used to be (see Faubion and Marcus 2009) is too big a question to be broached here, but one thing is clear: the study of Development as bureaucracy and ideology has rejuvenated anthropology by introducing to it new topics and methods. As an intellectual pursuit in its own right, it has emerged in conjunction with critiques of expert knowledge in colonial and postcolonial discourses (Mitchell 1988) and with the deployment of institutional ethnography by science studies (Latour 1993). Expert knowledge continues to be a domain that engages the anthropological imagination for fresh theoretical contributions (see Li 2007; Tsing 2005). Nor have the ethnographic and historical variations in Development been exhausted by the anthropology of development. On the contrary, genuinely comparative questions have barely begun to be asked. For example, the ways in which African development workers envisage Development through their personal ethical and pragmatic dispositions is likely to be influenced by the specific political histories of different countries (see, e.g., Englund 2006; Yarrow 2008).

It is not, therefore, Development that is problematic. Problematic is the anthropology of development with a small 'd' as a context of Development. The politics of recognition Baviskar describes so astutely may well take place in relation to the strategies of accumulation and legitimation associated with state power. But does not such a connection between development and Development make one a version of the other, rather in the way nationalism was once argued to be a derivative discourse among the Indian intelligentsia (Chatterjee 1986, 1993)? Examples of derivate discourse in the world of Development abound, particularly when the populist sensibilities among scholars and practitioners converge in their desire to define 'the poor' as the subjects of participation, grass-roots empowerment, indigenous knowledge and so on (see Englund 2011; Olivier de Sardan 2005: 110–125). As is well known, such a desire can have strikingly different consequences depending on the institutional and ideological configurations it draws on. Yet common to all configurations is the way in which they derive from Development's historically variable will to improve (Li 2007). As long as development with a small 'd' has the status of a context of Development, the anthropologist may lose sight of the myriad intellectual and pragmatic considerations poor people bring to bear on their circumstances.

Far from marking a return to the ivory tower, the development of anthropology may require an assault on academic specialization, such as when observations on the welfare functions of churches and burial societies in rural Africa uncover lacunae in the discipline of development studies (Jones 2009), or when development economics is shown to mask its theological roots (Bornstein 2005). Such interventions do more than contextualize existing knowledge. They provide an altogether different order of description and argument.

BIBLIOGRAPHY

Bornstein, E. 2005. *The Spirit of Development: Protestant NGOs, Morality, and Economics in Zimbabwe*. Stanford, CA: Stanford University Press.

Chatterjee, P. 1986. *Nationalist Thought and the Colonial World: A Derivative Discourse?* London: Zed Books.

———. 1993. *The Nation and Its Fragments: Colonial and Postcolonial Histories*. Princeton, NJ: Princeton University Press.

Comaroff, J. and J. L. Comaroff. 2006. 'Ethnography on an Awkward Scale: Postcolonial Anthropology and the Violence of Abstraction', in Paul Tiyambe Zeleza (ed.), *The Study of Africa*, vol. 1: *Disciplinary and Interdisciplinary Encounters*. Dakar: Council for the Development of Social Science Research in Africa, pp.75–100.

Englund, H. 2006. *Prisoners of Freedom: Human Rights and the African Poor*. Berkeley: University of California Press.

———. 2011. 'The Anthropologist and His Poor', in Erica Bornstein and Peter Redfield (eds), *Forces of Compassion: Humanitarianism between Ethics and Politics*. Santa Fe, NM: SAR Press, 71–93.

Englund, H. and J. Leach. 2000. 'Ethnography and the Meta-Narratives of Modernity', *Current Anthropology* 41(2): 225–248.

Faubion, J. D. and G. E. Marcus (eds). 2009. *Fieldwork Is Not What It Used to Be: Learning Anthropology's Method in a Time of Transition*. Ithaca, NY: Cornell University Press.

Jones, B. 2009. *Beyond the State in Rural Uganda*. Edinburgh: Edinburgh University Press for the International African Institute.

Latour, B. 1993. *The Pasteurization of France*, trans. J. Law. Cambridge, MA: Harvard University Press.

Li, T. M. 2007. *The Will to Improve: Governmentality, Development, and the Practice of Politics*. Durham, NC: Duke University Press.

Meyer, B., P. Pels and P. Geschiere. 2008. 'Introduction', in Birgit Meyer, Peter Pels and Peter Geschiere (eds), *Readings in Modernity in Africa*. Oxford: James Currey, 1–21.

Mitchell, T. 1988. *Colonising Egypt*. Cambridge: Cambridge University Press.

Olivier de Sardan, J. 2005. *Anthropology and Development: Understanding Contemporary Social Change*, trans. A. T. Alou. London: Zed Books.

Tsing, A. L. 2005. *Friction: An Ethnography of Global Connection*. Princeton, NJ: Princeton University Press.

Yarrow, T. 2008. 'Life/History: Personal Narratives of Development amongst NGO Workers and Activists in Ghana', *Africa* 78(3): 334–358.

PART IV

The Promise of Progress

CHAPTER 10

Development, Participation and Political Ideology in a Lebanese Town

Michelle Obeid

An Emissary for Change

> It became obvious to El Harid that there were too many players, too many agendas. . . . Frustrated university professors operating within the confines of a system that is not conducive to work in community development, local communities uneasy working with academia, research priorities too often disconnected from life's uncertainties. . . . As he ponders these issues, El Harid drops off to sleep and is dreaming again. (Hamadeh et al. 2006)

El Harid, the character of a cactus flower, was invented by a group of academic researchers who chose creative writing to reflect on their journey in a long-term development research project in one of the largest semi-arid towns of the north-eastern border of Lebanon. The choice of El Harid corresponds to the predicament of the land they studied. He is 'the drylands personified . . . he is there but no one can see him; he has potential but no one is interested. . . . He has silently witnessed the modern-day scenes unfolding around him, and finally he cannot stay quiet. He dreams of worst-case scenarios but is intent on change' (Hamadeh et al. 2006: xv). While attributed to the land and its emissary, the cactus flower, the desire for change characterizes the authors' own intentions. Throughout the account in *Research for Development in the Dry Arab Region: The Cactus Flower*, the authors share their experience by invoking El Harid. His sentiments become an echo of their own dreams, vision, disappointments and achievements.

This chapter explores the experience of a team of Lebanese professors at the American University of Beirut (AUB) who initiated a long-term 'participatory action research project' that despite many limitations is considered one of the model projects in the landscape of 'sustainable development' in the Middle East and North Africa. The chapter investigates notions of development in this particular cultural context, in which a historical moment after the Lebanese Civil War (1975–1990) provided an enabling environment for the founders of this project – and coincidentally the town-dwellers – to experiment with notions of change.

Development in the Middle East, as in other regions of the world (see Escobar 1995; Ferguson 1994; Fisher 1997; Mosse 2005), has undergone a painstaking critique in academic circles and public discourse alike. Development NGOs in the region, like their counterparts abroad, have been accused of deploying Western neo-liberal thought rooted in the private sector to resolve social problems, creating dependency, fostering class inequalities and perpetuating poverty. Perhaps most specific to the region is that the work of NGOs is evaluated through the regionally typical lens of what Carapico calls 'the three Ps': patrimonialism, patriarchy and primordialism (2000: 13). The very scant literature on rural development in Lebanon seems to endorse the mainstream critique, implicating development practitioners as well as privileged local stakeholders in use of the widespread institution of *wasta* (personal connections and favouritism)[1] to access funds and benefits and to consolidate existing inequalities (Makhoul and Harrison 2002), thus reproducing the patron-client relationships extensively discussed in literature on Lebanon (Hamzeh 2001; Joseph 1996, 1997). Although this critique is essential in addressing the efficacy of development, the overarching approach has tended to be confined by an 'Orientalist myopia' (Carapico 2000: 13). This has hampered our vision of a possibly more nuanced picture and distanced us from a diversity of questions that might interest both anthropology and development.

Recent voices have called for a rethinking of potential avenues of engagement between the two disciplines of anthropology and development. Gardner and Lewis, for instance, remind us that 'if anthropologists are to make politically meaningful contributions to the worlds in which they work they must continue to make vital connections between knowledge and action' (1996: 153). It is precisely this connection that this chapter explores. It sets out to understand the motivations, intentions and agencies that are behind people's involvement in development. Rather than concentrate on the 'failures' and 'immorality' of development, I follow anthropologists who have shifted attention to the 'personal choices and moral conundrums' (Yarrow 2008a: 335) underpinning development workers' commitment. These may give us a better idea of ideologies at play and the complex process of the construction of particular types of [moral] 'selves' in different cultural contexts (see Yarrow 2008a).

In the following, I outline the postwar Lebanese context that gave the idiom of 'development' political and ideological currency among actors of different backgrounds involved in the development project. Despite El Harid's apprehension of the coexistence of 'too many agendas', I argue that these multiple layers were mediated by a predominant agenda entrenched in an overarching moral project in which the personal and the national intertwined. It is through this constellation that ideas of development become meaningful. A focus on actors' motives and intentions will contest the regional literature's obsession with the 'three Ps' and advocate for a different picture framed by a longing to overthrow these loyalties, which are perceived to have deterred the progress of society.

Context: The Project

The Arsal project set out to analyse shifts in land use in the town of Arsal and to evaluate the sustainability of its existing farming systems. It aimed to develop technical and institutional mechanisms with the community for land use management at a time of increasing conflict between different land users. Starting before the Lebanese Civil War, the town underwent considerable transformations in livelihoods as residents gradually renounced their forefathers' traditional system of herding. Many shifted to fruit production, a transition that, in the absence of state control, allowed for diversification in livelihoods and the spread of informal (and illegal) ones towards the end of the war. These included smuggling across the Lebanese-Syrian borders and, mainly, a growing quarrying industry – most of it operating without licenses and depleting agricultural lands.

The Arsal project started out with a team of fourteen academic researchers from different disciplines within the AUB. Over time, the team expanded as the project sponsored postgraduate students researching the town, forged partnerships with national, regional and international bodies and secured more funding. I first joined the project when I was working towards a masters degree in 1996. My research interests focused on changing gender roles, a theme of interest to the project. Five years later, the project partially funded my doctoral degree, for which I conducted ethnographic research in 2002–2003. This time, I focused on themes broadly surrounding kinship, livelihoods and the political administration of the town. During the period of my research, the project rented a room for me on the premises of a local NGO, which was the main local partner. Although no specific tasks were asked of me, it was important that the project, as part of its vision for 'participatory research', have a resident researcher in the town.[2] My stay at the NGO allowed me to get to know its employees and volunteers. I attended formal meetings and had numerous discussions about the needs of the town, funding, the project and 'development'. I also grew to know a core group of the university team. In this chapter, I draw on my interactions with and knowledge of both the NGO workers and the university team, particularly two of the project founders. Further, I refer to the book *Research for Development*, from which the extract opening this chapter is taken.

The Arsal project produced a considerable number of academic documents – journal articles, thirteen master's dissertations, and two PhD theses including my own – as well as yearly progress reports. But the main researchers, with the support of the donor, wished to produce a different kind of publication as the project came to an end. The book *Research for Development* was aimed at a wider readership and hence was written in creative language, employing the fictional character of El Harid, who tells stories and recites poems throughout the account. Moreover, the book was translated into Arabic so that the initiative of 'participatory action research' could jumpstart a 'dialogue' within as well as without the region. Most importantly, the book, while discussing the complexities of development research, includes a self-reflexive and personal narrative with an emotive voice that describes the authors' personal frustrations, aspirations and sentiments. This particular point is key to this chapter's argument that the authors' vision of development was entangled in their personal lives and world view. The use of personal narrative invokes a sense of commitment and sacrifice that transcends the mundane view of development as mere 'project work'. As will be elaborated, this intertwinement lends credibility and authenticity to the discourse of development.

The Quest for Societal Change

In discussing the genealogies of commitment of Ghanaian activists, anthropologist Yarrow argues that his interlocutors' interest in development work was seen as the culmination of 'the conjunction of "life experience" and exposure to particular kinds of "ideology"' (2008a: 344), which activists privileged over individual gain. They demonstrated the 'sacrifice' entailed in their engagement by highlighting the risks involved, such as their safety and financial security, to the effect that 'struggle' became a main component of societal change. In a similar vein, 'ideology' was a core catalyst for both the founders of the Arsal project and those of the local NGO in the town. Despite dissimilar backgrounds and life experiences, when they met, their sociological differences were instantaneously diluted by a potent ideological denominator: their shared political affiliations during the Civil War and their common outlook toward societal change. In the following, I map out the backgrounds that had built up prior to the initiation of the Arsal project.

The University Professors

Like many other Lebanese, the main founders of the project felt that the Civil War had frozen their society in time. With the end of the war, however, they had hope for renewal and a strong motivation to take part in rebuilding society. 'We had been idle for a while, but now we were back with a vengeance. . . . Our mission was simple. . . . We wanted to replace death with life . . . and despair with hope. We knew we had something to give' (Hamadeh et al. 2006: 32). Their commitment to this ambitious project of change was imbued with their sense of sacrifice, perhaps twice over: first for having to leave their country because of the war, and second for having to readjust to a dysfunctional system when they chose to return. The two founding professors had similar historical narratives in which their educational background, technical knowledge, life in the West and political ideologies fed off each other. Both had participated in the Lebanese leftist activist scene of the 1970s and moved on to pursue their higher education abroad, where they completed their doctoral degrees and established careers in recognized international organizations.

It was precisely this success that prepared them to 'shake the academic world', which they perceived to be disconnected from the 'real needs of our communities' (Hamadeh et al. 2006: 32). The professors returned with a political approach that aimed for a more engaged academia. Their politics 'synergised with the new concepts which were flowering in the West at that time: "sustainable development", "appropriate technologies", "community participation" and "environmental conservation"' (ibid.). In the classroom, they wished to influence students 'on their way through a new life, where tolerance replaced bigotry' (ibid.: 33). In this account, we can see the overlapping of ideas derived from different domains, whereby seemingly technical concepts become tools to fight 'vices' such as bigotry that had nurtured enmities during the war.

These professors' commitment extended far beyond their academic work. Along with a few other colleagues, they founded a renowned 'scientific environmental' NGO that proactively engaged the 'non-specialist' grass roots. Together they established an exemplary demo-cratic and egalitarian structure that became a model to emulate among civil society organizations and attested to the centrality of participation in their thought. At an even more personal level, one of the professors chose to proceed with a controversial interfaith marriage, despite soci-etal and family disapproval. He then contemplated founding a move-ment for all the Lebanese who, like him, had rebelled against the forces of sectarianism and chosen civil marriage.[3] For these professors, there-fore, development was not about technical academic concepts removed from society. The seemingly specialized concepts were rather embedded in larger ideologies and pervaded different spheres of their lives. It is within this context that the professors and their team approached the Arsal project . But before moving to how the project came about, let us first address the ideologies at play within the town of Arsal.

The Local Townsmen

Towards the end of the Civil War, town residents had experimented with different forms of 'amal jama'i (collective action), the need for which arose from the town's border predicament and a historically contentious relationship with the Lebanese state, whose 'faces' generally seemed to oscillate between neglect and force (Obeid 2010a).[4] This neglect was compounded by the fact that the local municipality, which had been dissolved since 1964 after an outburst of inter-lineage violence, was rein-stated only in 1998 (Obeid 2006a). In the absence of local authorities, in 1986 town-dwellers formed a committee, Al-Lajna al-Sha'biyya (the Popular Committee), which took control of the town's local administra-tion. Its accomplishments included building roads, a secondary school, a medical centre and a water network (Obeid 2006a).

The committee was an extension of political party action, particu-larly that of leftist organizations active in the town.[5] One of the main features of these parties was that they operated at a national level and ensured movement of their membership. Zuhayr was one of the men with extensive party experience in the capital. His father had been a Communist before him, and Zuhayr joined the Communist Party as a teenager. He fought with its troops during the war and later was sta-tioned at the house of one of its leaders, whom he served as a personal driver for years. Zuhayr, who did not complete his formal education, considered the party to be his 'real school'. As he explained in his life history, 'aside from the ideology itself, the Party taught me a lot and gave me . . . the chance to be around people who were learned and cultured'. From them, Zuhayr learned the importance of *hiwar* (dialogue) an' concluded that 'we [Communists] had ethics (*akhlaq*) and remained decent, unlike other militias'.

These same ethics would later determine Zuhayr's choices upon his return to the town. With eight children to feed, he refused to work either in smuggling across the Lebanese-Syrian border or in any of the new quarries that some of his comrades had come to own. Unlike them, he did not want to 'sell out' and remained loyal to his values, which included the well-being of the environment. Zuhayr's choices at once invited the admiration and cynicism of his fellow townspeople, the latter for his naïve world view in an age of pragmatism. In his view, however, this only reinforced his commitment and gave it credibility.

By the late 1980s, a process of reverse migration had led many people to return to Arsal (Baalbaki 1997). Towards the end of the war, the town was in desperate need of development. It lacked infrastructure, social services, educational institutions and human capacities. Agricultural land faced the threat of an irregular and illegal quarrying industry born during the war in the absence of state control, while townspeople experimented with livelihoods in search for sustainability (Obeid 2006b). It was at that time that a group of men who, like Zuhayr, had returned to the town founded the first formally registered local NGO.[6] Their vision was based on an ethos of voluntarism, collective action and community work.

The experience of the NGO founders in Arsal seems to contest literature from the region that depicts the NGO world as a nucleus for reenacting 'primordial ties' and reifying class differences. Equipped with ideologies that crossed sectarian, familial and ethnic divides, the founders sought out a multiple-lineage membership at the outset of their project. This was a significant achievement in a town where extreme lineage loyalty had been known to be a source of violence. Moreover, despite the descent-focused nature of kinship and its patriarchal structures, the NGO founders believed that women should be partners in rebuilding society and were the first to introduce a women's economic and social programme. In later years, they encouraged women's representation and participation in their executive committee (Obeid 2010b). Thus, the NGO founders saw themselves as stretching the limits of patriarchy and familism, both predominant in their society.

Like the university professors, the engagement of the NGO founders was characterized by commitment and sacrifice. None were from privileged classes or even had stable employment, yet the time they dedicated to the NGO was voluntary. It was only when the NGO secured external funding that three of its key founders started receiving salaries, albeit often too low to make ends meet. But like Zuhayr, they refused to be involved in 'unethical' livelihoods and made choices that were consistent with the vision of their NGO. Their objectives revolved around a generic need for *tanmiya* (development), an all-encompassing term that originated before their return, while they fought for grand causes and sacrificed years of their lives in a vicious war. The effort put into the NGO, especially the amount of volunteering required, came at the expense of their personal lives and of securing better incomes for their families. Thus society was privileged over individual and even family gain.

The narrative of the NGO founders ought not to be seen as one that is intrinsically different from the life trajectories of others in Arsal, for commitment to political ideologies was not uncommon. In this sense, ideas promoted by NGO workers must not be seen in the light of their novelty. Rather, these ideas gained credence through their ability to survive and persist in the postwar years, a time when the majority were seen to be relinquishing their commitment to political parties and beliefs. The currency of these ideologies of change lay in their transferability from a failing medium, political parties, to a promising unexplored one, NGOs. It was in this context that the NGO founders encountered the prospect of a development project.

Serendipity and the Meeting of Minds

Initially the professors had intended to work in another village, but a serendipitous meeting with a herder diverted their attention to Arsal, where they discovered shifts in livelihoods that perfectly matched their research interests. With members of the local NGO, the professors immediately realized that 'we spoke the same language, that of development, poverty and equity, and also of environmental conservation, sustainability and capacity building. . . . We were made for each other' (Hamdeh et al. 2006: 36). Looking at the beginnings of the Arsal project and highlighting its uniqueness, a Lebanese professor exclaimed, '[unconventionally], the community [of Arsal] found us. We didn't have to go to them'. This was a testament to the 'naturalness' of the 'grass-roots approach' at a time when other development projects in the region worked hard on appropriating the 'dialect' (Abu-Lughod 2009) of 'bottom-up development'. The project seemed at once to be a response to local needs, the professors' research and ideological interests, and the agenda of the international donor that supported the project for the next ten years. Despite the diversity of backgrounds, there was a compelling meeting point: a belief in 'development' as a concept loaded with a political will for societal change. In what follows, I elaborate further the extent to which personal and political ideologies intertwined with technical concepts of development. In particular, I address the notion of 'participation', which was a medium for contradictory appropriations.

Contextualizing Participation

The uniqueness of the Arsal project in the development landscape of Lebanon (and the region) lay in its focus on participatory research: for the first time, students working in the project were encouraged to do field research with members of a community, who themselves were invited to take part in conducting the research. In addition, I lived in the town as the resident anthropologist. The international donor, as a result, took pride that the project 'did not arrive and disappear. In contrast to most field research in Lebanon, the researchers kept going back . . . and, to some degree, became a part of the community' (Rached and Navaro in Hamadeh et al. 2006: xi). This type of involvement was seen to be at the heart of participatory research. More importantly, the project was the first to formalize a platform that facilitated the participation of 'marginal groups'.

The currency of the 'participatory approach' in the Arsal project can be seen as a function of the ideologies at play when the project was initiated. Both the professors and the NGO founders were keen on dissolving hierarchies and schisms that stood in the face of societal change. 'Participation', 'bottom-up' and 'grass-roots' involvement, 'indigenous knowledge' and the engagement of a diversity of stakeholders seemed crucial to their quest.

The discourse and practice of participation in development have been thoroughly critiqued (Cooke and Kothari 2001; Mosse 2001, 2004), and by no means does the experience of the Arsal project dispute the limitations of the paradigm as outlined in this literature. Nevertheless, by focusing on questions of 'effectiveness', such critiques risk leading us to overlook the highly differentiated epistemological contexts in which actors deploy development concepts. In other words, analysis that focuses solely on the function of development overlooks why and how people engage with these concepts and what sparks their motivation. Development discourses may have global resonance, but they are mediated through local contexts in which their appropriation takes different forms. In the Arsal project, actors themselves eventually came to the realization that 'participatory research does not live in a vacuum and is never neutral. It diffuses into the existing system and is highly dependent on the context' (Hamadeh et al. 2006: 39). The fluidity of development concepts has been pointed out by anthropologists who argue that we need more sensitive analyses addressing the complex manner in which these concepts structure social, ideological and political contexts (e.g., Yarrow 2008b). Like other concepts, they can often be loose enough to allow for various appropriations and extended usage over different categories of people (Yarrow 2008b; Li 2001). Accordingly these concepts need to be deciphered through their cultural specificity. In the attempt to continue unravelling actors' motives and intentions, in the following I look at the local meanings associated with participation in Arsal.

In the first years of the project, participation was conducted 'informally' by ensuring the involvement of locals in different aspects of the research and tapping into 'indigenous knowledge' (Hamadeh et al. 2006; Zurayk et al. 2001). But as long as the project's main aim was 'research', the approach remained confined to a top-down framework, as the university team had more significant scientific capital. Participation took the shape of 'persuading' the locals into consensus, a point that resonates with Kelly's experience with the fieldworker whose role was to 'mobilize', to 'move participants, to affect their views, and generate awareness' (this volume).

With the growing demand for intervention over research, the project saw a need to establish more formal participatory structures. It aspired to contribute to the process of building institutions and empowering 'marginal groups' (*muhammash*), specifically women and herders, whom it sought to provide with a 'framework for participation with decision makers and a channel through which to express . . . and satisfy needs' (Hamadeh et al. 2006: 84–85). As a result, two cooperatives were established, the Herders' Cooperative and the Women's Food Cooperative.

As the project grew, an even more expansive structure was created, the so-called Local Users Network (LUN). The LUN was a 'loose structure' (see Riles 2000) 'extending beyond the community to involve all development stakeholders: the community, researchers, development project workers and the government'[7] (Hamadeh et al. 2006: 84–85). The diverse stakeholders required mediation, since they 'belonged to different cultural groups and to different organizational cultures' (ibid.: 45). The network was conceived as an ideal participatory communication platform that ensured the representation of 'traditional decision-makers as well as emerging forces' (ibid.: 46), the two constructed along an opposition that was, as we shall see, rather ambiguous. The 'traditional' is a category that deserves particular scrutiny: in certain contexts it was seen as a vice to be fought; in others it was portrayed as a virtue to be preserved. In both cases, it was a core concept in the local understanding of participatory development. The following explores the contexts in which these ambiguous understandings emerged.

'Tradition': Vice or Virtue?

The contradictory treatment of tradition can best be elaborated through its usage in the LUN. The network was portrayed as embodying a dual purpose.[8] On one hand, it built on local traditions and aimed to preserve them. On the other, it aimed to fight and change them. To understand this contradictory characteristic, we need to appreciate how and when traditions were considered worthy and, conversely, how and when they came to constitute a threat.

The LUN, being primarily a participatory communication platform that included 'traditional' as well as 'global' partners, relied on a variety of tools that catered for the different members. It produced a newsletter, videos and a website and utilized art and visual communication tools. These technological tools, however, were less accessible to the locals.[9] The project therefore saw its particular strength in the deployment of 'local traditional models of communication', the most important of which were interpersonal tools such as meetings, round table discussions and face-to-face interaction – considered a 'favoured form in the Arab World' (Hamdeh et al. 2006: 49). The LUN was seen as a variant of the traditional tribal *majlis* (meetings), this time extending beyond the community to involve all development stakeholders (ibid.: 45).[10] These meetings were based on dialogue and had a reconciliatory character that aimed at reaching consensus (see Antoun 2000). In this sense, this 'traditional' form was perceived as 'natural' and an agent of agreement in a context of diversity. The project was interested in reviving other such consensual institutions, for instance the *hima* (see Bocco 2000), a local system of range management in which communal lands and water resources were partially protected at different parts of the year in order to preserve rangelands and water (Baalbaki 1997). This system regulated land use and prevented the type of conflict that arose during the Civil War, when *hima* broke down among different land users. These types of tradition were perceived as worthy of preservation, as they served to regulate livelihoods and social relationships and were themselves based on participatory principles.

The discourse of preservation (*hifadh*) was also invoked whenever traditions related to an idea of an 'authentic' (*asil*) rural identity and heritage, now seen to be eroded by modernization as people moved away from their forefathers' livelihoods (mainly herding) and gradually embraced a consumerist lifestyle. In this perspective, traditions were valorized and even romanticized. These included rural customs that enunciated a collective ethos, such as marriage rituals and agricultural activities like the harvest, fruit picking or sheep shearing. With the help of the university team, the NGO organized ecotourism trips that included walks in the highlands, participating in ritual and agricultural activities, and eating with the locals. Both the NGO and the university team advocated preserving and refining local crafts like carpet and rug weaving. From this angle, 'tradition' was a vector for the participatory approach, since some of its practices possess what is seen as the essence of participation and promote the collective, the common good and an 'authentic' rural identity. But simultaneously – and paradoxically – 'tradition' was also spoken about as a hindering factor, not only to societal progress but also to the development project.

The starting point for the Arsal project was that it was dealing with a 'traditional society' (*mujtama` taqlidi*). This idea derived particularly from Arsal's familist history, mentioned earlier. In national leftist political discourse, loyalties such as familism and sectarianism were considered obstacles to the progress and development of the nation.[11] They were believed to have infected the political system and institutionalized divisions in Lebanon. The 'traditional' in this context came to have a negative connotation, even for the founders of the local NGO. Reminiscing on the beginnings of the project, its president said: 'We were very keen to work with the university project so as to try to boost our position in the local equation against traditional forces in the [town] . . . we saw the project as an opportunity to link with the outside world and create a dynamic process of social change in the town' (Hamadeh et al. 2006: 54).

When they symbolized extreme loyalties or 'backwardness', traditions were considered a vice that needed to be eradicated.

While members of the local NGO were able to overstep the power of tradition – as manifested in, for example, interlineage schisms – some of its aspects were essentialized and blamed for the inability to 'deliver' to the project. One often heard statements such as 'our capacities are limited' or 'the Arsali mind is too traditional to change', invoked to express obstacles within the NGO itself as well as within the 'community' within which it operated. One NGO member expressed his frustration to the university professor over being unable to fill out all the questionnaires assigned to him because 'traditional societies do not understand longitudinal studies! How do you expect me to convince a farmer why on earth I need to take details about his socio-economic background

one more time!' Tradition here was seen as an impediment to connecting to 'science', a domain outside the reach and interest of 'traditional
societies'. Tradition, therefore, was multi-natured, debilitating on one
hand and enabling on the other. It was at once aligned with and against
knowledge coming from outside. So how were these different natures,
functions and languages mediated by the different actors?

Identity Shifting and Translation

The discrepancy between different knowledges and languages within
the Arsal project was reconciled via the actors' ability to move between
registers of knowledge and identity through a process of 'translation'
(Lewis and Mosse 2006; Yarrow 2008b) that required the possession of
a 'multiple consciousness'.[12] This enabled people to oscillate between
layered understandings of the traditional, the local and 'outside' (barra),
a melange of urban, Western, global and scientific worlds. The local
founders of the NGO related to tradition in a varied manner. At times
they asserted their 'authentic' rural identity through appealing to their
local traditions. At others, they dissociated themselves from the 'vices'
of tradition by conjuring up ideologies and experiences they had cultivated beyond the boundaries of their town. Similarly, the university
professors, being Lebanese and having worked extensively with local
communities, identified with 'the local' and attempted to translate it
for the donor, whose knowledge was constituted 'outside'. But this was
a knowledge that they were able to decipher thanks to their education
and experience in the West. They were thus equipped to translate the
language of 'science' into 'traditional jargon' and vice versa. Arguably,
therefore, despite the local dichotomous framing of 'traditional us' and
the 'globalized outside', I suggest that it is more productive to appreciate the social and discursive uses of these categories and to view them
as fluid concepts. We can then decipher how actors move between and
appropriate them contextually.[13]

The local NGO found itself having to translate development concepts to the community with varying levels of success. This process
proved more difficult with the 'marginal groups', who were considered
the 'most traditional' in the town. Upon the establishment of the LUN,
the herders needed a lot of persuasion to join. One professor wondered
at the beginning,

> Is it really possible to involve the local community in a participatory
> manner while its traditional systems of communication are breaking

down under the pressure of a globalised world? . . . The pastoralists of Arsal, living relics of the ancient systems . . . see their traditional way of living falter around them, surrounded by unfriendly forces which they cannot grasp. Confronted with the outside world, they become either apprehensive or falsely accommodating. (Hamadeh et al. 2006: 104)

The university professors and the local NGO members embraced the task of 'translating knowledge' (Hamadeh et al. 2006: 104) to the herders. When the project advocated the establishment of cooperatives, the idea had to be 'sold' to the herders. This was accomplished through incentives such as free vaccination and four years of negotiation in which attempts were made to 'translate' from 'development jargon to traditional concepts' (ibid.: 104).

But this translation was not only channelled in a top-down direction. The university team also found itself having to translate local concepts to the donor. This was particularly articulated through a differentiated understanding and appreciation of gender roles in the town. While women were visibly active in their projects – the production of crafts and foods – and exhibited initiative and leadership skills, they were less visible in either the LUN or the formal managerial structures of their NGOs. While the local NGO and to a certain extent the university professors were pleased with women's engagement in this novel space, the donors were less satisfied and considered 'gender mainstreaming' the primary area on which the project ranked 'poorly' (Obeid 2010b). The university team felt it had to translate traditional gender dynamics to the donor. The professor believed the donors were working with different models that were impossible to transfer to the local community. He even laughed, for example, at the expectation of involving women in the Herders' Cooperative: 'We know women are empowered but we can't get them to be represented in the all-male Herders' Cooperative because it's not a women's space!'

While concepts of participation have a global resonance, their appropriation in the Arsal project reiterates the importance of factoring in local ideologies and experiences in our analysis. The Arsali example shows that 'participatory ideals' are fabricated from 'below' just as much as from 'above'. The example of the LUN sheds light on exercises in participatory development motivated by the creation of a communication process that is egalitarian, inclusive and representative. Key to this project was the ambivalent notion of 'tradition', at once an asset and a liability, an objective in its own right and a threat to be combated. These conceptions are best understood as interlocked in a web that weaves together the personal, political and professional trajectories of project actors, which in their turn are shaped by the interplay of global and local forces (see Friedman this volume).

Conclusion

The social science critique of development has succeeded in providing us with insights on some of the shortcomings of the processes of development. This chapter attempts, however, to go beyond critique as a starting point of engagement, the objective being 'an appreciation of the ethnographic complexities in which development becomes meaningful' (Yarrow and Venkatesan this volume). The material presented here attests to the importance of investigating 'development' as ideas and actions embedded in social realities. The particular Lebanese view of development as an encompassing idiom for societal change is best explored in the specificity of the postwar Lebanese context, when the country was undergoing a 'recovery period'. The atrocities of the war had sparked a moral mission among activists, whose personal and political ideological projects crystallized in idioms of development. Abstracting development concepts from this reality risks a misapprehension of why and how actors chose to engage with development in the first place.

One of the aims of this volume is to challenge the presumption that development concepts originate in Western thought and to question the axiom that development practice is guilty of consolidating unequal political relations. Literature on development in the Arab world has especially focused on types of inequalities specific to the region – 'patriarchal, patrimonial and primordial'. I have tried to show how a more nuanced picture might emerge once we shift our investigative lens. An examination of ethnographically emergent 'participatory' ideals in Lebanon reveals that development concepts are drawn upon to articulate alternatives to oppressive relationships rather than to perpetuate them – hence the focus on engaging 'marginal groups' and 'the grass roots' in the project. In this sense, I second the call in this volume to deconstruct the seemingly universal language of development to understand how ideas are appropriated locally and how certain concepts gain credence over others.

Rather than reducing development discourses to a 'single monolithic, univocal, hegemonic one' (Friedman this volume), we need to differentiate, even within the same ethnographic context, the underlying epistemological basis for espousing development concepts and acting upon them among different actors. The Lebanese case presented here elucidates the appropriation of global development concepts by two groups of Lebanese development workers brought together by an action research project, and the type of mediation and translation required between their different regimes of knowledge. When the object of study is 'development', a focus on actors' agencies, dilemmas and motivations is therefore likely to draw out the multivocality and the coexistence of numerous development discourses. It allows us to understand how different actors make links between knowledge and action, thus moving beyond an engagement whose starting point is critique.

NOTES

An earlier version of this essay was presented at the workshop Differentiating Development held in Buxton. I would like to thank the participants for their feedback. I would also like to thank the editors of this volume, Soumhya Venkatesan and Tom Yarrow, for their invaluable comments and Amit Desai for reading and commenting on my chapter. I am grateful to the Centre for the Advanced Study of the Arab World for the fellowship under which this essay was written.

1. For a discussion of *wasta*, see Rabo (1986, 2005).
2. Aspiring for 'integrated research', the Project took on board findings from my initial research to establish a women's cooperative in its second phase. The same, however, was not possible with my doctoral thesis, as the Project was over by the time I completed writing. See Green (this volume), for a discussion of differences in epistemic conduct and form between anthropology and development.
3. Since Lebanon follows the Personal Status Law for marriage, interfaith marriages are conducted in civil courts outside of Lebanon, usually in Cyprus.
4. There are several incidents of state violence in the town's recent history. Most infamous are those related to the 1958 Arab Nationalist–led rebellion against the regime and the aftermath of the municipal elections of 1963 (Obeid 2006a).
5. In particular, the Communists, the Arab Nationalists, the Ba'thists and some Palestinian factions became noticeably active in the town.
6. In order to register officially, NGOs must acquire a form known as "*ilm wa khabar*' from the Lebanese Ministry of Interior.
7. Over the period of ten years, the project forged several partnerships in Arsal with national, regional and international bodies including foreign embassies, United Nations agencies, three universities in the capital and three ministries and governmental bodies.
8. Compare with the oppositional usage of 'tradition' in the promotion of Vanuatu's *kastom ekonomi* (Rousseau and Taylor this volume).
9. The NGO had a website, but few of its members were computer-literate; even when they were, Internet connections in that part of the country were too slow.
10. Although technically speaking, Arsalis identified through lineage and not tribe, people resorted to a similar informal – though less ritualized – type of meeting particularly upon conflict or pressing matters that required decision-making (marriage, local elections, etc.).

11. This view also predominates in academic writing. For example, see Murad's analysis (2004) of tradition and the failure of municipalities in Lebanon.
12. See Yarrow (2008a) for a discussion of 'double consciousness' and the dual identity of aid workers in Ghana.
13. See Yarrow (2008b: 225) for a productive discussion on oppositional categories and their importance.

BIBLIOGRAPHY

Abu-Lughod, L. 2009. 'Dialectics of Women's Empowerment: The International Circuitry of the Arab Human Development Report 2005', *International Journal of Middle Eastern Studies* 41: 83–103.

Antoun, R. 2000. 'Civil Society, Tribal Process and Change in Jordan: An Anthropological View', *International Journal of Middle Eastern Studies* 32(4): 441–463.

Baalbaki, A. 1997. 'Transformations in the Pastoral Nomad System in the Village of Arsal', *Periodicals of the Institute of Social Sciences, Lebanese University, Beirut* 4: 67–84.

Bocco, R. 2000. 'International Organizations and the Settlement of Nomads in the Arab Middle East, 1950–1990', in M. Mundy and B. Musallam (eds), *The Transformation of Nomadic Society in the Arab East*. New York: Cambridge University Press, pp. 197–217.

Carapico, S., 2000. 'NGOs, INGOs, and DO-NGOs: Making Sense of Non-Governmental Organisations', *Middle East Report*, special issue, 'Critiquing NGOs: Assessing the Last Decade' 214: 12–15.

Cooke, B. and U. Kothari (eds). 2001. *Participation: The New Tyranny?* London and New York: Zed Books.

Escobar, A. 1995. *Encountering Development: The Making and Unmaking of the Third World*. Princeton, NJ: Princeton University Press.

Ferguson, J. 1994. *The Anti-Politics Machine: "Development", Depoliticization, and Bureaucratic Power in Lesotho*. Minneapolis: University of Minnesota Press.

Fisher, W. 1997. 'Doing Good? The Politics and Antipolitics of NGO Practices', *Annual Review of Anthropology* 26: 439–464.

Gardner, K. and D. Lewis. 1996. *Anthropology, Development and the Post-modern Challenge*. London: Pluto Press.

Hamadeh, S., M. Haidar and R. Zuraik. 2006. *Research for Development in the Dry Arab Region: The Cactus Flower*. Southbound Penang: International Development Research Centre.

Hamzeh, N. 2001. 'Clientalism, Lebanon: Roots and Trends', *Middle Eastern Studies* 37(3): 167–178.

Joseph, S. 1996. 'Patriarchy and Development in the Arab World', *Gender and Development* 4(2): 15–19.

———. 1997. 'The Public/Private: The Imagined Boundary in the Imagined Nation/State/Community. The Lebanese Case', *Feminist Review* 57: 73–92.

Lewis, D. and D. Mosse. 2006. 'Theoretical Approaches to Brokerage and Translation in Development', in D. Lewis and D. Mosse (eds), *The Ethnography of Aid and Aid Agencies*. Bloomfield, CT: Kumarian Press: 1–27.

Li, T. M. 2001. 'Locating Environmental Knowledge in Indonesia', in R. Ellen, P. Parkes and A. Bicker (eds), *Indigenous Environmental Knowledge and Its*

Transformations: Critical Anthropological Perspectives. Amsterdam: Harwood Academic Publishers, pp. 129–150.

Makhoul, J. and L. Harrison. 2002. 'Development Perspectives: Views from Rural Lebanon', *Development in Practice* 12(5): 613–624.

Mosse, D. 2001. 'People's Knowledge': Participation and Patronage: Operations and Representations in Rural Development', in B. Cook and U. Kothari (eds), *Participation: The New Tyranny?* London, New York: Zed Books, pp. 16–35.

———. 2004. 'Is Good Policy Unimplementable? Reflections on the Ethnography of Aid Policy and Practice', *Development and Change* 35(4): 639–671.

———. 2005. *Cultivating Development: An Ethnography of Aid Policy and Practice*. London: Pluto Press.

Murad, M. 2004. *Baladiyyat Lubnan: Jadaliyyat al-tanmiya wa al-dimuqratiyya* [Municipalities of Lebanon: Dialectics of Development and Democracy]. Beirut: Dar Al-Mawasim.

Obeid, M. 2006a. 'Close Bonds: Kinship, Politics and Livelihoods in a Lebanese Border Village', Ph.D. thesis. London School of Economics, London.

———. 2006b. 'Uncertain Livelihoods: Challenges Facing Herding in a Lebanese Town', in D. Chatty (ed.), *Nomadic Societies in the Middle East and North Africa: Entering the 21ˢᵗ Century*. Leiden: Brill Publishers, 463–495.

———. 2010a. 'Searching for the "Ideal Face of the State" in a Lebanese Border Town', *The Journal of the Royal anthropological Institute* 16: 330–346.

———. 2010b. 'The Production of Knowledge on Women, Gender, and Islamic Cultures: Non-Governmental Organizations in Lebanon', *Encyclopaedia of Women and Islamic Cultures*. Leiden: Brill Publishers, online publication.

Rabo, A. 1986. *Change on the Euphrates: Villagers, Townsmen and Employees in Northeast Syria*. Stockholm: Stockholm Studies in Social Anthropology.

———. 2005. 'Aleppo Traders and the Syrian State', in A. Rabo and B. Utas (eds), *The Role of the State in West Asia*. Istanbul: Swedish Research Institute, pp. 115–126.

Riles, A. 2000. *The Network Inside Out*. Ann Arbor: University of Michigan Press.

Yarrow, T. 2008a. 'Life/History: Personal Narrations of Development Amongst NGO Workers and Activists in Ghana', *Africa* 78(3): 334–358.

———. 2008b. 'Negotiating Difference: Discourses of Indigenous Knowledge and Development in Ghana', *Political and Legal Anthropology Review* 31(2): 224–242.

Zurayk, R. et al. 2001. 'Using Indigenous Knowledge in Land Use Investigations: A Participatory Study in a Semi-Arid Mountainous Region of Lebanon. *Agriculture Ecosystems and Environment* 86: 247–262.

CHAPTER 11

Kastom Ekonomi and the Subject of Self-Reliance

Differentiating Development in Vanuatu

Benedicta Rousseau and John P. Taylor

A recent set of projects undertaken in Vanuatu present a critique of development as it has been practised in that country over the past two decades. Coming variously under the umbrella terms *kastom ekonomi* and 'self-reliance and sustainability', these projects present indigenous economic practices, such as subsistence gardening and the exchange of 'traditional' wealth, as the logical, indeed natural way forward for this archipelago, which is relatively poor in both cash and exploitable resources. At first glance, this orientation suggests a problematic reification of 'tradition' as a resistant opponent to progressive modernity, and indigenous practice as the 'alternative' to a monolithic, homogenized concept of 'development'. Yet, as the chapters in this volume indicate, acceptance of such oppositions at face value can obscure the complex and productive relationships between categories placed in discursive opposition. In the context of our ethnography, we argue that ignoring such complexity may hinder our understanding of how the 'modern' epistemes of development and anthropology are being used in Vanuatu to challenge and reconfigure understandings of 'tradition' and 'progress' as inherently inhospitable bedfellows.

Our discussion focuses on two areas in particular: overlapping projects of subjective reform, and the shared use of knowledge practices. The process of promotion, acceptance and success of *kastom ekonomi* projects involves the intertwining of concepts and knowledge practices drawn from anthropology and development. Furthermore, it involves encouragement of reconsideration on the part of ni-Vanuatu who might be the subject of progress/development. While this echoes neo-liberal development policies recently promoted in Vanuatu, our case study indicates that such overlaps and cross-fertilizations do not end with entrapment in or repetition of such agendas. Rather, we suggest, *kastom ekonomi* and self-reliance and sustainability projects provide a means by which the indigenous can encompass modernity.

The Development of a *Kastom Ekonomi*

The idea for a *kastom ekonomi* originated as early as 1992 when a Van-uatu Cultural Centre (VKS) *filwoka* (fieldworker, indigenous anthro-pologist; see Bolton 1999), James Teslo, requested VKS support to set up what he called a 'pig bank' on his home island of Malakula. He aimed to help reinvigorate ritual and other *kastom* activities in the region, to which the exchange and ritual sacrifice of pig wealth is integral. Through the assistance of Tim Curtis (an Australian National University (ANU)-trained anthropologist working at UNESCO), Ralph Regenvanu (also an anthropologist by training [ANU] and at that time director of the VKS), and others at the VKS, this idea blossomed by 2004 into a much larger Traditional Money Banks Project through the acquisition of fund-ing from the UNESCO Intangible Heritage Fund and the Japanese gov-ernment (Vanuatu Cultural Centre n.d.a). By 2005 a project report had been completed and a meeting was held on the small island of Uripiv, off the coast of Malakula, to discuss ways 'to recognise and promote the tra-ditional economy as the basis for achieving national self-reliance'. This was quickly followed by the National Summit for Self-Reliance and Sus-tainability held in Vanuatu's capital, Port Vila, in July 2005 (Vanuatu Cultural Centre n.d.b).

The five-day National Summit for Self-Reliance and Sustainability was jointly hosted by the Malvatumauri National Council of Chiefs, the Vanuatu Cultural Centre and the Vanuatu Credit Union League. It generated thirty-six main recommendations in the areas of 'governance, national vision, land and land use, education, food security, energy, health, social security and maintenance of culture' (Vanuatu Cultural Centre n.d.b: n.p.). At the close of the meeting these were delivered to the republic's president and the minister of finance and economic man-agement and endorsed as the key objectives of a National Self-Reliance Strategy by the Malvatumauri National Council of Chiefs, sitting in full session on 26 July 2005. These ceremonial acts highlighted the growing legitimacy of the movement. Indeed, then Prime Minister Ham Lini also cited the strategy as one of the key future policy platforms of the government, later declaring 2007 the Year of the Traditional Economy. This, unprecedentedly, was repeated in 2008. This history entailed a continuing refinement of a materially oriented notion of culture. It also led to the development of an interesting new terminology focused on a linked opposition between traditional and nontraditional in relation to aspects of political economy, such as 'national self-reliance' and *kastom ekonomi*, as we discuss with reference to issues of subjectivity below.

Over the past five years, these terms have operated as generalized descriptors, indicative of an ethos as much as a concrete structure for action. For this reason, the activities undertaken in relation to these terms have not necessarily been carried out by the same actors, in the same locations, or with exactly the same aims in mind. Such projects have involved raising awareness through campaigns that circulate posters, leaflets and t-shirts and send teams to travel the length of the country to promote and discuss the issues concerned in both rural and urban communities; encouraging schools, hospitals and health clinics to accept traditional wealth and local produce in lieu of fees; discouraging land sales (to be implemented in government legislation); stipulating that only island food and produce be served at all government and other state events or functions; encouraging the performance of *kastom* exchange ceremonies at all levels of society; launching numerous area-specific projects to reinvigorate the production of particular items of material culture and food crops; removing cash from all *kastom* ceremonies and particularly from bride price; replanting coconut plantations for the production of biofuel; invigorating 'traditional governance' by, for instance, reinforcing systems of chiefly authority, instituting training programs for chiefs and using chiefs as probation officers; promoting, via the Ministry of Health, the research, use and exchange of *kastom* medicines; and reinvigorating historical environmental resource management techniques.

While important variations occur, projects that fall under the *kastom ekonomi* and self-reliance and sustainability banners are directed at promoting or utilizing aspects of 'traditional' economy and practice as a basis for achieving 'self-reliance'. Thus the notion of a *kastom ekonomi* is figured in opposition to a negatively conceived cash economy; it is also configured in opposition to the development industry, which is seen to be eroding the traditional economy and with it important indigenous values. It might therefore be seen to add a new spin to 'economic dualism' analyses, particularly through an apparently deliberate borrowing of terminology from the jargon of Western capitalism and development, even as it works to obscure commonalities with these. More generally, the fact that *kastom ekonomi* projects are often conceptualized at a national level suggests a reframing of the powerful political rhetoric of unity that was employed so effectively by the late 'Father of Independence', Walter Hadye Lini. But whereas *kastom* was previously envisaged as a cultural force providing unity with a space for difference, now the nation is to be united by economic factors. This distinction was constantly repeated in 2005 around the so-called Silver Jubilee celebrations of independence, with speeches and press releases from both the Malvatumauri and numerous politicians stating, 'we have political independence, but we are yet to achieve economic independence'.

Not surprisingly, given the rather haphazard growth of *kastom ekonomi* and related projects as well as the aetiological overtones that are often associated with the term *kastom* (Taylor 2010), many people found the ideas presented somewhat confusing. Some wondered, for instance, if they were meant to somehow go back to their pre-European *kastom* lifestyles, a fact that jarred with complex issues relating to Christianity and modernity (see Tonkinson 1982 for a discussion of similar confusion around the valorization of *kastom* in pro-independence political rhetoric). On 10 March 2007, a lengthy article by Ralph Regenvanu called 'Kastom Ekonomi, What Is It?' appeared in both of Vanuatu's main newspapers, *The Daily Post* and *The Independent*. This was intended to dispel such misunderstandings and to properly explain the full scope of ideas encompassed by these projects. What follows are excerpts from that article:

> The traditional economy ('kastom ekonomi' in Bislama) refers to the way in which our indigenous ni-Vanuatu societies are organised to look after the concerns and resources of their members. This is in contrast to the way the "Western", "Capitalist" or "cash" economy organises itself to look after the concerns and resources of its members. . . . The reality of Vanuatu today is that the traditional economy is by far the most important and predominant economy in the country. Far more people participate in the traditional economy, and to a significantly greater extent, than they do in the cash economy.
>
> In Vanuatu today, the great majority of people (roughly 80%), live in rural areas. Almost all of this 80% of the population:
> - live in settlements (villages) with other members of their traditional extended families, on land that is theirs under the rules of custom;
> - satisfy most of their food and other requirements using traditional methods and forms of land, sea and resource utilization (e.g. gardening practices), on their customary land and sea;
> - speak their indigenous language;

- are governed by traditional leaders (chiefs and chiefs' councils);
- have their disputes resolved within communities by traditional leaders using traditional dispute-resolution approaches; and
- have participated in custom ceremonies which cement their place as members of their community.

In addition, a large proportion of the other roughly 20% of ni-Vanuatu living in urban areas also participate in and rely on the traditional economy to a significant degree, utilizing kinship networks to access food and other resources and dealing with their disputes in the traditional way.

Today, even the most isolated rural dweller needs cash to pay for tea, sugar, kerosene, iron and steel implements and school fees. The fact that we are classified as a "Least Developed Country" by the United Nations, however, is based on the fact that the great majority of the population use only a tiny amount of cash in their lives. Their participation in the traditional economy is far more important and pervasive than their involvement with the cash economy. It is true to say, in fact, that the traditional economy constitutes the political, economic and social foundation of contemporary Vanuatu society. (Vanuatu Daily Post, 10 March 2007)

(What) Does a *Kastom Ekonomi* Oppose?

Regenvanu's description of *kastom ekonomi* portrays it as a pre-existing fact that can be positioned as an alternative to other possible formulations of the 'political, economic and social foundation of contemporary Vanuatu society'. This suggests an oppositional and/or resistant quality to *kastom ekonomi* and self-reliance projects. Indeed, within normative development accounts the aspects of Vanuatu life that Regenvanu (positively) highlights appear instead as obstacles. Like the majority of the so-called least developed countries of the Pacific island region, Vanuatu is relatively isolated in geographical terms from primary world markets. And in an extremely dispersed archipelago, such domestic markets as exist are further divided within. As such, Vanuatu has struggled to achieve what might be considered a 'viable' production economy (Tisdell 2002: 905–906) and relies heavily on foreign aid. It also lies within the fringes of what the Australian government, a primary source of that aid, has characterized as an 'arc of instability'. This includes the 'fragile' economies of neighbouring 'weak' or 'failed' states that make up Melanesia, most notably Papua New Guinea, Fiji and the Solomon Islands (see Dobell 2007).

The islands are mainly volcanic in origin with highly fertile soils, which means people in rural areas maintain rich and varied subsistence lifestyles. Most rural settlement comprises dispersed hamlets of around 50 to 300 people. Taro, yams and manioc are the primary staples, supplemented by a range of other garden crops as well as chickens, cattle and pig herds. The realities of transportation and other geographic limitations inherent to archipelago life contribute to poor access to education, health care and other services, and to a very low GDP per capita (in 2008 estimated at US$573 by the IMF for a rank of 170 out of 179 countries listed). Cash incomes are mainly derived from copra, timber, cocoa and kava production, which along with beef make up around 60 per cent of exports. Even so, as of 2003 services accounted for 77.5 per cent of the economy (including especially tourism and offshore finance), agriculture 13 per cent, and industry (including utilities) 9.5 per cent (Cox et al. 2007: 5).

Linked to the important tourism industry (Slatter 2006), coastal land sales to (mainly Australian, U.S. and New Zealand) 'investors' and 'sea-changers' have escalated dramatically in the last decade. This process of land alienation has contributed to an already increasing urban drift that has seen the population of Port Vila quadruple since 1980 to approximately 50,000. Unemployment among this city's extremely youthful population is high, at well over 50 per cent. Indeed, Vanuatu has the lowest 'formal-sector' employment in the Pacific region. The official working-age population is approximately 110,000, or 51.4 per cent at the 1999 census (Vanuatu Statistics Office 2000). Formal-sector employment in 2004 was estimated at 16,300, yielding an employment rate of 14.7 per cent. The United Nations 'Common Country Assessment' for Vanuatu (2002) has estimated that the working-age population will grow by 30 per cent in the next decade, which is far above employment growth. A 2007 AusAID-funded report stated that 'each year, 3,500 school leavers enter the workforce, but fewer than 1,000 new jobs are created' (Cox et al. 2007: 6).

Vanuatu has been governed by parliamentary democracy since gaining independence from a joint British and French condominium administration in 1980. The head of state is the president, who is elected by an electoral college consisting of members of parliament, presidents of the six provincial councils, and the Malvatumauri National Council of Chiefs. According to the Constitution (Section 52), the Malvatumauri, which is elected by district councils of chiefs, is supposed to advise the government on all legislative matters concerning land and ni-Vanuatu culture and language, although in practice this rarely happens. The Malvatumauri does, however, play an important role in conflict resolution at both community and state levels, especially through organization and oversight of *kastom* mediation and exchange processes (Westoby and Brown 2007).

In 1997 a structural adjustment program of 'economic liberalization' (including tax reform and 'macroeconomic stabilization') was introduced through the Asian Development Bank. This Comprehensive Reform Program (CRP), as it is called, was welcomed by many of Vanuatu's political and administrative elite, who agreed that the corruption-rife government was in crisis; however, opposition to it has also been used as a point of difference between parliamentary political parties. A large part of the programme was directed at 'right sizing' the civil service, and some 400 staff (10 per cent of the total) were retrenched. However, redundancies were applied in a somewhat arbitrary fashion, and many of the ambitious goals of the CRP were not achieved (Cox et al. 2007: 34). Even so, the five years up to 2010 have been relatively stable politically, and despite ongoing mismanagement and corruption issues particularly surrounding land sales and also bank fraud, Vanuatu maintained an economic growth rate of around 5 per cent before the recent global downturn. Part of this was due to the 2003 enactment of the Priorities and Action Agenda, aimed at supplementing the CRP (updated in 2006; see Government of the Republic of Vanuatu 2006), which forms the basis of government and donor decisions regarding the implementation of development projects.

In light of this potted view, Vanuatu is routinely characterized as 'in transition', and its economy, accordingly, as 'dualistic' (e.g., Cox et al. 2007; Tisdell 2002). Alongside the both negative and positive effects of exogenously derived political economy and the generalized material effects of 'modernity', the richly diverse traditional culture is recognized as very much alive, particularly amongst those rural populations who maintain strong kinship links and, through these, ties to ancestral land. Thus, as is true for many so-called developing countries, a profound reification of teleological narratives relating to the economic or social 'potential' imputed to Vanuatu may be used to highlight either positive hope or the generalized gloom-and-doom views that are often described under the catchphrase 'poverty of opportunity'.

Such narratives of progress and possibility were manifest, for instance, in a comprehensive AusAID development report titled *The Unfinished State: Drivers of Change in Vanuatu* (Cox et al. 2007). Arguing that 'managing change is at the heart of the development challenge in Vanuatu', this report outlined three possible future scenarios. The worst 'low case' scenario would entail a 'return to the political instability and mismanagement of the 1990s' (ibid.: iv). The 'high case' envisaged a situation in which 'more stable coalitions emerge, political competition becomes more issue-based and government is able to articulate clearer national development policies'. Here, a 'new generation is increasingly able to participate in both modern and traditional life' (ibid.: iv–v). Under the more likely 'medium case', a continuation of recent positive trends was forecast. However, 'the benefits of growth would accrue mainly to expatriates. Income differentials between the urban and rural areas would grow, increasing pressure on rural communities and accelerating urbanisation, with its accompanying social problems' (ibid.: iv).

These forecasts illustrate well the dichotomizing rhetoric that informs much debate around the future of development in Vanuatu. Contrasts are built between an underdeveloped rural population and a mis-developed urban population, and a mismanaged and weak public sector and an expatriate-dominated but potentially profitable private sector. These conceptual divisions are actualized in the economic motivations underlying recent aid donor focuses. For instance, the European Union is set on bolstering private-sector employment, with success to be measured through an increase in the number of active Vanuatu National Provident Fund accounts (each new account presumably demonstrating a newly "economically active" ni-Vanuatu). New Zealand, on the other hand, has rationalized its seasonal labour scheme as a means of creating a remittance economy, thus increasing cash flow into rural areas. At the same time, the dominance of exogenous ideas (and, often, participants) in development and the emphasis on "reform" in Vanuatu have aroused opposition. While organized opposition to neo-liberalism and associated reform at the regional level was largely absent until recently, as with the rest of the Pacific, those critiques that have been mounted have largely come either from or with the support of resident NGOs (Slatter 2007).

Finding Answers Within

The projects of *kastom ekonomi* and self-reliance and sustainability (S-RS) present something of a radical contrast to these more conventional approaches to development by shifting focus to the economic basis upon which such concerns are seen to rest. Indeed, the idea that Vanuatu may be 'developed' through its previously undervalued *kastom* economy – rather than seeking to bolster GDP though industry or private/public economic reform, for instance – has clearly anti-colonial, and indeed potentially revolutionary political overtones. By giving Western-style development discourse a creative new spin, the idea of a *kastom ekomomi* also implicitly presents an important critique of that discourse. It does so by turning 'Yali's Question' on its head. At the outset of *Guns, Germs and Steel*, biologist Jared Diamond describes a conversation he had in 1972 with a 'remarkable Papua New Guinean politician named Yali'. Questioning Diamond about the origins of the people of New Guinea, and about the material culture that Europeans later brought there, Yali posed to him the following question: "'Why is it,'" he asked, "'that you white people developed so much cargo and brought it to New Guinea, but we Black people had so little cargo of our own?'" (Diamond 1997: 1).

What is of course implicit and thus remains unquestioned in this conversation is an understanding of 'development' and 'prosperity' as measured by the yardsticks of industrialism, perceived relative technological 'progress', and the cash economy. Instead the aim is to draw the indigenous into a particular discourse of progress, hope and possibility (see Errington and Gewertz 2004 for a detailed critique of Diamond). Diamond's use of Yali's question also denies alternative interpretations of it that might consider it to be questioning the necessity of and rampant desire for 'cargo'. This is perhaps the angle that *kastom ekonomi* chooses to take: rather than progress based on exogenous values, it promotes activity within what it sees as specifically *indigenous* spheres of exchange and production. Of direct relevance to the aims of this volume, it also shows the potential value of 'traditional' forms of anthropological research to projects of sustainable development, precisely in cases where such linkages seem unapparent. It shows that anthropology and development practice are inextricably linked epistemological endeavours. Indeed, the *kastom ekonomi* and S-RS project is based, at least partially, on social scientific research and understandings (being also, in part, instigated by anthropologists). As such, it privileges the local over the global and seeks to revalue 'the traditional' (*kastom*) over narrowly defined ideas of 'progress' that are developed externally.

Overall, the *kastom ekonomi* and S-RS project is both ambitious and highly idealistic. Part of that idealism intersects and indeed draws upon two primary methodological and analytic anthropological tropes that have been subject to rigorous criticism and demystification within the 'post'-critiques of the 1980s and 1990s: namely, tradition and holism. In fact, the project can clearly be seen to reify ideas of cultural authenticity (which even so might positively feed into Vanuatu's valuable tourism industry). More perniciously, it appears to deny people access to the materiality of a 'modernity' (however that might be defined) that is perceived as emanating from outside forces. But the beauty of the project lies precisely in denying such negativity – in denying the apparent contradictions of modernity itself – by instead embracing the idea that 'the answer lies within'. These factors suggest that *kastom ekonomi* might

best be considered as a critically resistant assertion of national indigeneity, with the aim of providing an alternative to development as practiced
in Vanuatu over (at least) the past two decades.

Yet, as we outline below, to concentrate solely on these resistant qualities and accept the construction of holism at face value may obscure
similarities and overlaps between *kastom ekonomi* and other development projects that have promised 'progress' for Vanuatu. The projects
being undertaken through *kastom ekonomi* cannot be simply typified as
oppositional. For instance, the institutions of the state are not excluded
or resisted, but rather incorporated; there is considerable overlap too
with current regional development industry concerns, particularly
regarding sustainability, security and good governance; terms such as
'matrix' and 'platform' are used, which replicate the formal characteristics of other models for development, most notably the neo-liberal
Comprehensive Reform Programme discussed above. Rather than resisting or opposing development, *kastom ekonomi* resists the particular configuration of knowledge about Vanuatu that mainstream development
has used. Progress is not resisted, though; instead, *kastom ekonomi* pur-
sues an equally 'modern' project by reconfiguring knowledge in a way
that leads to a subjective reorientation by ni-Vanuatu that will better
produce progress for the nation. In the following section we chart some
of the entanglements that *kastom ekonomi* depends upon, focusing on
the role of anthropological and developmental knowledge practices and
projects of subjective reform.

Economies of *Kastom* and the Subject of Self-Reliance

The 1990s' developmental orientation towards 'good governance'
demanded a neo-liberal reform of the subject as a precondition to the
possibility of "successful" national change. In Vanuatu (as presumably
elsewhere) this was promoted to the general population through a variety of media exhorting ni-Vanuatu to reconceptualize themselves as
citizens and active participants in the newly introduced arena of 'civil
society'. The work of a local community awareness and development-
oriented theatre and media production organization, Wan Smol Bag,
provides representative examples of this approach: the narrative of the
film *Vot long Pati Ia!* (1999; translated into English as *Your Vote, Our
Party*) implicitly links electoral corruption and voter apathy to marital
infidelity, patriarchal domination and greed; and the cassette of songs
Democracy Dreams (1999) contains, amongst other tracks addressing the
ineffectiveness of the police and the fragility of coalition governments,

the song 'Jealousy', which recounts the abusive response of a man who sees 'his woman' talking to an old (male) school friend. These outputs, funded by good governance programmes of AusAid and DFID, made clear that reform was not just about state governance, and that 'good' demanded that virtue be evenly spread throughout the population. In such films and songs, the heroes or heroines were the ones who went against consensus-based views and actions (often equated with 'tradition' and frequently embodied by the archetypal patriarch and/or 'chief') – the ones who made their own choices. Participation in the process of change (reform) emanated from the independent thought of the individual, unbound from collective norms.

The particular 'subject of self-reliance' that is implicated by the *kastom ekonomi* movement stands in contradistinction to that of good governance. While the term 'self-reliance' itself calls to mind the potential sufficiency of the individual, parallels with neo-liberalism are undermined by the addition of the qualifying term 'national' in many documents relating to the project. This term serves two purposes (at least) in delineating the 'self', denoting simultaneously political collectivity and cultural difference. The ideal subject of self-reliance is thus the nation itself, but in the form that is most frequently found outside of the institutions of the state – the unconscious subject of 'the islands', the 'rural' or the 'grass roots'.

Speaking in 2005, Ralph Regenvanu summed up the response of this subject to the self-reliance and sustainability agenda: '[for] people in the islands, this stuff is like, "yes, so what? This is just natural."' The main obstacle in implementing self-reliance and sustainability – also envisaged under the term *kastom ekonomi* – is the 'resistant' subject. Regenvanu again:

> In Vila is where the main obstacles are, because ... it's this class that are well-educated and expect, kind of, western consumerist lifestyle benefits. And that's going to be the obstacle, I think. Because we're talking about banning rice, banning flour, and even when I tell [my partner] this, she's like, "you're crazy! No!" ... getting kids to learn their *kastom*, and that's not something that everyone wants anyway. But I think the main resistance is going to come from the policy makers and people who are already in that lifestyle in Vila, and especially people who have their kids growing up that other way. And for them it's going to be like, "well, my kids are going to be doctors and lawyers" ... and they've got their Playstations, and whatever, and it doesn't matter the fact that most people in the country would think this is a sustainable, good way to go, because certain people make decisions at

the top. . . . So it just depends how many of those people you can get within the administration that are willing to push it at all costs. (Interview, Port Vila, 9 August 2005)

In this formulation, the problematic subject is characterized as urban and particularly refers to those working in the public service; that is, those with power in terms of the apparatus of the modern nation-state. Occupying such a position is equated with a particular lifestyle, that of 'Western consumerism'.

Positioning self-reliance and sustainability as the alternative to Western consumerism highlights the strongly materialist orientation of *kastom ekonomi* projects. This is clear, too, when consideration is given to its historical development; starting with the original Pig Bank proposal of the early 1990s, moving into the Traditional Money Banks research project (2005), discussed in further detail at the Uripiv Workshop to Recognize and Promote the *Kastom* Economy as the Foundation for the Achievement of National Self-Reliance and emerging finally after the national summit as the National Self-Reliance Strategy. However, the desire to appear resistant to prior models of ideal development and the emphasis on the material bases of ni-Vanuatu culture should not obscure the commonalities of these projects with, for instance, the neo-liberally oriented good governance and reform strategies of the 1990s (outlined above). Of interest is these approaches' similar conception of an ideal subject: while good governance emphasized the rights-bearing subject, here it is the *kastom*-bearing subject. Both models imply that human beings have immanent capacities to realize particular subject forms, while acknowledging that this realization has to this point occurred unevenly through the population of Vanuatu. In addressing this discrepancy, both approaches involve the targeted use of particular presentations of knowledge to encourage subjective reform, thus implying that the same end result can be achieved through differential epistemological means.

While the initial Pig Bank proposal languished for a number of years, its first formalized, public presentation took shape in the report *Traditional Money Banks in Vanuatu* (Huffman 2005). Authored by the anthropologically trained former director of the Vanuatu Cultural Centre Kirk Huffman, this report conformed to the standards expected of a donor-funded survey document: it created a 'problem' through the presentation of academically informed accounts of indigenous practices. In highlighting the 'continued' production of 'traditional' wealth in certain areas of Vanuatu, it implicitly showed the current uneven functioning of the indigenous economy. This allowed for the broader project of using indigenous economic practices as the basis for national development – a project that needed to be engaged in evenly by all ni-Vanuatu – to appear as a possibility. The aesthetic properties of the report also reiterated the 'projectness' of the project, and the report itself was strategically directed towards those seen as most likely to recognize this form of legitimation. Recognizing this need for palatability, Regenvanu openly outlined the multiple deployments of knowledge in promoting the Self-Reliance and Sustainability agenda:

> The thing is, it's kind of obvious but you've got to make people see it in terms that they've been educated to understand. So you've got to present it in terms of economic self-reliance, which the economists and finance people are like, "Yeah, yep, economic self-reliance!" And then you realize, well, if we're talking about that, well, isn't this economic self-reliance? And you can see in Kirk's book when he did the survey that that's what he was saying as well; that it's kind of obvious but you have to make the policymakers realize that that's actually happening already. We don't have to create programmes to recognize what's already there. And that has been the big problem with *kastom* all this time, that *samting ia i stap finis* ['it's already there']. But you think, 'Oh, we've got to get someone else to come and teach us how to look after our reefs.' All this kind of stuff. (Interview, Port Vila, 9 August 2005).

The privileging of 'outside' knowledge emerges here as a point of frustration, but one that can be overcome through the skilful use of language and presentation, as in the report. This linguistic sleight of hand was extended too to the rest of the ni-Vanuatu population. Responding to playful questioning about how the terms 'self-reliance' and 'sustainability' might be translated into Bislama, Regenvanu emphasized that this was not a procedure he necessarily supported:

> We haven't actually converted it, but what's happened is that people have started talking about what's the term in [indigenous] language for this? . . . And I think that's what we want to encourage as well, that way to conceptualize it in the language of each community. They have to come up with it, because in Bislama there's no phrase for it. But part of that strategy, as well, is to encourage language, to encourage language conceptualisation. You know? Use your own term. Don't use MPA [marine protected area] or whatever, use your own language term for it; this is . . . the *ringi te suh* [Maskelynes language], or whatever. Because there are the words for it in the language. (Interview, Port Vila, 9 August 2005)

This approach points to a divergence between self-reliance and sustainability/*kastom ekonomi* and the neo-liberal reforms that preceded these initiatives, but also highlights ways in which the history of development in Vanuatu is tied to and informs the creation of modern indigeneity. During the late 1990s, terms such as 'transparency', 'accountability', 'civil society' and 'rights' became part of Bislama vocabulary, used with varied degrees of shared meaning (see Taylor 2008). This implicitly positioned these 'outside' concepts within the national culture of Vanuatu and thereby formed part of processes of differentiation amongst ni-Vanuatu: choice of vocabulary could imply affiliation with reform, a move away from the 'constraints' of *kastom*, and resistance to the perceived limitations of indigenous language for expressing engagement with transnational subject positions. *Kastom ekonomi* resists this transliterative tendency but similarly implies connections between language, subjectivity and reform.

There are parallels here with Goodale's (2006) notion of 'indigenous cosmopolitanism'. Discussed in the context of Bolivia, he points to the emergence of (broadly) political actors who exhibit the ability 'to bring together apparently disparate discursive frameworks as a way of reimagining categories of belonging . . . and, by extension, the meanings of modernity itself' (Goodale 2006: 634). We wonder, what might this ability look like in Vanuatu? Discussing his role in the *kastom ekonomi* project, then Secretary of the Malvatumauri Selwyn Garu pointed to aspects of his biography that made him particularly able to weigh up and amalgamate the ideas that informed the project. Contrasting himself to both other university-educated ni-Vanuatu who were not inclined to question 'outside' models of development, and those who had not experienced Western education, he stated:

> After completing university I came back to the island, so I had more understanding of what the culture is like. I can actually get what is coming from university and what is coming from outside, and I can piece things together in a shape that is going to work for us. So we hold onto the values, but the form of doing things may change. That's easy. But when we talk about the villager, the chief from Tanna, who's never been to even secondary [school] level, to be able to do that, that's the problem. (Interview, Port Vila, 1 September 2005)

Garu's description of his abilities suggests a reflexive engagement with alternative world views that has obvious resonances with the anthropological management of knowledge. This in turn suggests that, while self-reliance may be an innate capacity of ni-Vanuatu, realization of this involves a conscious act of recognition. The comparative element of his statement calls into question the idea that achieving self-reliance and sustainability does not involve change for the majority of ni-Vanuatu. While it does clearly aim to smooth out inequality at the material level, it rearranges difference to reflect access to, and the ability to successfully manipulate, knowledge and its formal properties. The success of *kastom ekonomi* depends on the simultaneous creation of a 'problem' that requires a project to address it, and denial of the same activities as *materially* problematic for the majority of ni-Vanuatu, for whom the message is 'don't change; carry on with what you're doing'. However, this necessitates reconceptualization of the relationship between types of knowledge, as described by Garu. And this results in an intertwining of knowledge practices that might otherwise be seen as epistemologically separate, drawn from anthropology, development and *kastom*.

Conclusion: Encompassing Modernity

This entanglement informed Regenvanu's schematic equation of formal presentation, intended audience and need for reform, yet the products and key ideas of *kastom ekonomi* circulated in less predictably rigid ways. Rather than 'naturally' already knowing what it entailed, examples from our 2005 fieldwork on Malakula and on Espiritu Santo in 2007/08 indicated a keenness on the part of ni-Vanuatu for ideas of self-reliance and sustainability, and of a *kastom ekonomi*, to be presented as 'project-like' and externally mandated/endorsed. For instance, Rousseau was asked to draft a speech for the president of the Malmetunvanu (Malakula island council of chiefs) on the topic of self-reliance, to be delivered at the Independence Day celebrations. She then (apparently) became the first 'outsider' to address a Malmetunvanu meeting, again on the subject of self-reliance. Interestingly too, when Rousseau photographed the Malmetunvanu president in his Lakatoro office, his chosen prop was a copy of the Traditional Money Banks report.

These examples could be enjoyed for their irony, or read critically as evidence of the success of neocolonialist development practices: the unconfident, passive local population trained to expect and accept leadership and endorsement from outside. However, it is more fruitful to consider them in terms of what they say about the position of *kastom* as both a domain of knowledge and a critical tool for evaluating possible courses of action in contemporary Vanuatu. The anthropologist as presenter/translator/interpreter of *kastom* is not a new phenomenon (see

Bolton 2003). Regardless of whether this might entail a personally dis-comforting and confusing experience for researchers, it tallies with the argument that the successful evocation of *kastom* requires its objectifi-cation (Rousseau 2004). In the case of projects such as those of *kastom ekonomi*, the anthropologist fulfils this role particularly well, being the ally of *kastom*[1] yet also someone connected to the generalized world of development by 'virtue' of being non-indigenous and (in most cases) white. This positioning suggests that the anthropologist is capable of the same weighing up of knowledge outlined by Selwyn Garu above.

The outcome of such an exercise, however, is not to reposition *kas-tom* in a further 'evaluative dualism' (Lindstrom 1982) with moder-nity, exemplified in this case by development, but rather to indicate the ways in which *kastom* can provide a better basis for 'progress'. Through its combination of formal characteristics of development (the 'prob-lem', the report, the deployment of expertise), knowledge practices of anthropology (cross-cultural translation, reflexive categorization and comparison of world views) and material indigenous practices (rear-ing tusked pigs, weaving mats, subsistence gardening), the realization of the ideas of self-reliance and a *kastom ekonomi* requires subjective change on the part of ni-Vanuatu through the reconsideration of how seemingly disparate epistemes can be united into a reformed *kas-tom* identity. *Kastom ekonomi* represents not so much the indigenous 'reclaiming modernity' (Goodale 2006), but rather the indigenous encompassing modernity in order to bring about positive change – the promise of progress.

NOTES

We would like to thank the Vanuatu Cultural Council for permission to carry out the research on which this chapter is based. Funding for fieldwork was provided by the British Academy (SG-40371) and the Wenner Gren Founda-tion. Our particular thanks are extended to our research participants in Port Vila and Luganville and on Malakula.
1. 'Anthropologist' is defined in the standard Bislama dictionary (Crowley 1995) as *man we i stadi long kastom* ('a person who studies *kastom*').

BIBLIOGRAPHY

Bolton, L. 1999. 'Introduction', *Oceania, Special issue, 'Fieldwork, Fieldworkers: Developments in Vanuatu Research'* 70(1): 1–8.
———. 2003. *Unfolding the Moon: Enacting Women's* Kastom *in Vanuatu*. Honolulu: University of Hawaii Press.

Cox, M., H. Alatoa, L. Kenni, A. Naupa, G. Rawlings, N. Soni, C. Vatu, G. Sokomanu and V. Bulekone. 2007. *The Unfinished State: Drivers of Change in Vanuatu*. Canberra: AusAID.

Crowley, T. 1995. *A New Bislama Dictionary*. Suva: Institute of Pacific Studies.

Diamond, J. 1997. *Guns, Germs and Steel*. New York: W. W. Norton.

Dobell, G. 2007. 'The 'Arc of Instability': The History of an Idea', in R. Huisken and M. Thatcher (eds), *History as Policy: Framing the Debate on the Future of Australia's Defence Policy*. Canberra: ANU E-Press.

Errington, F. and D. Gewertz. 2004. *Yali's Question: Sugar, Culture and History*. Chicago: The University of Chicago Press.

Goodale, M. 2006. 'Reclaiming Modernity: Indigenous Cosmopolitanism and the Coming of the Second Revolution in Bolivia', *American Ethnologist* 33(4): 634–649.

Government of the Republic of Vanuatu. 2006. *Priorities and Action Agenda, 2006–2015: 'An Educated, Healthy and Wealthy Vanuatu'*. Port Vila: Department of Economic and Sector Planning, Ministry of Finance and Economic Management.

Huffman, K. 2005. *Traditional Money Banks in Vanuatu*. Port Vila: Vanuatu Cultural Centre.

Lawrence, P. 1964. *Road Belong Cargo*. Melbourne: Melbourne University Press.

Lindstrom, L. 1982. '*Leftamap Kastom*: The Political History of Tradition on Tanna, Vanuatu', *Mankind* 13(4): 316–329.

Rousseau, B. 2004. *The Achievement of Simultaneity: Kastom in Contemporary Vanuatu*, Ph.D. thesis. Cambridge: Department of Social Anthropology, University of Cambridge.

Slatter, C. 2006. 'The Con/Dominium of Vanuatu? Paying the Price of Investment and Land Liberalisation'. Unpublished manuscript.

———. 2007. 'Treading Water in Rapids? Non-government Organisations and Resistance to Neo-liberalism in Pacific Island States', in S. Firth (ed.), *Globalisation and Governance in the Pacific*. Canberra: ANU E-Press.

Taylor, J. P. 2008. 'The Social Life of Rights: Gender Antagonism, Modernity and *raet* in Vanuatu', *The Australian Journal of Anthropology*, Special issue, 'Changing Pacific Masculinities', 19(2): 165–178.

———. 2010. 'Janus and the Siren's Call: Kava and the Articulation of Gender and Modernity in Vanuatu', *Journal of the Royal Anthropological Institute* 16(2): 279–296.

Tisdell, C. 2002. 'Globalisation, Development and Poverty in the Pacific Islands: The Situation of the Least Developed Nations', *International Journal of Social Economics* 29(12): 902–922.

Tonkinson, R. 1982. 'National Identity and the Problem of *Kastom* in Vanuatu', *Mankind* 13(4): 306–315.

United Nations. 2002. 'Common Country Assessment: Vanuatu', revised draft. Suva, May 2002.

Vanuatu Cultural Centre. N.d.a [c. 2004]. '"Traditional Money Banks in Vanuatu" Project: Executive Summary of the Survey Report'. Retrieved 13 June 2009 from http://www.vanuatuculture.org/documents/VKSUNESCOExecutive Summary.doc

———. N.d.b [c. 2005]. 'Vanuatu National Self-reliance Strategy 2020'. Retrieved 13 June 2009 from http://www.vanuatuculture.org/documents/Vanuatu%20 National%20Self%20Reliance%20Strategy%202020.doc

Vanuatu National Statistics Office. 2000. *The 1999 Vanuatu National Population and Housing Census Main Report.* Port Vila: Statistics Office, Republic of Vanuatu.
Westoby, P. and A. Brown. 2007. 'Peaceful Community Development in Vanuatu: A Reflection on the Vanuatu *Kastom* Governance Partnership', *Journal of Peacebuilding and Development* 3(3): 77–81.

CHAPTER 12

Intersection

Modes of Modernity

Norman Long

A common thread of both contributions to Part IV is the emphasis placed on 'people's projects' rather than projects designed and implemented by authoritative institutions that work within set policy templates and define their goals using standard 'development-speak' (such as 'sustainable development' and 'community participation'). The chapters by Obeid and Taylor and Rousseau make a stand against developmentalist hegemony by building their analyses 'from below', combining careful ethnographic observation with actor narratives that reveal from the 'inside' how particular development initiatives instigated by local protagonists come into existence and impact on the wider social context.

Both contributions resonate with my own earlier theoretical attempts to rescue questions of development from the grip of formal policy models and developmentalist notions of social change. From the mid 1980s onwards I championed a strong actor-oriented perspective for understanding issues of development intervention that focused on the everyday lives, commitments, negotiations and outcomes of the interactions of the multiple actors involved, and their relative capacities to transform and 'rewrite' both the means and ends of planned intervention and existing mainstream notions of 'development' (see Long 1984, 2001; Long and Long 1992). This theoretical approach embraces both 'directive' and 'non-directive' modes of intervention (Long 1980; Long and van der Ploeg 1989) and highlights the 'counterwork' that local groups perform vis-à-vis imported global notions of development and modernity. In such contexts, prevailing ideas and practices of modernity are appropriated, given new meanings and re-embedded in local lifeworlds, resulting in what Arce and I have termed 'multiple' or 'mutant' modernities (Arce and Long 2000a, 2000b: 17–18).

Obeid's and Taylor and Rousseau's chapters endorse the significance of such transformational processes initiated by different local groups and explore the complex intermingling of personal, collective and national values and attachments. The development projects discussed in these two chapters challenge the tendency to reify the notion of 'tradition' as resisting progressive modernity, as well as the idea of 'indigenous' practice as an alternative to the hegemonic concept of development. As they both suggest, there is an urgent need for a theoretical demystification of these phenomena. Both studies also make a strong case for a more 'engaged' type of anthropology that allows for a degree of activism through the sharing of knowledge and practice with the range of actors involved. As the authors reveal, understanding and participating in group action or *kastum ekonomi* and grasping precisely what self-reliance and sustainability entail for the actors involved leads to the additional insight that it is through these very means that local people construct their own modes of 'modernity'.

Here we can draw some comparison between Vanuatu and Lebanon, both of which face the problems of weak economies and low levels of income. Both cases reveal multiple layers wherein 'personal' and 'national' values and identities intertwine. It is through these constellations that ideas of development become meaningful. For the Lebanese professors described by Obeid, development was clearly not so much about technical and academic concepts removed from society, but rather how these specialized notions were embodied in larger civic ideologies that acted as motivators to transform an ailing society, one that had been through a civil war and suffered the repercussions of bigotry and intolerance. Likewise, Taylor and Rousseau's account pays close attention to how apparently competing or even contradictory discourses and practices – deriving, on the one hand, from 'indigenous' or 'subaltern' sources, and on the other, from global development debates – breed off each other to generate a rich combination of 'modernist' and 'counter-modernist' texts and practices. In no sense is this akin to the notion of 'economic dualism'. Nor does it conform to the model that depicts the interplay of 'informal' and 'formal' sectors of the economy. It goes beyond these to signal the cross-fertilization of a multiplicity of 'development' ideas and priorities, which require detailed, ethnographic research grounded in situated engagement with the various actors involved.

Following neatly from the discussion on 'doing and knowing' (Part III), both chapters offer a sophisticated account of how a multiplicity of development ideas and agendas cross-fertilize historically through a series of struggles between the various protagonists involved, including local political actors, government officials, academics and anthropologists. Hence both endorse a type of 'engaged anthropology' that allows for a degree of activism through the sharing of knowledge and practical endeavor with others, leaving open, of course, how these relationships should be made (see the recent edited volume by Hale, 2008).

We can all recall having to face testing moments during ethnographic research or consultancy work. My first fieldwork in Zambia in the 1960s, for example, required establishing close friendships within a congregation of Jehovah's Witnesses, to the extent that they once fixed a date for my baptism by total immersion in the local river. It took some clever manoeuvring to wriggle out of this and yet remain, as they put it, 'a person of good will', that is, someone interested and sympathetic but not fully committed to the faith. Such practical fieldwork dilemmas remain a leitmotif in both chapters and represent a strong critique of adopting either current international 'development-speak' or 'indigenous' categories and ideological stances for coming to grips with the development scenarios in today's global world.

BIBLIOGRAPHY

Arce, A., and N. Long. 2000a. 'Consuming Modernity: Mutant Processes of Change', in A. Arce and N. Long (eds), *Anthropology, Development and Modernities: Exploring Discourses, Counter-tendencies and Violence*. London and New York: Routledge, pp. 159–183.

——— (eds). 2000b. *Anthropology, Development and Modernities: Exploring Discourses, Counter-tendencies and Violence*. London and New York: Routledge.

Hale, C.R.(ed) (2008) *Engaging Contradictions: Theory, Politics , and Methods of Activist Anthropology*. Berkeley, Los Angeles and London: University of California Press.

Long, N. 1980. 'Some Concluding Comments', in D. Preston (ed.), *Environment, Society and Rural Change in Latin America*. London: John Wiley and Sons, pp. 235–248.

Long, N. 1984. 'Creating Space for Change: A Perspective on the Sociology of Development', *Sociologia Ruralis* 29(3–4): 168–184.

Long, N. 2001. *Development Sociology: Actor Perspectives*. London and New York: Routledge.

Long, N. and A. Long (eds). 1992. *Battlefields of Knowledge: The Interlocking of Theory and Practice in Social Research and Development*. London and New York: Routledge.

Long, N. and J. D. van der Ploeg. 1989. 'Demythologizing Planned Intervention: An Actor Perspective', *Sociologia Ruralis* 24(3–4): 226–249.

PART V

Forms and Effects

CHAPTER 13

Effecting Development

Bureaucratic Knowledges, Cynicism,
and the Desire for Development
in the Indian Himalaya

Nayanika Mathur

'You will find no development here. For that, go to the villages.' Throughout fieldwork in government offices in India, my explanation for what I was doing there – seeking to understand the operation of an ambitious anti-poverty scheme – was met with astonishment, for development (*vikas*) is not something that bureaucrats, at all levels, see as happening in their own offices. It is something that takes place without. Bureaucrats were not alone in wondering why I was 'wasting my time' with them and their routinized, workaday lives when I should be out in villages speaking to the beneficiaries of the rural development programme I was studying. Academics, including anthropologists, would often ask me, concernedly, if I had 'found my village yet'. Given anthropology's hoary tradition of producing village monographs in India, it was taken as natural that I should seek out this circumscribed space.[1]

In what is to follow, I work against the commonsensical assertions of both the anthropology of development and of development bureaucrats by seeking out development in an Indian government office. I locate the 'unstable term' of development (Edelman and Haugerud 2005: 1) in the discourse of agents of the state in a district in northern India. An ethnographic approach to office life exhibits its inhabitants' critical capacities to sophisticatedly analyse and articulate the practices and effects of development schemes. I argue that the technical rendition of standard development topics – poverty, unemployment – did not result in their depoliticization. On the contrary, stylized deconstruction of the project of development by state functionaries was buttressed by drawing attention to the politics of development planning and programming in India. The constant and critical deconstruction and politicization of 'development' led to a high level of cynicism within official circles. Somewhat counter-intuitively, cynicism with the Indian state's project of development coexists peacefully with officials' deep desire to embrace 'real' (*asli*) development as soon as possible.

The Desire for a New Developmental State

This chapter draws on the ten months I spent with government officials in a development office in a mountain district in the northern Indian state of Uttarakhand.[2] Officially detached from its parent state of Uttar Pradesh (UP) in November 2000 following a high-intensity period of lobbying and public agitation for it during the mid 1990s, Uttarakhand is a Himalayan state.[3] The public discourse that legitimized the creation of Uttarakhand was one that emphasized the geographical specificity of the mountains (*pahar*), which require a form of developmental effort very different from the types that 'work' in the plains (*maidan*).[4] This 'self-evident fact' was, it was claimed by the agitators campaigning for a new state, one that the development planners and implementers of UP, primarily plainsmen (*maidanis*) sitting in distant Lucknow, the capital of UP, were quite unable to comprehend (Mawdsley 1997). The creation of Uttarakhand was seen by many, including Ramachandra Guha, as 'perhaps the logical culmination of a century of popular struggle against forms of rule and types of rules inimical to the autonomous social development of the hills' (2001: 209).[5]

A particular discourse of development that reiterates the distinctiveness of the hills, its reduction to an 'internal colony' of UP in the postcolonial Indian state, the gross neglect coupled with exploitation of this remote region by UP, and the simplicity of the mountain people (*paharis*) is still in vogue in popular media reporting and in mundane everyday conversations, as well as in some academic analyses, to account for the imperative of creating Uttarakhand as a separate political entity. The popularity and proliferation of such a discourse bears testimony to the seductive desirability of the idea of development in contemporary India (cf. Pandian 2008) and its power to legitimate the idea of the state (Baviskar 1997: 195). Yet if one looks more deeply into the rhetoric of the separatist movement, 'the politics of legitimization' (Sinha 2003: 289) inherent in such a self-depiction – of mal-development of

present-day Uttarakhand caused by the indifference of external administration – becomes clearer. Tracing the genealogy of this particular
example of what she terms 'nonsecessionist regionalism', Emma Mawdsley (1997) shows that the pan-Uttarakhand demand for secession from
UP arose in direct response to the state's acceptance of a particular set
of positive discrimination policies that would reserve seats favouring the
state-defined category of the 'other backward classes' (OBCs) in educational institutions and government jobs, rather than due to a more vague
sense of requiring 'our type of development'. Given the caste composi-
tion of the mountain population, in which OBCs account for only 2–4
per cent of the total population, there was a fear that the region would
be flooded with outsiders, the *maidani* (plains people) who would, once
again, take away what legitimately belongs to the *paharis* (mountain
people): precious seats in institutes of higher learning and employment
in government positions (Mawdsley 1996).

My own fieldwork in Uttarakhand points to tangible and clearly articulated demands pinned to the new state. Following Mawdsley, this leads
me to suggest that the struggle for the new state was not as much an
indictment of the neglectful, non-performing, 'colonizing' state of UP as
it was a struggle by a constellation of groups to establish direct access to
coveted objects of desire – government jobs, educational opportunities,
and development funds. Thus 'the object of the Uttaranchal regional
struggle was the *capture*, not the *rejection*, of the state and thus state
power' (Mawdsley 1998: 49). To elaborate on this claim, I ask what
the (relatively new) state of Uttarakhand and its goal of development
(*vikas*) mean for subjects who are very much part of the apparatus of
the former and work to deliver the latter.

Guaranteeing Employment to the Rural Poor

I begin to answer this by recounting discussions woven around the implementation of one of India's largest anti-poverty schemes, the National
Rural Employment Guarantee Scheme (NREGS). The 'Guarantee', as
it was referred to in everyday bureaucratic parlance,[6] legally guarantees
employment for 100 days in a year at minimum wage to every rural
household that is willing to labour on a list of permissible public works.
One of the 'flagship schemes' of the present central government, the
NREGS is a critical development programme for the district authorities.
The district's development bureaucracy is headed by an official termed
the chief development officer (CDO). A district is further divided into
'development blocks' to facilitate the administering of development

assistance. Block development officers (BDOs) are responsible for the development work in the blocks in a position that mimics the CDOs in the district. At the level of the district, the mundane specificities of the Guarantee was handled by a specially designed NREGS 'cell' comprising four dedicated staff and an assortment of part-time functionaries. In this cell, where I was working as a non-participant observer, the Guarantee pervaded everyday chatter. On certain days it officially became the central topic of discussion. The monthly meetings held in the district office were one such occasion.

Monthly meetings were particularly poignant moments in the life of the office, for this was the one day in the month that was set aside for face-to-face interaction with members of every tier of the district's pyramidal development structure in order to minutely analyse and evaluate all the development activities underway in their combined area of command. They were convened in a large hall with a rectangular conference table at its centre. The CDO would occupy the position at the head of the table with his two deputies, the district development officer (DDO) and the project director (PD) of the District Rural Development Agency, seated on either side of him. The BDOs would cluster nervously around the head of the table, while other officers lower in the hierarchy sat on chairs placed at a slight distance from the table, along the walls of the room. Typically, the DDO would call out first the names of different development schemes in the district and then the names of blocks, at which point the BDO of the concerned block would stand up and reel out figures related to the assigned targets.

When the Guarantee was announced, all the BDOs would take out their monthly progress reports and give two key figures: 'number of households employment has been provided to' and 'money spent'. Almost always, the trinity at the head of the table would express their disappointment over these figures. The NREGS brought in vast amounts of money to the district. If this money was not spent on finding employment for the large numbers of rural unemployed, it signalled the failure of everyone in that meeting hall but especially the CDO, who was answerable to the tiers of government above him.[7] Hence, he and his two deputies would become particularly anxious about non-expenditure of the funds. If their subordinates gave any reasons for the non-performance of the NREGS, they would be blanked out or, more commonly, shouted down.

Unemployment remains the biggest grievance in the mountain districts of Uttarakhand, especially in the middle and upper Himalayan belt, where job opportunities remain minimal. Yet in private, everyone agreed that the Guarantee, with its focus on manual, unskilled labour, did not provide the type of employment that the residents of the villages of this Himalayan region wanted. Briefly put, BDOs found it extremely hard to generate demand for employment in manual labour at minimum wage in this high-caste, highly literate, female-dominated (due to men's emigration to the plains in search of jobs), geographically difficult terrain. This otherwise taken-for-granted fact of life in the district could never, however, be officially acknowledged. When even hesitantly suggested, the very idea would invite the ire of the higher officials, such as in the meeting held in November, snippets of which are reproduced below.

The Technical and the Political

Meeting Held on 27 November 2006

What follows is the response of the CDO to the BDO of X block in response to the very low expenditure noted in his monthly progress report (MPR) under the NREGS.

> CDO: Why is no work happening in your block?
> BDO (*very softly*): There is no demand, sir.
> CDO (*immensely irritated*): What do you mean there is no demand? I refuse to believe that!
> DDO (*shouting*): You are wasting the state's (*sarkar*) time!
> CDO: Begin work in two villages at the very least within a week. If you do not do so then I will hold you personally responsible for this failure.

The CDO, DDO and PD repeatedly exhorted their subordinates to make 'the people' (*janta*) understand the scheme. While the DDO and the PD were quite loud and rough, the CDO assumed a somewhat more polite mannerism involving repetition of the rules of the scheme. He kept focusing on the law that underpinned the scheme, the procedure whereby the people could be made to understand how beneficial the scheme was for them in this time of few employment opportunities, and the concrete and sequential measures government functionaries must take to operationalize the programme, all of which would culminate in the success of this initiative. In other words, he 'rendered it technical' (Li 2007: 123).[8]

The NREGS is, after all, a technical solution to the indisputably pressing problem of rural unemployment in the mountains. During these public assemblies the senior bureaucrats were careful to occupy themselves solely with these technicalities. An elision between the usage of 'technical' by development bureaucrats and anthropologists of development comes across in the frequent tossing-in of the English word 'technical' in these otherwise entirely Hindi-speaking meetings, with the understanding that only technicalities were worth discussing with superiors. On 28 November 2006, a couple of days after this particular meeting, for instance, a district-level workshop was held as part of a capacity-building initiative required to be conducted under the NREGS. At this event the CDO invited anyone from the NREGS staff to stand up and 'openly and fearlessly' tell him why they were not able to implement the scheme. Taking heart from this rather unfamiliarly inviting language, a few BDOs stood up to complain of infighting in their block offices, lack of motivation and time, insubordination, personality clashes and village-level politics, especially the absence of interest in the NREGS shown by elected members of local government bodies due to the slim possibility of 'eating money' from the scheme due to the stringent transparency clauses built into it.[9]

I was fascinated by these highly personalized accounts of the mundane politics of offices in the district. The CDO, DDO and PD, however, exchanged exasperated glances that clearly signified their disdain for these 'politics' (the English word was used).

> CDO (*dismissively*): I am not interested in these politics. You have to sort them out yourself. Don't eat up my head with them. Can you not see that I have more important things to think about rather than try to make peace between you and your *Pradhans* [village headpersons]? You are all grown men, not children, so please stop squabbling and get back to work on this scheme of national importance (*rashtriya mahatva*) and stop wasting my and *sarkar's* [the state/government] precious time. Further, here in the district I just want to hear of the technical problems faced by all of you.

In the meetings, the politics that was shot down referred to challenges, contestations, disputes and ill feelings at the local official level. Localized power struggles and the messiness of the everyday functioning of local bureaucracies – 'politics' – that did not adhere to Weber's ideal rational, modern bureaucracy were not, officially, to be considered serious factors impeding the implementation of a complex central plan of 'national importance'. Politics was utilized pejoratively by bureaucrats as something dirty and childish that must be somehow dealt with by these adults. In contrast, discussions of 'technical' problems – shortages of staff, lack of stationery and other material tools, lack of clarity on

precise procedures – were fit for the office and for the attention of superior officers.

Anthropologists, on the other hand, utilize the term politics in a
somewhat more celebratory fashion. 'Is politics the name for a relation
of power, or a practice of contestation? At what point does one slide into
the other?' asks Li (2007: 11). She settles on a definition of the practice
of politics as 'the expression, in word or deed, of a critical challenge'
(2007: 12). In private conversations, such a critical challenge was often
voiced to the project of development, the pretensions of the developmental state generally and the intentionality behind the Guarantee in
particular. Away from the formalized rituals of the bureaucratic world,
even though still within the physical space of the office, a macro understanding of the politics of poverty alleviation emerges. It is this understanding of politics – the type that occupies the critical branch of the
anthropology of development – to which I now turn.

The Politics of the Guarantee

The CDO, a member of the elite Indian Administrative Service (IAS),
was of the opinion that the NREGS was a very well-designed scheme,
and that problems in implementation arise due to the lack of staff, difficult terrain and poor connectivity of the mountains, 'lazy mountain-
men',[10] lack of 'capacity',[11] and rampant corruption in the state system.
If all these factors – technical and managerial – could be rectified, the
NREGS would work exactly as envisioned by the planners in New
Delhi, he believed. His opinion of the NREGS was quite different from
that of the levels below him, though of course nobody ever dared con-
tradict CDO *sahib* openly.

On my arrival in the NREGS cell in the district office, its inhabitants
did their utmost to relieve me of what they perceived to be my naïve
idealism about the scheme in particular, and state development (*sarkari
vikas*) more generally. The project economist (PE) told me on my very
first meeting with him, 'Such schemes come and go leaving nothing
behind. This is not development. Its just *sarkar* trying to show that it
is trying to develop the nation.' The section officer (SO) would often
tell me of how work used to happen in villages – through *shram daan*
(donation/free gift of labour). So, for instance, if a school was to be built,
all the men of the village would of their own accord volunteer their
labour power to its construction. Funds were amassed through door-to-
door collection. Those buildings still survive, for they were built with
care; they were not *sarkari* (government-like) in the least. He and the

rest of the older staff at the district office held these so-called development schemes through the expansion of the welfare state to have been
the ruin of the region. 'Ever since these subsidies by the government
began, they have totally ruined our honest mountain-folk for we have all
become too dependent on the state. Now everyone just wants subsidies,
they just want government money (*sarkari paisa*) by hook or by crook.
That is what Uttarakhand was made for, after all. For more *sarkari paisa*,
more *sarkari naukris* [more government money, more government jobs].'

For the middle and lower levels of the development bureaucracy,
the Guarantee would 'not work' (*nahin chalega*) – not only because
the *paharis* (mountain-people) were lazy [sic], although that was the
general perception of village men by most of their fellow *paharis*, but
because no *vikas* (development) could really happen when it was all on
paper, when it happened mechanically and procedurally from within
the confines of an office, when no one really honestly cared about development, when these programmes were mere exhibitory moves to convince the electorate that the government was genuinely interested in
development. The paperwork and procedure of the Guarantee, in the
opinion of officials, took over all other activities that might allow for
time to do 'real' (*asli*) development work, which would involve heavy
fieldwork, i.e., visits to villages.

BDOs in particular told me candidly that they never got the time to
go to villages to see what, if anything at all, was happening there. 'I am
so tied up with my papers only. This form, that register, that table, this
plan. After all, the Guarantee lives in these technical details. I am judged
by the neatness of my files and accounts, not by what is happening on
the ground', said one beleaguered BDO. The SO, who had handled similar employment generation schemes in the district for the past thirty
years, was bemused by my constant prodding on the scheme. For him
the point of the Guarantee was very clear. He meticulously explained to
me how such development schemes possess two lives: a *sarkari* (state-
like) one on paper in offices, and a real life (*asli zindagi*) in the villages.
The state, however, concerns itself only with the former, for that is what
counts as its measure of success. For the middle and lower levels of the
development bureaucracy, the fact of this dual life of the NREGS and
the Indian state's focus on what I term and study as the 'paper state'
(Mathur 2010) constituted clear evidence that the state did not really
'care' about development.

Over the course of my time in Uttarakhand, members of the state's
development bureaucracy laid bare the NREGS with succinct clarity.
It appeared that they understood, in a manner far superior to that of
the 'decoding anthropologist' (Mosse 2005: 6), the effects of 'rendering

technical'. The rendering technical of the NREGS was *not* its depoliticization, for development was understood and articulated always as a political problem resulting in large part from the historical neglect of the Himalayas (cf. Friedman this volume). The struggles that have characterized this region since precolonial times exhibit, to my mind, a very real understanding of the structural, historical inequalities of extraction of natural resources for utilization elsewhere and of the absence of any concerted effort to work for the betterment of everyone in the mountains. In the context of the NREGS, it would seem that for the operators of the development apparatus implementing it, the practice of identifying deficiencies to be rectified and then working (ostensibly) on the solutions did not, as Ferguson would have it, make it function as an 'anti-politics machine'. Ferguson rightly points out that the development apparatus 'insistently reposes political questions of land, resources, jobs, or wages, as technical "problems" responsive to the technical "development" intervention' (1994: 25). However, his account fails to illuminate the extent to which development workers are aware they are doing this – the practice of rendering technical – and recognize that in doing so, the identified problem – in this case, rural unemployment in the Indian Himalayas – will not be ultimately eliminated.

Expanding *Sarkar* in Uttarakhand

The other strategic effect that Ferguson claims results from the 'anti-politics machine' is that 'it is a machine for reinforcing and expanding the exercise of bureaucratic state power' (1994: 256). As do other governmental programmes, the NREGS leads to an expansion of the state bureaucracy, hence increasing 'the extent and reach of a particular kind of exercise of power' (ibid.: 274). However, in the Uttarakhand case this did not happen, as Ferguson claims for Lesotho, 'behind the backs or against the wills of even the most powerful actors' (ibid.: 18). Rather, development workers of the district considered a tangible benefit of the scheme to be that it was recruiting more young locals. Not only did the scheme become an employer itself, but also, through the employment of these new petty state agents, state money was able to make its way into the remote villages of the district.

The stated objective of the NREGS is to enhance livelihood security in rural areas.[12] Whatever was happening with the development funds within the village was considered an altogether different story, one that need not necessarily concern officials as long as their books were in order for the scrutiny of the paper state.[13] As it stood, state money (*sarkari paisa)* released under the head of the NREGS was going into these villages through the aid of the new recruits and the expansion of the district bureaucracy. These two effects of the Guarantee were seen by its primary implementers to be beneficial to the district. This was most certainly not the intent of the planners of this development scheme in New Delhi, who operated under the neo-liberal dictums of cutting India's 'bloated bureaucracy' and eliminating corruption through transparent governance.[14] But was it perhaps these unintended effects of the NREGS, and not the achievement of the bullet-pointed aims in the operational guidelines, that allowed it to flourish?[15]

It is striking, and thus bears repeating, that I found absolutely no evidence to suggest that an expansion of the state in Uttarakhand was leading to a 'squashing of political challenges'. Poverty, the state, lack of development and neglect of the hills continued to be discussed and debated hotly in the media, in everyday life in the district and, as I discovered, within the state offices of the district. It was precisely this critically appraised aspect of state development schemes that led their primary implementers in the district to attach to them the prefix 'useless' *(bekaar).*[16] Development schemes launched by the non-caring state were considered useless on a number of accounts: they did not match the expectations of the populace, they did not take into account the real needs of the region, they maintained structural inequalities such as those between the plains and the mountains or the rich and the poor, and so on. What particularly chafed the bureaucrats was the profound inefficiency of the Indian state's development apparatus, the very same system in which they themselves were deeply embroiled.

One day a veteran accountant decided to empirically prove why government *(sarkari)* schemes are *bekaar.* He brought out the ledger of development schemes in the district, which gave a rough approximation of the funds allocated to each of them in one financial year by the state, added them up and then divided them by the number of households in the district. The figure that popped up on the calculator at the end of this arithmetical exercise was Rs 53,000. He turned to me triumphantly, for he had proven once and for all the utter illogicality of government development schemes. 'Just distribute this money directly to each household per annum. *Automatic poverty elimination.'*

The Cynical Babu

For weeks afterwards, the figure of Rs 53,000 was thrown at me as the answer to poverty elimination in the hills, on the presumption that this was the solution I had been seeking during my months in the office. I was earnestly entreated to write a letter to Sonia Gandhi[17] telling her to forget her 'pet scheme' (the NREGS) and instead consider this solution of direct cash transfer to the poor. An unrelenting cynicism, then, pervades the development bureaucracy of the district. By cynicism I refer, firstly, to the dictionary definition of the word as 'an attitude of scornful or jaded negativity, especially a general distrust of the integrity or professed motives of others'.[18] Secondly, I use the term following Navaro-Yashin (after Zizek), who claims people can 'see through ideological pretensions and consciously verbalise critique. . . . And yet (and this is the point), the same people take actions upon the world as if they did not know, as if they were deluded by ideology, as if ideology were reality. This is cynicism' (2002: 159–160). The bureaucrats I worked with compellingly analysed and articulated the state's effecting, and effects of, development – including, and perhaps especially, their own part in this process. They were able to see through the ideology of development, the prime legitimizing tool of the state, especially in Uttarakhand, where the creation of the new state premised precisely on this plank remained fresh in everyone's minds.

Why, one might wonder, do officials then continue to work within the system of the state, which they consider morally bankrupt and utterly inefficacious in the deliverance of its stated aim of 'development'? The question is merely rhetorical, for the answer is self-evident. Scepticism of 'the state' and 'development' is all very well, but it does not vanquish the reality of the lives of the bureaucrats, as of all other Indians, which take place within the hegemonic, gargantuan, material structure of the Indian state. It is within this world of the state that bureaucrats live their everyday lives and from which they derive their livelihoods. Critical awareness of the state apparatus's limitations in delivering on its stated objectives does not prevent one from working within and with it. As Navaro-Yashin writes, 'the signifier "state" can remain intact, in spite of public consciousness against it, because a material and tangible world has been organized around it' (2002: 171). Referring to Turkey, she convincingly argues that it is, in very fact, the prevalence of cynicism that allows the state to endure: 'As long as what I will call the *everyday life of statecraft* is maintained, the state is reproduced. *A pretence to normality* is coeval with a critical consciousness about state' (2002: 179, emphasis in original).

It was precisely the everyday life of statecraft with its pretensions of normalcy that allowed functionaries to continue working within the folds of the state on the project of development. Cynicism was ever-present in the ironical attitude adopted by *babus* to state-led development and in their acceptance of their own culpability in upholding this farce.[19] Irony took many forms, often veering towards the theatrical. For instance, many a dull hour was filled by the comical reading aloud of news items from local newspapers, especially if the story concerned the misdemeanours of a fellow colleague from the Vikas Vibhag (Development Department) or an exposé of corruption in the higher echelons of the state. Another favourite text that served as a script for ironical performances was the operational guidelines (OG) of the NREGS issued by the Ministry of Rural Development (MoRD) in New Delhi.

Once, a ludic moment was spun around reading the following objective of the Guarantee: 'Fostering conditions for inclusive growth ranging from basic wage security and recharging rural economy to a transformative empowerment process of democracy' (Government of India 2008: 2). The elocution was rendered in a sardonic tone, accompanied by rolling of eyes and expressive hand gestures, to indicate the absurdity of grandiloquent state claims such as this, which litter the official documentation on the Guarantee. At all other times, the OG was treated as a Holy Grail whose minutest terms must be seen, officially and on paper, to have been abided by. After all, the implementation of the scheme was premised upon the rules and regulations printed within it. At more relaxed moments, though, this very same document would be whipped out as an example of the Kafkaesque absurdity of bureaucracies. These moments of reversal point to the self-reflexive irony that officials often exhibited. The irony was directed not solely at the state but also at one's own self through an attitude of 'rueful self-recognition', which Herzfeld (1997) terms 'cultural intimacy'. Whilst filling up ledgers, writing letters, crunching numbers, creating spreadsheets, giving speeches, sitting in meetings, attending workshops and other such familiar bureaucratic everyday rituals, officials would gently, ruefully, mock their own selves and their own acts.

Catching Up with Development

A striking counter to what I would describe as the ruling trope of cynicism regarding development and the state in the district is the coexistent hope for progress and aching desire to 'bring development' to the *pahar* (mountains). At first blush, the hope and desire for development contradicts my depiction of the cynical babu. Yet scepticism towards the state's practice of implementing development by means of plans and programmes does not negate the proliferation of a desire for development or obliterate the hope in it. Talk of *vikas* and of progress is all-pervasive in Uttarakhand. The very word development, *vikas*, contains within itself a promise of a better future. Stacey Pigg notes that, 'embedded in the Nepali usage of *bikas* is what I call an ideology of modernization: the representation of society through an implicit scale of social progress' (1992: 499–500).

In the mountains of Uttarakhand too, the word *vikas* evokes powerful images of an evolutionary move towards a modernity that can be sighted from afar in the plains (*maidan*) and in the big cities of India. The plains, it is believed in Uttarakhand, have been allowed to grow up, while the mountains are trapped in an adolescent innocence. As Gupta notes, 'if there is an enduring trope in development discourse, it is that which equates "development" with adulthood and "underdevelopment" with infancy and immaturity' (1998: 11). An economist in the district office explicitly couched the developmental condition in the Rostowian schema when he complained of how the plains have 'taken off', while most of the Himalayas of Uttarakhand are stuck either in the pre-take-off period or, if really 'remote' and 'backward, even in 'traditional society'. In such a scenario it is imperative to develop, to catch up somehow. Unfortunately, according to the vast majority of the development bureaucrats, the form of development that *sarkar* was bringing forth – token schemes such as the Guarantee – was not the way to do so. The hope of a form of *vikas* – the 'real' (*asli*) type, not the banalized state (*sarkari*) type that they work on daily in their routinized official worlds – remains afloat. Development, then, is differentiated by members of the state's development apparatus.[20]

Conclusion

This chapter has attempted to portray the complex world of bureaucratic engagements with development programmes. Immersion in the quotidian world of development bureaucrats renders the assumption of the 'superiority of anthropological knowledge' (Yarrow and Venkatesan this volume) unsustainable. Rather, my ethnography shows that the terms that anthropologists and development practitioners play with – the political, the technical, the state, development, plans, documents – share more in common than conventional anthropological wisdom would have us assume. Annelise Riles (2001) dwells on the 'uneasy tone' that characterizes much ethnographic writing on current knowledge practices. The unease stems from the fact that 'it always has been the subject's job to produce the symbols and the anthropologists job to do the analysis, so to speak. Yet what is one to make of a subject . . . that one

encounters already analyzed?' (2001: xiv). Similar to Riles's experience
with development institutions in Fiji, what I encountered in the offices
of Uttarakhand was a series of practices that were already coherently
analysed and presented upfront to me. In such a scenario, what constitutes 'my job'? 'The achievement', Riles declares, 'lies not in the discovery of new knowledge but in the effort to make what we already know
analytically accessible' (2001: 18). The attempt of this chapter has been
precisely this – to portray the everyday acts of deconstruction of development schemes that might officially be rendered technical but remain
highly politicized for their practitioners. The deeply politicized nature
of development and access to opportunities; the constantly voiced need
for the mountains to catch up on the evolutionary path of progress, led
by the plains; and scepticism about the current model of state-led development coupled with the critical capacities of agents of the state make
for what I have termed the 'cynical *babu*'. Cynicism might dominate the
environs of development offices, but it simultaneously shares the stage
with the desire to develop that envelopes the Himalayan portion of this
northern Indian state.

NOTES

I am extremely grateful to Harri Englund, Monique Nuijten, Megan Rivers-
Moore, all the participants of the 'differentiating development' workshop
held in Buxton in 2008 and, especially, the editors of this volume and David
Sneath for their comments on drafts of this piece.

1. This correspondence between bureaucratic and anthropological categories of
   what constitutes the correct field site for an aspiring anthropologist highlights
   the proximity of these two seemingly disparate knowledge-practices (Riles
   2006).
2. In order to maintain the privacy of my informants, I have chosen to keep the
   name of the district anonymous.
3. Ninety-three per cent of its landmass is classified officially as mountainous.
   Of the thirteen districts of the state, three are in the plains area. However,
   the population in the plains, particularly in the larger cities, is expanding
   exponentially, leading to a fear of the 'emptying out of the mountains' as
   people migrate down to the plains in search of employment and access to
   education and health facilities.
4. The state presently known as Uttarakhand was born in 2000 with quite a different name: Uttaranchal, or 'the blessing of the North'. This was the name
   favoured by the ruling Bharatiya Janata Party (BJP) in 2000 as, supposedly,
   it diluted the regionalism inherent in such a demand for regional autonomy.
   Uttarakhand, on the other hand, means literally 'a piece of the North', which
   was felt to be somewhat threatening to the notion of the singular nation-state
   of India. The Indian National Congress party, which was in power in Uttaranchal till 2007, ordered a reversion back to the name of Uttarakhand just

before it went in for reelection. By this point, we had all become habituated to Uttaranchal, and indeed, many continue to employ this supposedly alien signifier on a daily basis, leading to no small amount of confusion about what is, after all, the best name to utilize for this state in everyday encounters. I shall refer to the state as Uttarakhand.

5. The popular struggles include the iconic Chipko, which has been variously defined as an environmental movement (Bhatt and Kunwar 1982), an eco-feminist movement (Shiva 1988) and a peasant movement (Guha 2001); concerted anti-liquor demonstrations by women; and the more recent protests against the construction of a dam that led to the submergence of the almost two-centuries-old town of Tehri and its many outlying villages in late 2005. Guha qualifies this assessment of the formation of the new province in the mountains by cautioning against a repetition of the practices of the former state, which in his opinion would only exacerbate protests against the 'indigenous' rulers.

6. I shall be using both the acronym NREGS and the shorthand Guarantee.

7. For the financial year 2008/09 the district received a budget of Rs. 1,022.26 lakh just for the NREGS. (One lakh in the Indian numbering system equals one hundred thousand).

8. Li explores the operation of rendering programmes technical by studying how 'new sets of programs identified an arena of intervention, bounded it, dissected it, and devised corrective measures to produce desirable results' (2007: 123).

9. The metaphor of 'eating money' in Hindi refers to the 'leakage' of development funds via corrupt practices.

10. The inherent laziness of the *pahari* men was a trope that echoed across the state bureaucracy even among *pahari* officers themselves. In contrast, *pahari* women were always celebrated for being quite the opposite, hardworking and diligent. Parry makes a parallel observation on the perception of men in the state of Chattisgarh in India as being *kamchor* (work-shy) in contrast to the 'Stakhanovite reputation' of Chattisgarhi women (1999: 115).

11. The English words 'capacity', 'participation', and 'gender' have moved from the global discourses of development into the local lexicon of non-English speaking development practitioners in the district.

12. Government of India (2008). *Operational Guidelines for the Implementation of the National Rural Employment Guarantee Scheme (NREGS)*: 3rd Edition. Ministry of Rural Development. New Delhi, GoI. Available at: http://nrega. nic.in/Nrega_guidelinesEng.pdf

13. 'The village' was seen as a bit of a black box from the vantage point of the district office – a space where government funds were swallowed up with little or nothing to show for their utilization other than, of course, the copious production of the deemed state documents (see Mathur 2010).

14. Indeed, the biggest problem in the implementation of the NREGS in the district was the very low administrative budget that was ordained for it – only 2 per cent of the total amount spent – which meant that funds had to be juggled or diverted from other, less strictly monitored schemes to meet the salaries of the additional personnel employed with the NREGS. In the end, the administrative budget was doubled to 4 per cent to cope with the massive pressures exerted on the extant bureaucratic system by the stringent requirements of transparency and accountability that distinguish this programme.

Bureaucrats continued to complain that this amount was not enough, but it appears that the Ministry of Finance in New Delhi was unwilling to accede to a greater budget than this for the programme during the period I was in Uttarakhand.

15. Looked at thus, Ferguson (1994) was absolutely right to suggest that it is the unintended consequences of development projects that allow 'failed schemes' to be replicated over and over again.

16. In that sense, the development officials can be seen to be falling into the school of thought described by Mosse as abiding by a critical view of policy that 'takes the failure of development interventions as self-evident' (2005: 4).

17. Sonia Gandhi is the president of the Indian National Congress and the chairperson of the United Progressive Alliance (UPA), the ruling coalition of political parties in the Indian parliament at present. The NREGS, as the UPA's 'flagship programme', is widely considered to be a product of Gandhi's penchant for state welfarism.

18. Taken from the American Heritage Dictionary of the English Language (Fourth Edition), 2006. Retrieved 25 April 2009 from http://dictionary.reference.com/browse/cynicism

19. *Babu* is a colloquial Indian term for government functionaries, often used disparagingly to connote the implicit problems of sloth and corruption that are commonly associated with Indian bureaucrats. In the British Raj it referred to native Indian clerks who could write in English. I utilize the term *sans* the pejorative connotations that are commonly associated with it.

20. In a sense, the differentiation follows the one between Development with a big D and development with a small d, as elaborated by Baviskar (this volume).

BIBLIOGRAPHY

Baviskar, A. 1997. 'Tribal Politics and Discourses of Environmentalism', *Contributions to Indian Sociology* 31(2): 195–223.

Bhatt, C.P. and S. S. Kunwar. 1982. *Hugging the Himalaya: The Chipko Experience*, Gopeshwar: Dasholi Gram Swaraj SamitiEdelman, M. and A. Haugerud. 2005. *The Anthropology of Development and Globalization: From Classical Political Economy to Contemporary Neoliberalism*. Oxford, UK: Blackwell Publishing.

Ferguson, J. 1994. *The Anti-politics Machine: "Development", Depoliticisation and Bureaucratic Power in Lesotho.* Cambridge: Cambridge University Press.

Government of India. 2008. *Operational Guidelines for the Implementation of the National Rural Employment Guarantee Scheme (NREGS): 3rd Edition.* New Delhi: Ministry of Rural Development.

Guha, R. 2001. *The Unquiet Woods: Ecological Change and Peasant Resistance in the Himalayas.* New Delhi: Oxford University Press.

Gupta, A. 1998. *Postcolonial Developments: Agriculture in the Making of Modern India.* New Delhi: Oxford University Press.

Herzfeld, M. 1997. *Cultural Intimacy: Social Poetics in the Nation-State.* New York and London: Routledge.

Li, T. M. 2007. *The Will to Improve: Governmentality, Development and the Practice of Politics.* Durham, NC, and London: Duke University Press.

Mathur, N. 2010. 'Paper Tiger? The Everyday Life of the State in the Indian Himalaya', Ph.D. dissertation. Cambridge: University of Cambridge.

Mawdsley, E. E. 1996. 'The Uttarakhand Agitation and the Other Backward Classes', *Economic and Political Weekly* 27: 205–210.

———. 1997. 'Nonsecessionist Regionalism in India: The Uttarakhand Separate State Movement', *Environment and Planning A* 29(12): 2217–2235.

———. 1998. 'After Chipko: From Environment to Region in Uttaranchal', *Journal of Peasant Studies* 25(4): 36–54.

Mosse, D. 2005. *Cultivating Development: An Ethnography of Aid Policy and Practice.* London: Pluto Press.

Navaro-Yashin, Y. 2002. *Faces of the State: Secularism and Public Life in Turkey.* Princeton, NJ, and Oxford: Princeton University Press.

Pandian, A. 2008. 'Devoted to Development: Moral Progress, Ethical Work, and Divine Favour in South India', *Anthropological Theory* 8: 159–176.

Parry, J. 1999. 'Lords of Labour: Working and Shirking in Bhilai', *Contributions to Indian Sociology* 33(1–2): 107–140.

Pigg, S. L. 1992. 'Inventing Social Categories through Place: Social Representations and Development in Nepal', *Comparative Studies in Society and History* 34(3): 491–513.

Riles, A. 2001. *The Network Inside Out.* Ann Arbor: The University of Michigan Press.

———. 2006. 'Introduction: In Response', in A. Riles (ed.), *Documents: Artefacts of Modern Knowledge.* Ann Arbor: The University of Michigan Press, pp. 1–40.

Shiva, V. 1988. *Staying Alive: Women, Ecology and Survival in India.* New Delhi: Kali for Women.

Sinha, S. 2003. 'Development Counter-narratives: Taking Social Movements Seriously', in K. Sivaramakrishnan and A. Agrawal (eds), *Regional Modernities: The Cultural Politics of Development in India.* New Delhi: Oxford University Press, pp. 286–312.

CHAPTER 14

The Transformation of Compassion and the Ethics of Interaction within Charity Practices

Catherine Trundle

Charity and development are linked by the shared goals of intervention and improvement. Despite the similar intentions and effects involved in both practices, development and charity have largely remained separate objects of analysis in the social sciences. In this chapter I question such a division of academic labour, and show that the problem of critical distance associated with anthropology's treatment of development is equally prevalent in current analytic engagements with charity. Furthermore, I argue, studies of charity offer insights that extend and broaden current debates within the anthropology of development by providing examples for how ideas and actions, and detachment and engagement, are complexly interlinked. Ethnographically, this chapter describes American expatriate volunteers at a church charity food bank in Florence, Italy, who provided food to poor and undocumented migrants. By considering theories of development through the lens of this case study, like Yarrow (2008), I argue that the complex ethical practices of development and charity practitioners are too often ignored by anthropologists, who tend to overlook the 'small politics' of daily practice that are often submerged beneath the discursive realm of 'big politics' (cf. Jensen and Withereik this volume). This hides the range of ways development is enacted and apprehended by all those involved in its performance, making it a phenomenon of multiplicity (Mol 2002).

Notes for this section begin on page 224

If anthropology is to move beyond a post-structuralist critique of development, then it must explore 'dialectical encounters' (Friedman this volume), that is, the quotidian issues and problems that development practitioners and recipients face through which development ideals are transformed into practice. Taking such an approach, I seek to destabilize a division, common within the analysis of both charity and development, that exists between knowledge and action, and means and ends. I argue that for the volunteers of this study, ideology and discourse emerged largely from the iterative daily acts of, as my participants said, 'getting the work done'. By focusing on the *form* of charity work (cf. Jensen and Wintheriek this volume) and configuring it as the most important moral domain through which compassion could be enacted, volunteers came to value an ethic of *disinterested equality*. This challenges an underlying assumption within development practice, which values 'engagement' and considers 'detachment' to be morally suspect. Moreover, this case study unsettles the distinction between detached knowledge and engaged action that often separates anthropology from development, illustrating that for food bank volunteers, the two domains were experienced as inseparable.

Charity and development are differentiated by distinct historical origins. In Western contexts the former emerged from Judeo-Christian institutions, while the latter was born from modernist and secular roots.[1] Yet this distinction has long since eroded. As early as the mid nineteenth century, the burgeoning 'relief' and 'alms' sectors in the Euro-American world gave way to the domain of 'charity.' Charity proponents regarded their new approach as a 'scientific', modern 'technique' of improvement that required expert knowledge and training (Gardner and Lewis 1996: 3–10). Here we see echoes of a rhetoric that would later infuse development discourses: 'Through the carefully planned and coordinated actions of professional charitable . . . societies, scientific charity would do what poor houses alone were unable to accomplish – repress pauperism, reform the character of the needy, and restore the poor to a life of self-sufficiency' (Bartkowski and Regis 2003: 40).[2]

Frequently charity and development are distinguished with regard to the temporal and spatial frames within which they operate: charity is assumed in public discourses to be largely located in the West[3] and responsive to immediate needs, while development operates within 'developing nations' and is focused on the long-term and sustainable. Yet these divisions also prove to be erroneous. For example, Save the Children offers programmes with similar aims to support poor children and increase school attendance in both Britain and Zimbabwe. Yet while the projects in the former country are framed as charitable work or even welfare, those in the latter are cast as development. Child sponsorship programmes such as World Vision are legally and socially configured as charities in donor countries. When such funds reach destination countries, however, they go towards projects defined as development. Furthermore, the sponsor's giving is framed as an immediate and affective form of support for a suffering child. Yet such giving is also reworked so that it comes to build 'sustainable independence' for an entire 'target community' (see for example Bornstein 2005). Such divisions are thus largely lenses for constituting global differences rather than reflections of distinct practices. Increasingly, the tropes of development – 'empowerment,' 'partnership' and 'long-term support' – are included in the discourses of charity (see, e.g., Bialecki 2008; Zelizer 1994), while the charitable 'impulse' (Bornstein 2008) to help immediate suffering is interwoven into the fabric of modern aid programmes. Attention to the relational networks and flows in rhetoric shows a mutable and dynamic link between charity and development practices on a global scale.

Despite the critique of such concepts as the 'third' or 'developing' world, charity and development remain divided as distinct terrains for analysis along both territorial and disciplinary lines. Anthropologists have concentrated on 'third world' development, leaving to sociologists the study of Euro-American charity and welfare regimes. Yet in the last decade we have witnessed the fusion of the charitable imperative to give with the goals of development in many guises. *Voluntourism* allows untrained young people to travel abroad to participate in development projects (see, e.g., Simpson 2004; Wearing 2002), while in Britain one can give the gift of a goat destined for a 'needy' person in the 'third world.' Such gifts promise instant and direct philanthropic giving designed to simultaneously develop independent livelihoods.[4] Slippage between the categories of charity and development in many ethnographic contexts calls such categories as analytic devices into question.

Like development, charity has typically been analysed in the social sciences as a form of action through which status inequality is upheld and social order is maintained (see, e.g., example Blau 1964; Caplan 1998; Heilman 1975; McCarthy 1990; Mindry 2001; Simmel 1971 [1908]). Studies have, therefore, sought to 'uncover', often with ironic effect, the oppressive consequences of practices professing to lessen human suffering. While such critiques have served the valuable purpose of exposing contradictions between discourse and practice, they have, through the method of discursive deconstruction, tended to assume that the researcher's models more effectively reveal truth and power than do any practical modes of knowledge used by participants (Mosse 2004; for example see Ferguson 1990: 17).

Rather than seeking to expose the underlying and unjust discursive 'logic' of charity work, this chapter details the complex and transforming ideas that guide charity workers at the 'street level' (Lipsky 1980). In his study of development programmes in India, Mosse argues that within such projects, 'the logic of political mobilization and the logic of operations are different' (2005: 16). In contrasting developmental policy and implementation practices, Mosse asks, 'What if the things that make for good policy are quite different from those that make it implementable? What if the practices of development are in fact concealed rather than produced by policy?' (ibid.: 2). In a different context, I ask what the difference is between charity action as understood through knowledge systems that aim to inspire volunteers, enable Christian compassion and place charitable action within a theological frame, versus charity action that aims to 'get the work done', as volunteers often referred to it? I seek to show not only that, as Mosse argues, '[i]deas have to be understood in terms of the institutions and social relationships through which they are articulated' (ibid.: 10–11), but also that for volunteers, constituting their guiding ideals through the process of 'doing' was one of the key moral practices involved in enacting charitable compassion.

The Food Bank, 'the Generous' and 'the Hungry'

The St James Church is an American Episcopal Church, attended by American expatriates, tourists and students, as well as other English-speaking nationalities. Its food bank (*banco alimentare*) was open once a week throughout the year. It was run by a small core of about eight volunteers who attended every week. Caitlin, an American woman heavily involved in the church, oversaw the event. Nearly all of the volunteers were female Americans of retirement age who were married to Italian men. Most were long-term residents of Tuscany (twenty years or more). During fifteen months of fieldwork in Florence, I became a volunteer for the food bank.

Between forty to eighty people collected a food bag and chose items from the tables of used clothing each week. Only 10 per cent were Italians, and nearly all of these were elderly men and women living on small state pensions (*pensionati*). The remaining recipients were immigrants, the three largest groups being Romanians, Poles and Peruvians. This group also included migrants from other parts of Eastern Europe, North Africa and the Philippines. Many were undocumented migrants who struggled to speak Italian.[5]

When I asked the rector, the food bank organizer and volunteers why the church had established the food bank and what their aims were for such a project, their answers commonly centred on what it meant to be both a Christian person and an Episcopal church. At mass, the rector's sermons clearly articulated this Christian obligation to parishioners. 'Jesus says to us', he stated one Sunday, 'today this Scripture is to be acted out in your presence.' In one of his sermons he preached:

> Luke's blessing is simply to say this, 'that the Kingdom of God is theirs' means concretely that the gospel, the Christian message, and hence the church, belongs to them, the poor-hungry-weeping. Any ministry by religious organizations or religious people to the church of the poor – the real church – must work to make these hopes of Jesus come true in our lifetime, in our global village. . . . He is raised, blessed forever, in the poor-hungry-weeping Ones, and in our sisters and brothers persecuted and perishing.

'The poor,' in such a theological tradition, were conceived to be the physical embodiment of Christ. Working closely with the poor was, therefore, a way of both emulating Christ and of being physically and socially near to such embodied spiritual virtue. The Christianity espoused by the rector was, as he phrased it, 'earthly' and based in the here and now. Being a good Christian entailed emplacing oneself in one's immediate material and social world rather than a far-off heavenly realm of future salvation. Distinctions between faith and action, and prayer and service, were ideally annulled (cf. Bartkowski and Regis 2003: 143).

The food bank organizer, Caitlin, was a devout Episcopalian. As was so for many of the volunteers, compassion lay at the heart of her explanation for volunteering: 'It's just what you do, as a Christian, Following Jesus's example, [being] compassionate to those who need it, regardless of who they are.' Such ideas and motivations stemmed from the need to enact a Christian identity, and such an identity was focused on fusing both the spiritual salvation of self and the material salvation of an already spiritually virtuous 'needy other' into one project. It was scripture, bible group readings of the parable of the 'good Samaritan', sermons and volunteer meetings that provided the knowledge systems to understand and articulate charitable action.

Studies of charity and development commonly nuance the ideal of compassion by placing it in dialogical tension with other contrasting ideas, to point out 'ideological discrepancies' (Elisha 2008: 157). For example, within U.S. Christian charity projects, an ethic of compassion must often contend with neo-liberal ethics of accountability and empowerment (Elisha 2008), self-sufficiency and judgment (Bartkowski and Regis 2003), or shrewd fiscal stewardship (Bialecki 2008). Yet such contrasts place discourse and ideology as causally prior to social interaction and actions. While ideologically configuring discourses of compassion within church networks, food bank volunteers equally reworked their aims through the valued process of 'doing' – through, as Mosse states, 'the collaborations and compromises that practical action brought' (2005: 79) to the ministry. I argue thus that the ideal end goals and tangible results of their actions came to be understood within the framework of iterative and unfolding action. In place of a sense of outcomes and purpose (spiritual, economic, social), in performing charity work the volunteers focused their energy and conceptual work on the *means* of charity work.

The Morality of Form

In this chapter I define action outside of the common paradigm driven to reveal the purpose of endpoints. Like Georg Simmel's understanding of the relationship between means and ends in modern society (2003 [1907]), I draw attention to the realm of aesthetics within action, whereby actors focus on the *form* of action as an ethical domain. Simmel argues that a constant awareness of purpose is an exhausting endeavour. In everyday life and in repetitive acts, ends fade from the view of consciousness and cease to be the driving force of action.

> If the consciousness of purpose remains alive then it is . . . a process that consumes the organic strength and intensity of consciousness. The general practicality of life will therefore tend to eliminate it, since . . . it is basically no longer necessary for the teleological guidance of our actions . . . [T]he ultimate link of our practical sequences, which can be realized only through the means, will be better realized the more our strength is focused and concentrated on producing these means . . . if we are constantly conscious of the final purpose then a certain amount of strength is withdrawn from the labor by means. The most expedient attitude is that of the complete concentration of one's energy on that stage of the sequence of purposes that would be realized next. (Ibid: 230–231)

Correspondingly, as this chapter demonstrates, the realm of aesthetics can powerfully generate the direction of action and become teleological in itself.

The relationship between means and ends in development practice can be complex, contradictory or conflated. Aid workers often attempt to juggle an 'ethics of interaction' with recipients and an 'ethics of outcomes', which leads humanitarian work to become 'compromised action' (Feldman 2007: 693). Yet such 'tensions' suggests a conceptual separation between equally valued and visible 'means' and 'ends' that often does not play out so neatly. In this case study what constituted the most important moral work within charity volunteering was not the resolution of compromise between two discrepant spheres, but the creation of new ends out of means, a process that renders such a division less salient to an understanding of participants' experiences. As Riles's study of NGO networks shows, action can become an aesthetic form that generates its own effects. 'Networks do not refer to a reality outside themselves' (2001: 22).

The main organizer of the food bank, Caitlin, had worked for this ministry for over twelve years. She remembered that the original 'clients' of the food bank were a group of some ten to twenty local, elderly Italians. She described this as a harmonious time when the givers and receivers of charity developed personal, unique bonds of affection for each other. After twelve years, their names and personal characteristics rang clearly in her memory. Caitlin's memories of these early stages of the food bank contrasted with her recollection of its more recent past. Beginning in 1997, she explained, immigrants slowly became the primary group of charity recipients. 'We started getting all the Albanians', she said 'and that was hairy, we were a bunch of women, and it never got totally out of control, but we would give the bags out through the gate.' The majority of the new recipients were young or middle-aged men, and the small group of volunteer women soon began to experience a sense of physical threat, especially as the recipients increased and began to outnumber them at least three to one, Caitlin explained.

The food bank volunteers' sense of unease corresponded to a nation-wide moral panic regarding the perceived threat new immigrants posed to the social and cultural fabric of Italy. Caitlin described many Albanian food bank recipients during this time as always demanding more goods or different items from what the volunteers had.[6] At this point, Caitlin said, the quiet and informal atmosphere of the food bank disappeared. As the number of food bank recipients rose, so too did their ethnic diversity. Instead of a relatively small and homogenous group of poor, elderly Italians, the volunteers were now giving food out to a great variety of nationalities, ages and backgrounds, and many did not have a common language in which to communicate. This, she explained, led to more competitive interaction between food bank recipients, and a tenser atmosphere. The volunteers found they now had less time to spend with each recipient. What was perceived by many volunteers to be an increasingly 'demanding atmosphere' led many to withdraw from relationships with recipients and to act defensively and sometimes coldly with them. A new anonymity, she recalled, entered the social relations of charity.

Many volunteers had suffered from what in volunteer sector parlance has been termed 'compassion fatigue' (Elisha 2008: 155). The volunteers found they had become emotionally desensitized after repeatedly hearing the same stories of need. Their cynicism also stemmed from what many described as years of being verbally abused, as well as a sense of constantly being 'duped' by untrue stories. As Caitlin explained,

> Now it is a different atmosphere, now we get cheese thrown at us, people would get stuff out and throw them at the ground. There was a couple of times when I would just take the bag back and say, 'If this is your behaviour, then give it back, because there is someone who needs it more than you obviously.' Because I would not be afraid of these people.

Belligerence and defiance, I was told, begot belligerence and defiance. In response to a situation in which the volunteers felt they were 'losing control, a new 'ethic of interaction' developed. As the recipients attempted to shape the food bank into a realm that more closely met their own needs and desires, so the volunteers were forced to adjust their procedures and understanding of their own action. Caitlin recalled that in order to effectively give out food and diffuse the tension between recipients, the food bank volunteers soon developed a clear set of rules for recipients to follow. The volunteers' control over the moral tone of the event, which in previous times had involved receivers of charity conforming to particular ideals regarding gratefulness and passivity, had lost its hold. I was told that now the food bank recipients – often in competition with each other – refused to recognize their relatedness as recipients, a charity category.

Similar memories were recounted to me by several of the long-term food bank volunteers. Such shared narratives of the past were part of an important reflexive process that helped the volunteers to frame their own responses to changing circumstances in ways that made the present ethic of interaction seem logical, moral and unavoidable. Such memories emphasized the co-created, specific and situated origins of current volunteer behaviour that had emerged at the coalface of charitable work. For such women, compassion was largely a puzzle of enactment, emergent and understood within cumulative and small acts rather than the lens of doctrinal theology.

In order to continue to 'be Christian' towards 'the poor,' the volunteers focused their attention on providing a consistent and sustainable service. In settling into the routine of charity work, the volunteers expressed one key concept through which such ordered relationships were enacted and made meaningful. A phrase repeated often was that charity involved 'getting the work done.' At its core, this phrase expressed what I shall term an ethic of 'disinterested equality'. Theories of bureaucracy are a useful starting point in explicating such an ethic. As Weber argues, bureaucracy develops best 'the more completely it eliminates from official business love, hatred and all purely personal, irrational and emotional elements which escape calculation' (1978: 975). Peter Blau points out that in order to treat each 'client' equally, bureaucrats must disengage and become aloof, to avoid offering favourable treatment to some clients over others (1956: 30). Weber argues that disinterest is inherent to bureaucracy and emerges from above, from ministers and policy (1978). Post-Weberian approaches have attempted to insert cultural nuance and agency into such theories by showing how bureaucrats transform policies of 'indifference' (Herzfeld 1993) through practice and develop their own systems and sets of rules against such top-down pressures towards disinterest (see, e.g., Lipsky 1980).

Correspondingly, James Scott (1998) argues that development projects fail because they rely solely on what he terms *Techne* – abstract and universal knowledge. Such knowledge is schematic and contains within it all the causal explanations necessary to be self-contained and self-perpetuating. *Mētis*, by contrast, he defines as local and informal knowledge that represents 'a wide array of practical skills and acquired intelligence in responding to a constantly changing natural and human environment' (ibid.: 313). Such knowledge relies on 'feel', the adaptive skill gained through iterative 'doing'.

Scott's model, like other models of bureaucracy discussed above, argues that the logic of bureaucratic behaviour comes from a structural level above everyday human action. Despite inserting agency, adaptation and resistance into accounts of agents' responses to bureaucratic pressure, 'bureaucracy' as a trope with *Techne* qualities remains largely untouched. In this case study, however, disinterested equality emerged at the level of *Mētis* rather than *Techne*. Such impersonality was a response to the contests and collaborations at the heart of everyday social interaction, which both givers and recipients had a hand in shaping, rather than simply a response to a governing structure or ideology.

This calls into question an assumption in many models of bureaucracy. Mitchell (2002) argues that the social sciences and development often produce a similar effect: the tendency to bifurcate reality from representation, and acts and objects from ideas, which hides the complex interaction of practices, contingencies and forms of agencies. In this case study, the volunteers did not understand or experience the impersonality of their practices as concealing or tidying the underlying complexity of their world and dividing the ideal from the real. Rather, impersonality was held to be built out of the intimate interactions of actors, as ideals and acts were fused by the moral method of 'making do'. Rather than seeing distance and detachment as an ideational endeavour removed from practical action (as anthropology has often assumed in order to distinguished itself from development), the food bank volunteers offer us a challenging model that fuses engagement with detachment, and ideas with action.

A large number of 'rules' regulated the food bank space. According to the volunteers, these 'rules' aimed to guarantee the smooth running of the event and the equitable distribution of clothing and food. First, volunteers ensured that recipients lined up outside a locked gate and, once the food bank was open, entered only in groups of four. The bounded path that the recipients travelled through the front of the church grounds to collect their bag, browse through the clothing and then exit through a different gate was clearly marked by tables and volunteers. Each recipient was given one food bag. Volunteers often complained that if they turned their backs from this job they would soon see recipients attempting to take a second bag. These rules were not installed with regard to an overall planned structure of management, but had developed one by one in an ad hoc and reactive way, in response to the 'ineffectiveness' of the charity system. The volunteers were firm with those who lingered over the clothing longer than five minutes, asking them to leave. Libby, a volunteer, often felt frustrated that the first few groups would take large piles of clothing, leaving only a few items for the remaining recipients. 'It's just not fair', she often said to me with a defeated sigh.

Food bank recipients often complained that the donations they received – four items of food and a few pieces of used clothing – were not enough to meet their needs. Those who arrived last asked why it was that they could not have another bag when there clearly were leftovers. Most volunteers refused to give more, unwilling to set what they saw as a dangerous precedent of asking and of unequal access. Often recipients would attempt to explain their particular social situation to a volunteer – their inadequate housing or the number of children that they had to support – in order to ask for more. Against the anonymity of the category 'the poor', individual recipients attempted to insert themselves into such relationships as unique and unequal cases of need. At the same time, recipients were careful to watch all attempts other recipients made to garner more from the food bank than the rules permitted. If they witnessed any such behaviour, they would immediately seek equal treatment. Between such responses the volunteers felt caught in a double bind.

In most cases the volunteers would reply to requests for extra items by firmly stating that the displayed goods were all that was available. This was despite the often large number of bags of goods downstairs donated for food bank recipients. If the volunteers did try to meet diverse needs, the resulting interaction often discouraged them from breaking the rule of disinterested equality again. 'Things just get out of hand', Caitlin explained to me. On one occasion a volunteer listened patiently to a Filipina's story. It was raining, and the woman had holes in her shoes. The volunteer felt empathy for her and went downstairs to the storeroom. Upon reappearing with several pairs of shoes in her hand, the volunteer found herself surrounded by a group of Romanian women who pulled the shoes out of her hands, saying, 'We need shoes too.' Unable to think of anything else to do, the volunteer threw a too-small pair at the Filipina woman for her to take. With a defeated shrug, the volunteer observed that doing a favour for one of them was too difficult: the others, she said, just became too angry.

The pressure to be 'fair' and treat each recipient equally, then, came as much from those who received support as it did from the volunteers. Ironically, the ethical logic that givers used to maintain a manageable space was co-created and utilized by charity recipients as the acceptable rationale to make claims, even as recipients complained that such an ethical logic was unfair and unresponsive. In such a situation, rules to enforce equality became a bind to prevent givers from extending the support they offered as well as a protection from recipients' attempts to extend the orbit of charity into areas of support that recipients themselves sought to define.

When I asked why the volunteers directed so much of their energy towards enforcing the rules, their response was simple: it was because the recipients broke them so often, they said. This was an answer that displaced the centrality of their own agency, placing it in dialogical tension with recipients' agency. Such explanations also show that the volunteers' focus temporally and spatially limited charity work to the realm of immediate social interaction, bracketing out questions regarding wider life histories of need or long-term charity support. Perhaps, one volunteer told me, they might have had more time to consider individual stories of need were they not constantly dealing with recipients' attempts to 'outwit' them.

As a volunteer, I observed many incidents when recipients attempted to subvert the rules of the food bank. Some brought in large bags and tried to hide the first food bag they received in order to gain another from a different volunteer. Others left and returned twenty minutes later, hoping the volunteers would not remember they had already been through. The volunteers found these attempts to 'dupe' them annoying and kept a close eye on those who had a reputation for such behaviour. Volunteers labelled food bank recipients known to use clever tactics for garnering more goods 'furbo/a' (cunning, sly).

On one occasion a Nigerian woman had been let in by a parishioner before the food bank opened. She sat quietly on a bench pushing her baby in a pram. She explained to me that she needed a food bag and baby food, as she had a doctor's appointment for her baby at the time the food bank opened. She also asked for women's and baby clothes. Two volunteers soon told me she had done this before and was lying about the appointment. I was allowed to give her the food bag and the baby food, but they explained that if the other food bank recipients saw her rifling through the clothes they would get angry. The Nigerian woman then told me that her appointment was in fact at ten-thirty and she would wait for the food bank to open. When I reported this to the other volunteers they rolled their eyes, one saying, 'We knew it, they're always doing this.'

The volunteers had also seen recipients later selling the clothing and food on the streets. Some recipients even discarded the clothing once they turned the corner: Not having had much time to look through the clothing, and wanting to get hold of it before other recipients did, they often left the food bank without properly examining their chosen items. The volunteers tended to shrug defeatedly, admitting that they could not control what recipients did with the charity goods. The volunteers thus proclaimed the limits of their power to determine the outcome of their giving, and instead focused on the realm of charity that they did have firm control over – the site of the food bank – making sure that at least there, recipients would conform to a charitable ethos. Compassion as enactment thus entailed a resigned realism that refused to allow disappointment and potential failure to disrupt the flow of action.

Disinterested equality cannot be explained simply with reference to the assumed unequal exchange lying at the heart of charity. The previous patron-client relations of the food bank, which had been decidedly unequal, were seen to produce less distance and more personable, stable interaction than when giver-recipient relationships became more open to negotiation. If one structural rule could be invoked here, it is Mauss's: gift giving creates relations, but only if recipients accept the gift (1990 [1924]). In this case study, the recipients partially rejected the material gifts offered, complaining that they were insufficient, while also rejecting the non-material gifts of sentiment that would have allowed givers to enact compassion as theologically configured. In such a context, the relational power of the giver over the recipient was destabilized. Volunteers felt thus unable to enact compassion as a type of affective love, and instead, in the midst of unstable relational exchanges and negotiations, realized compassion in ways that emphasized the virtue of detachment and pragmatism.

Conclusion

At the St James food bank, what appeared to be a lack of empathy from the volunteers – an ethos that was in stark contrast to their stated aims and goals for volunteering – was in part a protective strategy to avoid destabilizing the continuity of complex charity relations. Such a mode of interaction avoided enraging food bank recipients and prevented volunteers and recipients from entering into morally complex relationships that had no clear boundaries. Satisfaction was gained from the harmony of a job smoothly executed without the interruption of too many moments of disorder. On the ground, Christian compassion translated into being fair, and being fair meant being disinterested. Yet this ethnography also demonstrates that the volunteers only partially controlled the frameworks of charity interactions. Even if volunteers desired to offer affective Christian love, they felt that recipients had ways, such as rule breaking or open hostility, of rejecting the non-material gift of intimacy that volunteers could offer.

A widespread criticism of bureaucracy is that its agents become so concerned with enforcing the rules that they forget what the organization aims to achieve. Sharp discrepancies can arise between a bureaucratic organization's mission statement and the treatment of its clients. This is often associated with the myriad levels of organizational complexity that distance planners from recipients (Herzfeld 1993; Scott 1998). In this case study, however, distance was created out of the complexities of charitable giving that were both small-scale and face-to-face. It was, ironically, an ideology of Christian compassion demanding emotional engagement – which existed at a distance from social interaction – that called for a lack of distance. This case study challenges the distinction between detachment and engagement within both anthropology and development, illustrating one method by which such ideals coexist as inseparable and dependent aspects of both knowledge and action.

Constant preoccupation with the smooth-running form of charity work had multiple and complex effects. It enabled an ethos of disinterested equality that allowed charity work to continue, despite conflicts, disappointments and fatigue. Disinterested equality was the means by which compassion came to be configured as a lived practice. Yet it simultaneously discouraged volunteers from addressing hard questions regarding the charity's successes or failures, or the long-term effects on individual recipients' lives. Detachment was not simple. It was neither simply a form of discursive power that perpetuated an unequal social system nor an emancipatory alternative to such systems.

In this chapter I have explored how volunteers understood and experienced the development of impersonality, and have taken their reflections seriously as a springboard into new understandings of charity and development. This provides one example of how we can broaden ideas of what counts as development by destabilizing its definitional, ethnographic and theoretical boundaries (see also Kelly this volume). At first appearance, this narrative of charitable giving might appear as an example of the difference between voluntary and 'ad hoc' charity services as compared to large-scale and professional development projects that are strongly focused on outcomes and successes. Yet attention to the everyday practices of practitioners, who must implement ideals, reforms and programmes through specific means, as well as to the discrepancies and connections between such spheres, is vital for studies of charity and development alike. Even in highly planned programmes, where end goals are writ large in the multiple levels of planning, implementation and assessment, how might practitioners develop new ends out of the means of daily interaction that transform and contrast with the planned programme? Such a question takes seriously both the influence recipients have on the enactment of such schemes of human improvement, and the practitioners' creative response to such effects.

Furthermore, how might we critically engage with the assumption, existing in both development and anthropology, that the small-scale and face-to-face are domains through which impersonality can be overcome? The current epistemologies of development and anthropology praise 'partnerships' (Jensen and Withereik this volume), 'participation' (Cooke and Kothari 2001) and 'engagement' while distrusting 'detached' interaction, and leave little room for considering alternative ethical approaches. By contrast, I argue, we should seriously explore enactments of impersonal relationality that stress the positive value of detachment, treating them as important forms of contemporary knowledge and action. Such studies could give rise to alternative models of 'detached engagement' that would perhaps be useful to anthropology in rethinking its engagement with the word of development, and to development in rethinking its current moral tropes of enactment.

NOTES

1. Christian charity became a widespread practice in medieval Europe (Davis 1996). Associated with the moral worth of the donor, such giving was seen to promote salvation, piety, compassion and fraternity (Henderson 1994; Davis 1996). Charity's social reach related to its configuration as a voluntary lay practice rather than a specialized profession. By contrast, 'development' professed to be scientific, secular, technological and reliant on expert, specialist knowledge, key qualities of a post-WWII modernization project aiming to achieve 'economic growth' and 'human progress' in the 'third world' (Gardner and Lewis 1996: 3–10).
2. The relationships between missionization, charity and development are long-standing, and many influential religious agencies, such as CARITAS and the Catholic Relief Agency, are major global development players.
3. Anthropologists have never, however, confined the notion of charity to the West. Most anthropological studies of charity have been carried out in non-Western countries. See for example Laidlaw (2000), Bornstein (2007) and Benthall (1999).
4. See details on the Oxfam website: www.oxfam.org.uk/shop/Hub.aspx?catalog =Unwrapped
5. About 10 per cent of the Commune of Florence's registered *residenti* were immigrants. There had been a steady growth since 2000, when it stood at around 5 per cent. Of these immigrants, 2006 data confirmed that Albanians made up the largest group at 14.2 per cent, while Chinese accounted for about 12.6 per cent. Romanians stood at 8.2 per cent, Filipinos 8.4 per cent, Moroccans 6.4 per cent, Peruvians 6.3 per cent, and Poles 1.7 per cent, and Americans at 1.4 per cent) (Comune di Firenze 2006). These figures do not, however, account for the large number of undocumented migrants living in Florence.
6. Italy experienced two 'Albanian emergencies'. In 1991 tens of thousands of Albanians fled to neighbouring countries as their state's economic and political systems collapsed, leading to mass shortages of food. In 1997 an Albanian government–endorsed Ponzi scheme, in which two-thirds of Albanian citizens had invested, collapsed, leading to civil unrest. Tens of thousands of Albanians fled to Italy as refugees (Pettifer and Vickers 2007: 1–36). While the Italian state provided many with material support and migration permits, many also faced expulsion, detention and discrimination (Campani 1993: 526–528; Vasta 1994: 84–85). The Albanian food bank recipients' more 'demanding attitude' thus likely reflected their sense of vulnerability as migrants in Italy, and real levels of need that the food bank's offerings were not meeting.

BIBLIOGRAPHY

Bartkowski, J. and H. Regis. 2003. *Charitable Choices: Religion, Race and Poverty in the Post-Welfare Era*. New York and London: New York University Press.

Benthall, J. 1999. 'Financial Worship: The Quranic Injunction to Almsgiving', *The Journal of the Royal Anthropological Institute* 5(1): 27–42.

Bialecki, J. 2008. 'Between Stewardship and Sacrifice: Agency and Economy in a Southern California Charismatic Church', *Journal of the Royal Anthropological Institute* 14(2): 372–390.

Blau, P. M. 1956. *Bureaucracy in Modern Society*. New York: Random House.

———. 1964. *Exchange and Power in Social Life*. New York: John Wiley and Sons, Inc.

Bornstein, E. 2005. *The Spirit of Development: Protestant NGOs, Morality and Economics in Zimbabwe*. Stanford, CA: Stanford University Press.

———. 2007. 'No Return: A Brief Typology of Philanthropy and the Sacred in New Delhi', in K. Inaba and R. Habito (eds), *The Politics of Altruism: Caring and Religion in a Global Perspective*. Cambridge: Cambridge Scholars Press, pp. 165–179.

———. 2008. 'The Impulse of Philanthropy', *Enacting Improvement Conference, Cambridge, 6 October 2008*. University of Cambridge, U.K.

Campani, G. 1993. 'Immigration and Racism in Southern Europe: The Italian Case', *Ethnic and Racial Studies* 16(3): 507–535.

Caplan, L. 1998. 'Giving and Receiving: Anglo-Indian Charity and its Beneficiaries in Madras', *Contributions to Indian Sociology* 32(2): 411–431.

Comune di Firenze. 2006. *Migranti Le Cifre: edizione aggiornata con dati al 31.12.2006*. Retrieved 4 September 2007 from http://www.comune.firenze.it/servizi_pubblici/stranieri/immigra.html

Cooke, B. and U. Kothari (eds). 2001. *Participation: The New Tyranny?* London and New York: Zed Books.

Davis, S. 1996. 'Philanthropy as a Virtue in Late Antiquity and the Middle Ages', in J. B. Schneewind (ed.), *Western Ideas of Philanthropy*. Bloomington and Indianapolis: Indiana University Press, pp. 1–23.

Elisha, O. 2008. 'Moral Ambitions of Grace: The Paradox of Compassion and Accountability in Evangelical Faith-based Giving', *Cultural Anthropology* 23(1): 154–189.

Feldman, I. 2007. 'The Quaker Way: Ethical Labour and Humanitarian Relief', *American Ethnologist* 34(4): 689–707.

Ferguson, J. 1990. *The Anti-Politics Machine: Development, Depoliticisation and Bureaucratic Power in Lesotho*. Cambridge: Cambridge University Press.

Gardner, K. and D. Lewis. 1996. *Anthropology, Development and the Post-modern Challenge*. London: Pluto Press.

Heilman, S. 1975. 'The Gift of Alms: Face-to-Face Almsgiving Among Orthodox Jews', *Urban Life and Culture* 3(4): 371–395.

Henderson, J. 1994. *Piety and Charity in Late Medieval Florence*. Oxford: Clarendon Press.

Herzfeld, M. 1993. *The Social Production of Indifference: Exploring the Symbolic Roots of Western Bureaucracy*. Chicago: University of Chicago Press.

Laidlaw, J. 2000. 'A Free Gift Makes No Friends', *Journal of the Royal Anthropological Institute* 6(4): 617–634.

Lipsky, M. 1980. *Street-Level Bureaucracy: Dilemmas of the Individual in Public Services*. New York: Basic Books.

McCarthy, K. D. (ed.) 1990. *Lady Bountiful Revisited: Women, Philanthropy and Power*. New Brunswick and London: Rutgers University Press.

Mauss, M. 1990 [1924]. *The Gift: The Form and Reason for Exchange in Archaic Societies*, trans. W. D. Halls. London: Routledge.

Mindry, D. 2001. 'Nongovernmental Organizations, "Grassroots," and the Politics of Virtue', *Signs* 26(4): 1187–1211.

Mitchell, T. 2002. *Rules of Experts: Egypt, Techno Politics, Modernity*. Berkeley: University of California Press.

Mol, A. 2002. *The Body Multiple: Ontology in Medical Practice*. Durham, NC, and London: Duke University Press.

Mosse, D. 2004. 'Is Good Policy Unimplementable? Reflections on the Ethnography of Aid Policy and Practice', *Development and Change* 35(4): 639–671.

———. 2005. *Cultivating Development: An Ethnography of Aid Policy and Practice*. London: Pluto Press.

Pettifer, J. and M. Vickers. 2007. *The Albanian Question: Reshaping the Balkans*. London and New York: I. B Tauris.

Riles, A. 2001. *The Network Inside Out*. Ann Arbor: University of Michigan Press.

Scott, J. 1998. *Seeing Like the State: How Certain Schemes to Improve the Human Condition Have Failed*. New Haven and London: Yale University Press.

Simmel, G. 2003 [1907]. *The Philosophy of Money*, trans. T. Bottomore and D. Frisby. London and New York: Routledge.

———. 1971 [1908]. 'The Poor', in D. Levine (ed.), *On Individuality and Social Forms: Selected Writings*. Chicago and London: University of Chicago Press, pp. 150–178.

Simpson, K. 2004. 'Doing Development: The Gap Year, Volunteer-Tourists and a Popular Practice of Development', *Journal of International Development* 16: 681–692.

Vasta, E. 1994. 'Rights and Racism in a New Country of Immigration: The Italian Case', in J. Wrench and J. Solomos (eds), *Racism and Migration in Western Europe*. Oxford: Berg, pp. 83–98.

Wearing, S. 2002. *Volunteer Tourism: Experiences that Make a Difference*. Oxon and New York: CABI.

Weber, M. 1978 [1956]. *Economy and Society: An Outline of Interpretive Sociology*, trans. E. Fischoff et al. Berkeley.: University of California Press.

Yarrow, T. 2008. 'Life/History: Personal Narratives of Development in Ghana', *Africa* 78: 334–357.

Zelizer, V. 1994. *The Social Meaning of Money*. New York: Basic Books.

CHAPTER 15

Intersection

The Art of Balance, or Else . . .

Alberto Corsín Jiménez

O urs is a society of balances, of equilibriums and resting points. The
macro is balanced by the micro, the local by the global, the self by
the other. Our liberal, plural society is a balanced society, insofar as we
can accommodate new (minority) perspectives to net out and balance
existing (majority) perspectives. Gift giving is balanced by debt honour-
ing, and the donor by the beneficiary. Society is never outstanding: there
is always a balance that tricks the social back into its proper whole.

Balances evince symmetries and commensurabilities. In the language
of liberal pluralism, the commensurable looks very much like a partner
in commensality, too. In John Rawls's famous theory of justice, it is
our partnership in mutual ignorance that defines the inaugural conditions for all future political and juridical contracts. Because we are all
originally interchangeable (that is, commensurable) as socio-economic
actors, we are therefore also taken for commensals in the same polity. The new digital economy takes the fantasy of liberal commensality
one step further. If in the Rawlsian model the liberal polity followed
a contractarian programme, in the digital age it has become a self-
performative engine: gift givers and gift takers turn economic commen-
surability (file sharing) into sociological commensality (peer exchange),
or so digital evangelists argue.

Theories of political ethics and freedom have long partaken of the proportional fantasy of ecumenical commensurability/commensality. In this
context development and progress are but classic teleological exemplars
aiming for an elusive utopian whole – an imaginary country of plenty
where we all live in harmony and balance. Catherine Trundle's charity

workers idealize benefaction as *compassion un-interreptus*; Nayanika
Mathur's bureaucrats take ironic distance from the fantasy of development as *coitus interruptus*. The interruptions gesture towards encompassing histories of hope, for the history of political ethics is indeed full
of what I have elsewhere called 'autarkic justifications': minima mora-
lias that posit an elemental moment of balance to the human condition
(Corsín Jiménez 2008: 10). These are the foundational endowments
that are required to complete or balance out the integrity of the human
project: contemplative reason (Aristotle), primary goods (John Rawls),
the capability to function (Amartya Sen) or the inalienability of property rights (Robert Nozick). They remainder-out human life by positing
a missing weight that completes it: to produce human life as a rounded,
balanced whole.

Aesthetics of Form

That the discourses of political sociology, economy and justice are
inflected by the imaginary of balancing should not come as surprise,
however. The oldest known meaning of the word *logos* is, precisely, balance or proportion. Holding the world to account – balancing its multi-
farious meanings and tensions – is what the work of reason accomplishes.
The reasons that people give for their actions, the terms through which
they make sense of their world, are but measured im/balances of their
existence. We proportion the world as we apportion and accommodate
to its ongoing irruptions. We reason through the world via exercises
in dis/proportionality. The art of balance yields the *aesthetic of form* of
worldly experience.

However, balancing and proportionality are cultural categories,
ones that are deeply entrenched in Euro-American habits of thought.
They dictate in profound ways our expectations of *logos*, of reason and
accountability, although they do not, of course, hold universal validity.
Anthropology's claim to theoretical status rests precisely on this capacity to elucidate modes of reason and engagement in/with the world that
do not rely on proportion, but rather proportion or tend towards other
aesthetics of form.

A corollary of the Euro-American art of balance is its epistemic per-
suasiveness. It is very difficult to show or point to an epistemic effect
in social theory that does not work as a netting-out effect of something
else. Insofar as one of the aims of social theory is the production of analyses, it becomes very difficult not to think of analyses as levelling mechanisms: the output of abstraction that levels the input of the empiric; the

simplex on the other side of the complex. There are few arguments in social theory that work as free-fallers; most stand squarely and assuredly atop a hill. Some manage as cliff-hangers. The art of balance, or else . . .

Take, for example, critique. As Yarrow and Venkatesan show in their introduction, critique has always been presumed to social theory. Anthropology's encounter and engagement with development *had* to produce critique, or else be seen as falling short of its authentic epistemic/knowledge mission: anthropological knowledge as counterbalance to developmental practice. Without critique, there can be no point (to anthropology). Yarrow and Venkatesan's alternative reads instead as a courageous cliff-hanger, a form of analysis that is internal to the engagement (between anthropology and development). The terms of such internal engagement are spelt out by ethnography. If the internal relation is rich, the anthropology is self-enhancing, resulting in 'anthropologies with development in them', as they put it. But what form does an analysis that is internal to itself take? How can we see it for an *analysis* and not simply for a singular and contextual relational engagement between (say) anthropology and development? If ethnography works analytically (tenuously, in cliff-hanger mode, but analytically nonetheless), what form of knowledge performs the counterbalance?

Perhaps the ethnographic counterbalance is *itself*, in the guise of (yet more) ethnography. The ethnography that is balanced by ethnography is of course (anthropological) *comparison*. All ethnography is singular, contextual and emergent, but it can work analytically nonetheless because it refers to other ethnography. In its fashioning as a unique piece of description ethnography does not require, nor does it depend on, a proportional imagination. The ethnographic world does not have to net out. Its terms of description are internal to those who inhabit it at the time of reportage. 'Getting the work done' in charity work, as reported by Trundle, collapses for instance any presumed distinction between 'detached [anthropological] knowledge' and 'engaged [developmental] action'. Knowledge and action no longer stand in proportional (inverse) relation. Instead, ethnographic analysis deploys a *form* that is internally fashioned by its own descriptive register; it does not require balance to function as an analytical effect.

Anthropological Baroques

If critique works as an intermediation between knowledge and action, perhaps it is fair to redescribe the anthropology of critique as the cultural perspective of 'double vision': a perspective from which knowledge and action may be uncoupled or coupled back again for novel perspectival effects. We see through knowledge to its actions and explain actions back to knowledge – except that certain bodies of knowledge are very often weighed as capacitating of their own accord, and certain sets of actions impress us with their reflexive power. The intermediation, as noted, works both ways.

Nayanika Mathur, for instance, finds this type of intermediation among her bureaucratic informants in the shape of cynicism. The cynics 'see through the ideology of development' and yet do so by becoming the very optical mediators of such knowledge. Cynicism is the form of (self-)knowledge through which the social agency of the state is reproduced. The image recalls Annelise Riles's noted description of networking as a bureaucratic and sociological form. As she puts it, 'networkers deploy the *optical effect* of Network form as a "fulcrum or lever" that generates *alternative inverted forms* of sociality by projecting an image of each – Network and "personal relations" – *from the point of view of the other*' (Riles 2001: 115–116, emphases added). Thus the optics of networking and cynicism enact the perspectivism of double vision that characterizes the culture of late liberalism: forms of knowledge that double back on themselves, generating their own reversible effects – their own 'inside-outs', in Riles's wonderful formulation.

Optics, double vision, the aesthetics of form, the pulsations of effects: these are all idioms of analysis that exude a certain mannerism, a splendour of formalization, a baroque aesthetics. In an important essay, David Mosse has recently observed how the ethnographic study of public policy and professional communities operates upon anthropological knowledge to work an uneasy relationalization of that very knowledge (Mosse 2006). Whereas anthropologists are intent on producing knowledge, the professionals with whom we work demand that we produce (novel) relationships with them. Perhaps we entered the field as outsiders (academics) but are in time recast as insiders (colleagues, advisors). The inside-out of knowledge is thus confused by new or unexpected exit and entry points (Mosse 2006: 936–937). Analytical forms pop up where we least expect them: in a document, an email, a cynical statement. It would seem that the art of balance demanded by ethnography (as opposed to that of critique, or of proportional social theory at large) is cajoled into existence by a profusion of form.

Echoing Leibniz, the new ethnographic sensibility must remain alert to the self-perpetuating complexity of form: 'Every bit of matter can be conceived as a garden full of plants or a pond full of fish. But each branch of the plant, each drop of its bodily fluids, is also such a garden or such a pond' (Leibniz 1991: 228, cited in Kwa 2002: 26) Forms elicit their own hopeful connections and extensions: drops that become gardens or swell into ponds. Perhaps the present move to learn how to differentiate ethnographic developments signals a return of such a baroque epistemology where interruptions, if scrutinized, contain self-proliferating economies of hope – ethnography, that is, as critical hope.

BIBLIOGRAPHY

Corsín Jiménez, A. 2008. 'Introduction: Well-being's Re-proportioning of Social Thought', in A. Corsín Jiménez (ed.), *Culture and Well-being: Anthropological Approaches to Freedom and Political Ethics*. London: Pluto Press.
Kwa, C. 2002. 'Romantic and Baroque Conceptions of Complex Wholes in the Sciences', in J. Law and A. Mol (eds), *Complexities: Social Studies of Knowledge Practices*. Durham, NC, and London: Duke University Press.
Leibniz, G. W. 1991. *Monadology*, trans. N. Rescher. Pittsburgh: University of Pittsburgh Press.
Mosse, D. 2006. 'Anti-social Anthropology? Objectivity, Objection, and the Ethnography of Public Policy and Professional Communities', *Journal of the Royal Anthropological Institute* 12(4): 935–956.
Riles, A. 2001. *The Network Inside Out*. Ann Arbor: The University of Michigan Press.

CONTRIBUTORS

Amita Baviskar is a sociologist at the Institute of Economic Growth, Delhi. Her research focuses on the cultural politics of environment and development. Her first book was *In the Belly of the River: Tribal Conflicts over Development in the Narmada Valley*. Her subsequent work further explores the themes of resource rights, subaltern resistance and cultural identity. She has edited *Waterlines: The Penguin Book of River Writings*; *Waterscapes: The Cultural Politics of a Natural Resource*; *Contested Grounds: Essays on Nature, Culture and Power* and (with Raka Ray) *Elite and Everyman: The Cultural Politics of the Indian Middle Classes*. She is currently writing about bourgeois environmentalism and spatial restructuring in the context of economic liberalization in Delhi.

Alberto Corsín Jiménez is a senior scientist at the Spanish National Research Council (CSIC). Previously he was dean at Spain's School for Industrial Organisation (EOI) and university lecturer in social anthropology at the University of Manchester. He is the author of *The Strabismic Polity: an Anthropological Essay on the Political Optics of Modernity* (forthcoming) and editor of *Culture and Well-being: Anthropological Approaches to Freedom and Political Ethics* (Pluto 2008) and *The Anthropology of Organisations* (Ashgate 2007).

Veena Das is Krieger-Eisenhower Professor in the Department of Anthropology at John Hopkins University. The abiding concerns of her research are to understand the working of long-time cultural logics in contemporary events as well as moments of rupture and recovery. She is the author of a number of books, including *Mirrors of Violence: Communities, Riots and Survivors in South Asia*; *Critical Events: An Anthropological Perspective on Contemporary India* and *Life and Words: Violence and the Descent into the Ordinary*.

Harri Englund is a reader in the Department of Social Anthropology at the University of Cambridge. He has written and edited several books about liberalism and the moral imagination in Africa, including *Prisoners of Freedom: Human Rights and the African Poor*.

John T. Friedman is an associate professor in sociocultural anthropology at Roosevelt Academy (Utrecht University) in the Netherlands. His research focuses on the state, customary law, politics and development in (post-)apartheid Southern Africa. He is author of *Imagining the Post-Apartheid State: An Ethnographic Account of Namibia* (Berghahn Books, 2011) and is currently co-editing *Debating Development: Controversies in the Theory and Practice of International Development* (Pearson-Prentice Hall, forthcoming).

John Gledhill is Max Gluckman Professor of Social Anthropology at the University of Manchester, a member of the Academy of Social Sciences and a fellow of the British Academy.

Maia Green teaches anthropology at Manchester University. She got her Ph.D. at the London School of Economics in 1993. Her original research explored the constitution of popular Christianity in Southern Tanzania. Recent work continues to assess the impact of institutional forms and knowledge practices in relation to traditional healing and anti-witchcraft practices, international development and poverty. She is also involved in international development as a practitioner, having worked in the U.K. Department for International Development as a social development adviser and undertaken consultancies for a range of international organizations.

Maria Gabriela Hita is an adjunct professor of sociology and the coordinator of LIDES, the Laboratory for Research in Social Inequalities of the postgraduate social sciences programme at the Federal University of Bahia. She has conducted extensive research on the kinship and family structures, social networks and forms of association of the residents of the poorer neighbourhoods of Salvador, Bahia, and is currently completing a monograph on the matriarchal family amongst poor Afro-Brazilians

Casper Bruun Jensen is associate professor at the Technologies in Practice group of the IT University of Copenhagen. He has published in *Configurations, Science, Technology and Human Values* and *Social Studies of Science*. He is the editor (with Kjetil Rödje) of *Deleuzian Intersections:*

Science, Technology and Anthropology (Berghahn Books, 2009) and the author of *Ontologies for Developing Things: Making Health Care Futures Through Technology* (Sense, 2010).

Ann Kelly is a lecturer in the Department of Global Health at the London School of Hygiene and Tropical Medicine. She holds a Ph.D. in anthropology from Cambridge University. In collaboration with the Anthropologies of African Biosciences (AAB) group, her research examines how the community, polity and society are conceptualized by international public health. Her ethnographic fieldwork in Tanzania, Benin and The Gambia explores the production of scientific facts in Africa, with special attention to the built-environments, material artefacts, genres of memory and practical labours of experimentation. She has published on the ethics and epistemics of entomological experimental design, malaria control interventions and ways rural, urban and domestic spaces are configured to manage the flow of human, parasite and mosquito populations.

Norman Long is professor emeritus of the sociology of development at the University of Wageningen, the Netherlands; adjunct professor of the sociology of development at China Agricultural University, Beijing and honorary professorial fellow of the White Rose East Asia Centre at the University of Leeds. He is best known for his actor-oriented/interface analysis of processes of development policy intervention and the dynamics of social change. He has carried out detailed ethnographic research in Central Africa and Latin America (Peru and Mexico) and over the past ten years has contributed to postgraduate training and rural development research in China. Key publications include (with Ann Long) *Battlefields of Knowledge* (Routledge, 1992); (with Alberto Arce) *Anthropology, Development and Modernities* (Routledge, 2000); *Development Sociology: Actor Perspectives* (Routledge, 2001) and (with Ye Jingzhong and Wang Yihuan) *Rural Transformations and Development: China in Context* (Edward Elgar, 2010).

Nayanika Mathur is an Affiliated Lecturer at the Department of Social Anthropology, University of Cambridge. Her recently completed doctorate from the same Department is an ethnography of a government development office located on the Indian borderland, incorporating her research interests in the anthropology of the state, space and development; bureaucracy and documentary practices; neo-liberalism and policy making; and big-cat protectionism.

Annemarie Mol is professor of anthropology of the body at the Amsterdam Institute for Social Science Research. She has published *The Body Multiple* and *The Logic of Care* and recently co-edited *Care in Practice. On tinkering in clinics, homes and farms*. Currently she is working on a project called 'Eating bodies in Western practice and theory'.

Michelle Obeid lectures in Social Anthropology at the University of Manchester. Her research interests are focused within the Middle East and Arabic-speaking world and include the state and borders, kinship and gender relations, mobility and displacement.

Benedicta Rousseau is a McArthur Research Fellow in anthropology at the University of Melbourne. She trained in social anthropology at the University of Auckland before completing her Ph.D. at the University of Cambridge. She has carried out fieldwork in various locations in Vanuatu since 2000, looking at indigenous leadership, the interplay between *kastom* and state courts, election campaigning and the lived experience of provincial government. Over the past ten years she has taught a range of topics within anthropology at universities in England and New Zealand. Her current research traces the concept of development as understood, remembered and physically actualized on the island of Malakula (Vanuatu) since 1960.

John Taylor (Jack) is a lecturer at La Trobe University, Australia. He holds a masters (Auckland) and Ph.D. (Australian National University) in social anthropology and is the author of *The Other Side: Ways of Being and Place in Vanuatu* (2008) and *Consuming Identity: Modernity and Tourism in New Zealand* (1998). His research interests are focused primarily within the Pacific region and include public and popular culture, tourism, kinship and gender relations, religious cosmologies and ritual, colonialism and neocolonialism.

Catherine Trundle is a lecturer in cultural anthropology at Victoria University of Wellington, New Zealand. She completed her Ph.D. in social anthropology at Cambridge University. Her doctoral research ethnographically examined English-speaking migrant groups in Florence, Italy, with a focus on charity volunteering. She is the co-editor (with Brigitte Bönisch-Brednich) of a volume entitled *Local Lives: Migration and the Politics of Place* (2010). Her current research explores the claims for state compensation and health benefits made by Commonwealth nuclear test veterans.

Soumhya Venkatesan lectures in social anthropology at the University of Manchester. She is the author of *Craft Matters: Artisans, Development and the Indian nation* (Orient Blackswan, 2009).

Brit Ross Winthereik is associate professor at the Technologies in Practice group of the IT University of Copenhagen. She has published in *Science, Technology and Human Values, IT and People, Common Knowledge* and *Comparative Sociology*. Her current research explores instruments for knowledge production in the development aid sector, in environmental work, and in the academy.

Thomas Yarrow lectures in socio-cultural anthropology at Durham University. He is the author of *Development Beyond Politics: Aid, Activism and NGOs in Ghana* (Palgrave Macmillan, 2011) and the co-editor of *Archaeology and Anthropology: Understanding Similarity, Exploring Difference*.

INDEX

accountability
  expectations of, 228
  mutual, 89, 94–95
  relationship with governance, 48
  research into, 96
  transparency and, 89, 182, 207n14,
    214, 228
action
  and engagement, 35, 219
  as aesthetic form, 215–216
  charitable, 213, 214
  cynical, 203
  in development, 7, 8, 13–15
  relationship to knowledge, 13–15, 26–27,
    43, 45, 52, 58–61, 100, 211, 229–230
  research, 47
Action Aid, 74
activism
  and 'engaged anthropology', 188–189
  environmental, 110
  in Brazil, 110, 118
  in Ghana, 154–155
  in India, 128, 136
  in Lebanon, 155, 165
  influence on development methods,
    47, 50
actor-oriented perspective, 187
Adivasi, 127–130, 138, 140, 141n1
  poor, 130, 135, 136, 140
aesthetics
  of action, 215, 216
  of charity, 13
  of collaboration, 91, 96
  of form, 228–230
  vs. political representation, 61
aid workers, 27, 167n12, 216
affect, 59, 61, 75, 212, 216, 222. *See also*
  love, sentiment

Africa, 36, 87, 97, 146–147
  North, 152, 213
  South, 30
  Southern, 27
  water pumps for, 87, 105
  West, 79, 81n4, 81n5
agency
  and cynicism, 230
  and disinterest, 118
  and ethics, 78
  and transgression, 136
  denial of, 34, 114
  local, 35, 38
  neglect of, 58
  relationship with structure, 25, 26, 34, 60
Al-Lajna al-Sha'biyya, (the Popular Com-
    mittee), 156
Albanian , 216, 224n5, 224n6
American University of Beirut (AUB),
    152, 153
anthropological knowledge, 81n1, 81n3
  absence from development practice,
    42–44, 54
  as counterbalance to development prac-
    tice, 229
  as representation, 59
  assumed superiority of, 7, 205
  form and content of, 61
  of development, 35
  relevance to development, 53
  subjectivity in construction of, 6, 44
  See also action
anthropology
  activist, 219
  applied, 24, 28, 67, 145
  as scientific discipline, 59
  circumscribed, 73
  critique of, 4, 8, 59

www.ingramcontent.com/pod-product-compliance
Lightning Source LLC
Chambersburg PA
CBHW060032030426
42334CB00019B/2295